An Introduction to
Southeast Asian Studies

An Introduction to Southeast Asian Studies

Edited by

*Mohammed Halib and
Tim Huxley*

Tauris Academic Studies
I.B.Tauris Publishers
LONDON · NEW YORK

Published in 1996 by Tauris Academic Studies,
an imprint of I.B.Tauris & Co Ltd
Victoria House, Bloomsbury Square, London WC1B 4DZ

175 Fifth Avenue, New York NY 10010

In the United States of America and in Canada
distributed by St Martin's Press
175 Fifth Avenue, New York NY 10010

A full CIP record for this book is available from the British
Library

A full CIP record for this book is available from the Library of
Congress

ISBN 1 86064 351 5

Library of Congress catalog card number: available

Set in Monotype Ehrhardt by Ewan Smith, London

Printed and bound in Great Britain by
WBC Ltd, Bridgend, Mid Glamorgan

Contents

Contributors

Mohammed Halib, Associate Professor, Department of Southeast Asian Studies, University of Malaya, Kuala Lumpur

Lewis Hill, Lecturer in South-East Asian Social Anthropology, Centre for South-East Asian Studies, University of Hull

Michael Hitchcock, Professor of Tourism, University of North London (formerly Senior Lecturer in South-East Asian Development Sociology, University of Hull)

Tim Huxley, Senior Lecturer in South-East Asian Contemporary Political History and Director, Centre for South-East Asian Studies, University of Hull

Hong Lysa, Senior Lecturer in History and Deputy Co-ordinator, Southeast Asian Studies Programme, National University of Singapore

Victor T. King, Professor of South-East Asian Studies and Dean, School of Social and Political Sciences, University of Hull

Duncan McCargo, Lecturer in Politics, University of Leeds

Geoffrey E. Marrison, Honorary Fellow, Centre for South-East Asian Studies, University of Hull (formerly Director and Keeper, Department of Oriental Manuscripts and Printed Books, British Library)

Michael J. G. Parnwell, Senior Lecturer in South-East Asian Geography, Centre for South-East Asian Studies, University of Hull

Robert H. Taylor, Professor of Politics and Pro-Director, School of Oriental and African Studies, University of London

John Walton, Lecturer in South-East Asian Economics, Centre for South-East Asian Studies, University of Hull

Acknowledgements

The editors would like to thank Professor V. T. ('Terry') King (Director of the Centre at Hull between 1988 and 1993, and subsequently Dean of the School of Social and Political Sciences there) for his unflagging encouragement of this project. Terry King also provided particular advice to Lewis Hill and Michael Hitchcock on their chapter on anthropology, as did Daniel Arghiros (ESRC Research Fellow at Hull) and Professor P. E. de Josselin de Jong. Dr Jonathan Rigg, Reader in Geography at Durham, Dr Ulrich Kratz, Reader in Indonesian and Malay at the School of Oriental and African Studies (London), and Dr Charles McGregor, long-standing friends of the Hull Centre, together with Dr Lester Crook from I.B.Tauris and Dr Clive Christie and Pauline Khng from Hull, all made extremely helpful comments on drafts of various chapters. The British Council in Kuala Lumpur provided generous assistance through the funding of visits to Hull by Mohammed Halib, who also wishes to acknowledge the University of Malaya's support for his involvement.

Mohammed Halib and Tim Huxley
Kuala Lumpur and Hull
November 1995

Abbreviations

ADB	Asian Development Bank
ASEAN	Association of Southeast Asian Nations
ANU	Australian National University
BEFEO	Bulletin de l'Ecole Française d'Extrême Orient
BIES	Bulletin of Indonesian Economic Studies
EFEO	Ecole Française d'Extrême Orient
ESCAP	Economic and Social Commission for Asia and the Pacific
ESRC	Economic and Social Research Council
FAO	Food and Agriculture Organization (UN)
FAS	Field of Anthropological Study
IMF	International Monetary Fund
ISEAS	Institute of Southeast Asian Studies (Singapore)
JMBRAS	Journal of the Malayan Branch of the Royal Asiatic Society
JSS	Journal of the Siam Society
KITLV	Koninklijk Instituut voor Taal-, Land-en Volkenkunde (Royal Institute of Linguistics and Anthropology, Leiden, Netherlands)
LDC	less-developed country
LSE	London School of Economics
MIT	Massachusetts Institute of Technology
NGO	non-governmental organization
NUS	National University of Singapore
UM	University of Malaya
SOAS	School of Oriental and African Studies (London)
ZOPFAN	Southeast Asian Zone of Peace, Freedom and Neutrality

Introduction

Mohammed Halib and
Tim Huxley

This volume is intended to help advanced students of Southeast Asian Studies wishing to explore the background to, and the present state of, the more important academic disciplines in relation to Southeast Asian Studies. While the authors of the eight disciplinary chapters have each adopted an individual approach to some extent, they have all attempted to draw out the most important themes in their own discipline's approach to the region, highlighting significant milestones in the literature. In most cases, they have also attempted to assess the current disciplinary 'state of the art'.

Southeast Asian Studies has in recent years emerged as one of the healthiest branches of area studies. The most immediate explanation for this lies in the attractiveness of the region to the current student generation in Europe, Australia, the United States and Japan, as well as Southeast Asia itself. The region's economic dynamism, the growing concern over human rights and environmental issues, and actual and potential conflicts (in Cambodia, East Timor, Burma and the South China Sea, for example) have all focused external media attention on Southeast Asia during the 1990s. Within Southeast Asia, economic success has bred an atmosphere of confidence and the beginnings of a sense of region – at least at the elite and middle-class levels. Direct contact has also stimulated student interest: with the massive expansion of affordable air travel, the region has come within reach of Western tourists and 'travellers'; Southeast Asians are also beginning to travel more widely within their own region. Many Western students are also attracted to the region's religions and to its material culture. At the same time, governments outside Southeast Asia have recognized its economic dynamism by encouraging and funding research on the region; some Southeast Asian governments have also encouraged Southeast Asian Studies for policy-related reasons.

Southeast Asian studies worldwide

Southeast Asian Studies programmes have evolved from disparate origins. In the United States the efforts of one man, Lauriston Sharp, played a crucial role in the foundation and development of Southeast Asian Studies as a field of study in its own right. In the words of George McT. Kahin:

> It was he [Lauriston Sharp] who realized the need to develop the study of Southeast Asia in the United States and acted on that conviction, providing the leadership for the establishment of a program dedicated to that goal at Cornell and directing it during the first critical decade of its growth. Without him there would have been no Southeast Asia Program at Cornell, nor would the study of Southeast Asia have advanced nearly so far in this country as it has (1994: 2).

After a series of negotiations, a grant made available by the Rockefeller Foundation enabled the initiation of Cornell's Southeast Asia Program in 1950. Forty-five years later, Cornell is still regarded as the Mecca of Southeast Asian Studies in the United States, although several other US universities have since started their own programmes. Yale, for example, was given a grant for the establishment of Southeast Asian Studies at the same time as Cornell, 'officially to promote a healthy competition but also to preempt any charge of partiality' (Kahin 1994: 3). The United States' growing global role, and particularly its strong strategic interest in the region in the era of the first and second Indochina wars, led to substantially increased government funding for Southeast Asian Studies between the late 1950s and early 1970s, and this allowed the establishment of important programmes at such universities as Michigan, Northern Illinois and Wisconsin-Madison.

Victor T. King has identified four distinct phases in the development of 'non-Western studies' in Britain, 'each one initiated by an official enquiry into and a report on national needs' (King 1990: 2). Following the Reay Committee's Report (1909), the School of Oriental Studies was set up in 1917, becoming the School of Oriental and African Studies (SOAS) in 1938. The establishment of SOAS was closely related to Britain's imperial interests in Asia and Africa, and particularly the need for expertise in the relevant vernacular languages. Though the 'pre-Second World War period was relatively insignificant for the academic study of South-East Asia' in Britain, the practical importance of Oriental Studies generally was established, and a more coherent scholarly approach to the study of the East was initiated (King 1990: 2).

After the Second World War, three important government-initiated reports shaped the development of Southeast Asian Studies in the United Kingdom: these were the Scarbrough Report (1947), the Hayter Report (1961) and the Parker Report (1986). Summing up these reports, King notes that the rationale for Area Studies was implicit in each of them:

> a common theme running through all three reports is the importance to the nation of the study of non-Western peoples and cultures, the dangers of an overly Europe-centred view of history, culture and world affairs, and the particular problems arising from British ethnocentrism. What is also stressed, though less directly in the Hayter Report, is the practical application of area studies programmes, though these utilitarian considerations were subordinated to strong arguments, even in the Parker Review, for the importance of a base of scholarship in area studies (1990: 4).

Southeast Asian Studies in Britain was a clear beneficiary of all three reports. In particular, following Hayter, funding was made available for the establishment of a Centre for South-East Asian Studies at Hull (in 1962). A similar centre was also set up by the University of Kent in 1978.

While the post-Hayter period from the early 1960s to the late 1970s might credibly be recalled as Britain's 'Golden Age of Area Studies', the 1980s may well be remembered as the 'Dark Age' (King 1990: 4, 12). During the 1980s funding became scarce, centres began losing their staff, and most regrettably at the end of the decade the decision was taken to close Kent's Centre of South-East Asian Studies.

Helped to some extent by the modest but welcome boost in funding that followed the Parker Review, which precipitated the establishment of a lectureship in Indonesian and Javanese (together with a number of 'training fellowships') at SOAS and two additional posts at Hull, Southeast Asian Studies is now thriving again in Britain. Both SOAS and Hull offer undergraduate as well as postgraduate Southeast Asian Studies programmes. Within Southeast Asian Studies, SOAS's greatest strengths lie in the breadth and depth of its courses in Southeast Asian languages and literatures. While Hull offers courses in Indonesian and Thai, its primary focus is on the social sciences and humanities, including applied anthropology, sociology, geography, modern history and politics. The Hull Centre now has a staff of twelve, teaching around a hundred undergraduates and thirty postgraduates, many of whom are Southeast Asians.

In continental Europe, there are important loci of Southeast Asian scholarship within various universities and other institutions. Major centres include the Royal Institute of Linguistics and Anthropology

(KITLV) at Leiden in the Netherlands, Leiden University's Centre of Non-Western Studies, the Centre for Asian Studies Amsterdam, the Nordic Institute of Asian Studies in Copenhagen, the Ecole Française d'Extrême Orient in Paris, and the Institut für Asienkunde in Hamburg. The European emphasis is on research and postgraduate teaching in the context of Asian Studies as a whole, rather than on providing coordinated, multidisciplinary undergraduate programmes in Southeast Asian studies specifically.

For geographical, political and, more recently, economic reasons, there is a greater concentration of Southeast Asian scholarship and university teaching in Australia than in any other country outside the region. A Centre of South-East Asian Studies was established at Monash University (Melbourne) in 1965, and there is a great concentration of Southeast Asianists in every conceivable discipline at the Australian National University (ANU) in Canberra. The ANU's Research School of Pacific and Asian Studies is committed to research and postgraduate training, but the Faculty of Asian Studies provides undergraduate courses, particularly in Southeast Asian languages. Since the 1980s, many Australian universities have established Asian research and teaching programmes, relating to Southeast Asia to a greater or lesser extent. Of the more recently established Centres, Murdoch University's Asia Research Centre stands out for the high quality of its work.

Inside the region itself, Southeast Asian Studies programmes and centres have been created to satisfy a variety of needs. In Malaysia, although the idea of replacing the University of Malaya's Faculty of Arts with a 'School of Southeast Asian Studies' had been mooted as early as 1961, it was not until 1976 that UM's Programme of Southeast Asian Studies was started. Both internal and external reasons prompted the establishment of this programme. Within the university, concern had been felt over Arts Faculty students' rather limited and superficial knowledge of the rest of Southeast Asia. Courses dealing with the region were already offered, but only within disciplinary departments; there was little cross-disciplinary access. But the establishment of the programme – the first in the region – also reflected perceived national foreign policy requirements. The withdrawal of US forces from Vietnam in 1973, and the communist victories throughout Indochina in 1975, accentuated the ASEAN governments' interest in concepts of regional cooperation and self-reliance. The decision by ASEAN's first Summit Meeting in 1976 to promote Southeast Asian Studies reflected a realisation that great mutual understanding within the region required a sound knowledge base (Bahrin 1981: 100–1).

The establishment of the Institute of Southeast Asian Studies (ISEAS) in Singapore in 1971 was partly precipitated by the city-state's wish to project a Southeast Asian rather than Chinese national identity. But although it has sponsored a number of Singaporeans through postgraduate study in universities overseas, ISEAS has never itself been involved in teaching, even at postgraduate level. However, there had long been strong Southeast Asian components in many arts and social sciences courses at the National University of Singapore (NUS), which established a coordinated, multidisciplinary Southeast Asian Studies Programme in 1993.

Some problems in teaching Southeast Asian Studies

Undergraduates and postgraduates involved in Southeast Asian Studies can draw on insights into the region from a wide variety of disciplines, ranging from languages through the humanities (literature, archaeology and history) and geography to the social sciences (anthropology, sociology, economics, politics and international relations). But the teaching of Southeast Asian Studies poses interesting and peculiar problems, both within and outside the region. Advocates of area studies, including Southeast Asian Studies, have always insisted on the multidisciplinary or interdisciplinary character of the field: a comprehensive understanding of a region or country requires the study of its language, literature, people, culture, history, geography, politics and economics. However, in Centres of Southeast Asian Studies, the academic staff are usually essentially disciplinary specialists with specific interests in Southeast Asia. This may create a problem: 'disciplined' academics teach 'multidisciplinary' undergraduates who tend to lack disciplinary 'backbone'. For this reason, some universities (such as Cornell) offer Southeast Asian Studies only to postgraduates, who are expected to have developed their disciplinary 'spine' as undergraduates. In other universities (such as Hull), the problem may be mitigated by many undergraduates' tendency to 'stream' themselves towards specialization in anthropology, sociology and geography or, alternatively, history and politics, participating in non-Southeast Asian courses in these disciplines offered by other departments.

In the realm of language teaching, another difficulty may exist. Language is an integral part of Southeast Asian Studies and students are usually expected to reach a certain level of proficiency in speaking and writing at least one Southeast Asian language. But while it is perfectly acceptable for an undergraduate in the United Kingdom or United States to choose to learn Malay or Indonesian, this is not usually a valid option for Malaysian students of Southeast Asian Studies, for most of whom these languages are the mother-tongue (or, in the case of Indonesian, a closely related dialect). At UM's Department of Southeast Asian Studies, for example, students are expected to choose from Filipino, Thai, Vietnamese, Burmese and Javanese. Similarly, research on Malaysian topics is highly discouraged among Malaysian students of Southeast Asian Studies.

Exploring the literature

Across all eight disciplines investigated in this volume, several common features stand out. First, the contributions of Western writers dominate every discipline's English-language literature on Southeast Asia, to which Southeast Asians have only relatively recently begun to contribute significantly. A related point is that Southeast Asians have tended to research and write on their own countries: the number of true 'Southeast Asianists' in the region remains limited. Thus a large part of local scholars' work on the region has involved Indonesians, Thais and to a lesser extent Malaysian scholars writing in their national languages about their own countries, and being published 'locally'. Nevertheless, ISEAS in Singapore has done much to facilitate, encourage, sponsor and publish scholarship on Southeast Asia by Southeast Asians in English for an international as well as regional readership: its success is clearly reflected in the bibliographies of several of this book's chapters.

The second feature that stands out from the literature is a concomitant of the first. Western-derived concepts have dominated practically all writing in the humanities and social sciences that has related to Southeast Asia. Local scholars have primarily been trained in the West; those who have been trained locally have been supervised by those trained in the West. Thus, Western concepts and theories, grounded firmly in traditions that emphasize cultural interpretations of the region and processes of modernization, have been perpetuated. Both foreign and local scholars have called for an 'indigenized' approach in the social sciences and for the writing of 'autonomous' history. Indeed, most academic researchers (Western as well as local) now routinely attempt to avoid ethnocentrism and 'orientalism' in their scholarly work on Southeast Asia.

Third, post-colonial scholarship relating to Southeast Asia has not been applied evenly throughout the region. The relative political openness of Indonesia, Malaysia, the Philippines, Singapore and Thailand has facilitated research across a wide disciplinary range. This openness has been manifested in the ease with which foreign scholars have routinely been able to secure research permits to work in the ASEAN countries. These states have certainly been studied much more intensively than Burma, Cambodia, Laos and Vietnam, where political restrictions and conflict have severely constrained scholarship and research since the 1960s. Not only have outside researchers been prevented from gaining access, but postgraduate students in the humanities and social sciences from these countries have not been sent abroad to study. By way of contrast, large numbers of students from the ASEAN countries have written postgraduate theses on their own countries (and occasionally other parts of the region) in American, Australian and British universities. Southeast Asian scholars have generally been restrained in their criticism of their own countries' political, economic and social systems, but, when allowed at all, scholarship in the communist and socialist Southeast Asian states has been directed strictly towards the requirements of the state. Quite often, data and information relating to Burma and the Indochinese states have been inaccessible, and extended fieldwork by foreign scholars has usually not been permitted – or has been too dangerous.

A fourth feature is the minimal impact that work on Southeast Asia has had on wider theoretical debates. This is in stark contrast with, for instance, scholarly work on Latin America – particularly that associated with the 'dependency theorists' of the 1960s and 1970s – which had a profound effect on theoretical and conceptual constructs in the social sciences. The relative lack of research on mainland Southeast Asia (Thailand excepted) may have hindered theory-building in the social sciences with regard to the region as a whole.

Fifth, while this volume (like much teaching and research on the region) is neatly divided up into disciplinary chapters, it is clear that some of the most important themes in scholarship on Southeast Asia cross disciplines. In particular, 'development' and its down-side 'under-development' are common themes running through the disciplines of economics, geography, sociology, anthropology and politics. Writers in several or all of these disciplines concern themselves with developmental sub-themes such as poverty, urbanization, the peasantry and rural development, civil society and political development. Often it is extremely difficult to place a certain piece of writing firmly and exclusively in one discipline: the literature on political economy, for example, is important in economics and sociology as well as in politics. Disciplinary boundaries are arguably becoming out-dated and irrelevant to the analysis of many important Southeast Asian themes.

A sixth point is that in the more 'modern' disciplines – particularly sociology, politics, economics and international relations – the boundaries of Southeast Asia as a useful region for analysis are being challenged by developments in the real world. In economic terms, links across the wider 'Asia-Pacific' region are much more significant than those within Southeast Asia. Moreover, industrialization and urbanization are creating commonalities in social and political trends throughout East Asia. For example, Thailand's halting democratization in the face of military-led reaction has much in common with recent developments in South Korea and Taiwan. In security terms, the growing strategic reach of China, and the increased salience of territorial disputes in the South China Sea, mean that Southeast Asia should no longer be seen as a discrete 'regional security complex'. At the level of political and intellectual elites, there is a growing sense of 'Asian-ness', which transcends the boundaries that have defined Southeast Asia since the 1940s.

The future of Southeast Asian Studies

In the future, Southeast Asia will continue to offer the student and scholar of the region an almost infinite array of potential research topics. The region's current economic boom is adding to the list of themes worthy of investigation: some of the more recent innovations in research at SOAS and at the Hull Centre, for example, include cross-disciplinary work on Southeast Asian business culture and management, on environmental issues, and on the arms trade in the region.

Many Southeast Asianists working on the region's economics, politics and international relations, while retaining a focus on Southeast Asia and its constituent states and societies, are attempting to place their work in the context of East Asia as a whole.

It seems clear that as their countries become richer and more closely inter-linked in economic and political terms, Southeast Asians will play a much greater part in research on their own countries and other parts of the region. The need to 'understand thy neighbour' has surfaced repeatedly at recent regional conferences. Remarks by Professor Shaharil Talib (Head of UM's Department of Southeast Asian Studies) encapsulate the up-beat mood amongst regional scholars:

> Southeast Asian Studies by Southeast Asians must have an open agenda. It is open because it deals with our ancestral heritage and life of those yet to be born. It is open because the region has been always open before colonial partition. It is open because the peoples, cultures, capital, technology and commodities have moved to markets in the region and beyond ... The deconstruction of the field of Southeast Asian Studies of the open agenda will be a task shouldered by Southeast Asians. International funding, research and training institutions must return to their drawing boards and plan with their hands on the table in collaboration with Southeast Asians who will spearhead the field (1994: 9).

Such is the challenge for the rising generation of Southeast Asianists, within as well as outside the region. Several of the chapters in this volume (notably those by King, and McCargo and Taylor) make suggestions regarding the future relationship between Southeast Asian and Western scholarship on the region.

Fortunately, a firm basis of collaboration between Southeast Asianists inside and outside the region already exists, and this can be built on. For example, the Hull and UM Centres have cooperated in several areas since the 1980s, against a background of scholarly collaboration between the two universities dating back to the Hull–Malaya exchange agreement of the late 1960s. Many Hull students taking the four-year undergraduate degree in South-East Asian Studies and Language have taken advantage of the opportunity to spend part or all of their third year at UM. The Hull and UM Centres have also cooperated on a variety of research and writing projects, including the production of this volume. We hope that there will be further scope for such endeavours in the future.

Bibliography

Bahrin, Tunku Shamsul (1981), 'Southeast Asian studies in Malaysia', in Tunku Shamsul Bahrin, Chandran Jeshurun and A. Terry Rambo (eds), *A Colloquium on Southeast Asian Studies* (Singapore: Institute of Southeast Asian Studies, 1981).

Hall, D. G. E. (1981), *A History of South-east Asia*, fourth edn (London: Macmillan).

Kahin, George McT. (1994), 'Lauriston Sharp (1907–93)', *Southeast Asia Program Bulletin* (Cornell University, Ithaca, NY), Fall 1994.

King, V. T. (1990), *Between East and West: policy and practice in South-East Asian studies in Britain* (Hull: Hull University Press).

Shaharil Talib (1994), 'Post-Graduate Studies in Southeast Asian Studies: An Open Agenda' (paper presented at the international symposium on Social and Cultural Development in the Context of Economic Growth in Asia, Hanoi, 24–26 November).

1 Anthropology

Lewis Hill and
Michael Hitchcock

Introduction

The study of the anthropology of Southeast Asia can appear to be a daunting task at the beginning. There is no standard textbook covering the whole area to ease one into the vast literature, the nearest approach being the encyclopaedic studies from the Human Relations Area Files, compiled and edited by Frank LeBar et al. (1964, 1972 and 1975). These volumes have the convenience of a structured approach to the description of ethnic units in the area, and condensed notes on the knowledge accumulated about its many peoples over the 150 years or so prior to publication. They are essential and invaluable reference works. For linking this ethnography to a broader anthropological perspective one has to turn to textbooks covering parts of the area, such as those by Kroeber (1943), Peacock (1973), Provencher (1975) and Keyes (1979). An enormous amount of research has been published since these were written, but it is largely of a specialized nature, concentrating on particular problems and single peoples or states. Bringing this research together into a new overview daunts the professionals, but at least we can see attempts to cover broader subjects in studies such as *The Peoples of Borneo* (King 1993) and *The Khmers* (Mabbett and Chandler 1995) in a recently launched series. The volume of research and its explosion in many local languages may mean that no one individual will attempt the task, but the quality of international cooperation today is such that we can expect to see a collaborative work in the future. In the meantime, it is still possible to get some grasp of the whole by perceiving the patterns that persist in Southeast Asian cultures, shared traits that exist beneath the superficial diversity. This chapter attempts to offer an introduction to some of the works that have established those patterns. The authors are only too aware of this survey's limitations.

The term 'Southeast Asia' has come to denote the southeastern region of the continent of Asia, the lands that lie to the south of

China and to the east of India. 'Southeast Asia' is essentially a political rather than an anthropological concept, and has its origins in the military campaigns of the Second World War. Anthropologists have never been entirely satisfied with the term because the political borders of the region frequently cut across ties of ethnicity and religion, and largely reflect colonial spheres of influence. Despite reservations about the use of 'Southeast Asia', the term has gradually gained acceptance in anthropological circles, though not without substantial modification. In ethnographic terms parts of northeast India, southern China and Taiwan can be said to belong to Southeast Asia, whereas Irian Jaya has much in common with the Melanesian world. Links can also be drawn between Southeast Asia and Madagascar far to the west, and the numerous island cultures of the Pacific to the east. Generally speaking, however, anthropologists usually think of the region in terms of the Southeast Asian peninsula, including southern China to the 33rd parallel, and the vast Indonesian Archipelago.

The Indonesian Archipelago alone extends for almost 5,000 kilometres from east to west and – if the Philippines are included – measures approximately 2,000 kilometres from north to south. Rivers such as the Mekong (Lanchang in China) have long provided arteries for trade, as well as definitions of political borders. Mainland Southeast Asia is flanked by oceans; few locations are more than 200 kilometres from the sea. Historically, the seas brought the region's diverse peoples into contact with one another. The South China Sea might, for example, be compared with the Mediterranean as a catalyst for trade and cultural interchanges. The region is flanked by the Pacific to the east, hence the collective term 'Pacific Asia' for the countries of Northeast and Southeast Asia. Monsoon winds also permitted trade across the Indian Ocean and historical contact with India exerted a great influence on the region's development.

Much of the region is also very rugged and mountainous. There are mountains along the borders of Laos, Burma (Myanmar) and Thailand, an area known as the 'Golden Triangle' because of its association with the cultivation of opium poppies. A ridge of mountains divides Vietnam from Laos, and is the home of distinct ethnic minorities. The Indonesian Archipelago lies along an extremely active seismic zone, which can be traced through Sumatra and Java eastwards until it curves north to Ternate and then re-emerges in northern Sulawesi, from where it continues into the Philippines. The fertility of many Indonesian islands, especially Java, owes much to the periodic eruptions that have coated the land in layers of rich ash.

There are many unresolved questions concerning the early human settlement of Southeast Asia. Research on language, archaeology and anthropology, combined with new techniques in genetic fingerprinting, is, however, helping to shed some light. Archaic European terms such as 'Indo-Chinese', which classify the inhabitants of Southeast Asia as halfway between Indians and Chinese, are increasingly shown to have little analytical validity. What is clear is that Southeast Asia is one of the world's oldest sites of human settlement.

The remains of *Homo erectus* in the Solo river valley show that Java was inhabited at least a million years ago. Recent finds suggest an even earlier period of settlement. What remains unclear is how these ancient hominids relate to us, and whether or not they were the ancestors of modern Southeast Asians. During the Ice Ages, when the polar ice-caps grew and sea levels fell, mainland Southeast Asia was linked to the islands by dry land. Modern humans, who were hunter-gatherers and possessed relatively advanced stone tools, travelled down this land bridge. Australia and New Guinea, though connected to each other, remained cut off by sea from Southeast Asia. These hunter-gatherers must have developed seafaring skills in order to settle those regions. The human settlement of Australia commenced between 60,000 and 40,000 years ago, and aboriginal myths provide tantalizing clues about how this was accomplished. Humans probably brought to Australia its second placental mammal, the sandy-coloured dog known as the dingo. Semi-feral dogs still accompany human beings in canoes on hunting trips to offshore islands in eastern Indonesia. As the world warmed and the sea levels rose, Australia and New Guinea became separated from one another by water. The populations that remained in Southeast Asia began to diverge from their proto-Australian neighbours as they mingled with newcomers from elsewhere in Asia.

Language families

It used to be held that much of Southeast Asia's early history could be understood in terms of waves of migrations from northern Asia. In the archipelago, both linguistic and material-cultural features have been attributed to immigrants from southern China who settled maritime Southeast Asia from 3000 BC onwards (Bellwood 1985: 98). These people have been associated with a rectangular axe culture encountered by archaeologists, and were probably skilled farmers and craftsmen. They also knew the arts of weaving and pottery.

The newcomers, according to Bellwood (1991), spoke ancestral versions of the Austronesian languages that are encountered in the archipelago today. These Asians may have originated in southern China around Taiwan, and appear to have settled in the Philippines before moving on to Java (2000–500 BC). The spread of languages need not invariably be associated with identifiable waves of migrations since language and material culture could have been spread through interaction, especially trade.

Nevertheless migrations did occur, and Austronesian-speaking seafarers did go on to colonize the far-flung islands of Micronesia and the Pacific. Some intrepid seafarers also sailed around the Indian Ocean, and Arab writings mention a people known as the *waqwaq*, who lived on the eastern and western fringes of the Indian Ocean (Hitchcock 1992–3: 62). By the time Arabs began to publish geographical accounts of the ocean, Southeast Asian peoples were already established in Madagascar. The Malagasy peoples, especially the Merina of the interior, speak languages that closely resemble those of modern Indonesia, the closest parallel being Ma'anyan in Borneo (Kent 1970: 47). Malagasy seafaring triumphs were eclipsed by those of the Arabs, and their last attempt at supremacy seems to have been an attack on the Arab base in Pemba around AD 945–46 (Sutton 1990: 66).

The Austronesian language family comprises between 500 and 700 languages, spoken by over 200 million people in a vast geographical region ranging from Madagascar to Easter Island, and from Hawaii to New Zealand. This family includes the languages of Micronesia, Melanesia, Polynesia and coastal New Guinea, as well as the languages of the Philippines, Indonesia, Malaysia (excluding Mon-Khmer) and Madagascar. Speakers of Austronesian languages are also encountered in the highlands of Formosa (Taiwan), southern Thailand (Pattani), and in pockets in Vietnam and Cambodia (the Chams).

The term Tai is given to a family of around forty languages encountered in an area centred on Thailand, which extends northeast into Laos, north Vietnam, southwest China, and northwest into Burma and India. The spelling 'Tai' is used to avoid confusion with Thai, the largest member of the group. The link between Tai and other Asian languages remains unclear, although there may be connections with both the Sino-Tibetan and Austronesian families. Rigid definitions of Southeast Asia's boundaries are especially inappropriate in the case of the Tai peoples. Myths of origin point to an ancestral home to the south of the Yellow River in China, though the precise history and archaeology remain uncertain. Generally speaking, the Tai peoples are wet rice farmers located in the valleys alongside the main river systems of mainland Southeast Asia. The Tais may have settled the area gradually, rather than in identifiable waves of colonization.

As is the case with the Austronesian and Tai families, the speakers of so-called Austro-Asiatic languages are also scattered over a wide area. The family comprises over one hundred languages, spoken mainly in Southeast Asia but also further west in the Nicobar Islands and northern India. The largest group within the family is Vietnamese. Mon (in Burma and Thailand) and Khmer (in Cambodia) are spoken by comparatively large populations of settled farmers, but many related languages are spoken by minority groups on the fringes of the large agrarian cultures in Assam, Burma, Thailand, Laos, Cambodia, the Nicobar islands and the Malay peninsula. These minorities commonly engage in swidden farming ('slash-and-burn' or shifting cultivation) and foraging in the upland regions (Mabbett and Chandler 1995: 4–5). 'Khmer' denotes the language of Cambodia and the people who speak it. The Khmers were provided with written characters and the institutions of court culture during the period of Indic influence (Mabbett and Chandler 1995: 3). Despite these foreign borrowings, the Khmer language remains distinct from the languages that have influenced it, and is recognizably Southeast Asian. The Mon-Khmer group cannot readily be linked to a single economic or social system, and speakers of these languages include the builders of Angkor Wat and various hunter-gatherer cultures of the Malay peninsula.

Among the later arrivals in the Southeast Asian mainland were speakers of Sino-Tibetan languages, chiefly the Burmese. They conquered and partly absorbed many of the previous inhabitants of Burma, notably the Mons. Other rather diversified groups – known by general names such as Garo, Kuki, Chin, Naga, Kachin and Karen – occupied the mountainous borderlands between Burma and Bangladesh, India, China and Thailand. Miao (Hmong) and Yao (Mien) also fall into this family of languages. The Tibeto-Burman-speaking hill peoples are mainly small groups of patrilineal clans practising swidden cultivation, and contrast markedly with the state-organized wet rice cultivators of the plains.

Traditional states and religion

In those parts of Southeast Asia where there is ample rainfall, up to three crops of rice a year may be cultivated with irrigation. Historically, the bountiful harvests achieved with wet rice agriculture facilitated the growth of large court and bureaucratic systems, especially in Burma, Vietnam, Thailand, Cambodia and Java. Along the coastlines of many Southeast Asian countries can be found fishing and trading communities who share a common culture with other maritime peoples. Some, like the Malays and Bugis, spread throughout the archipelago, mingling with other trading peoples and founding powerful kingdoms. In the more remote areas, however, there are peoples who possess distinctive local systems of knowledge and belief, though there is pressure to assimilate with more dominant groups. These small-scale cultures are encountered both in the outer islands and in the remote forests and mountains of the interior. Most practise swidden cultivation and keep domestic animals; a tiny minority are engaged in hunting and the collection of forest products.

Buddhist pilgrims made their way home to China from India via Southeast Asia, and it is clear that direct communications had been established across the South China Sea by the fifth century AD. One of the most important early Southeast Asian kingdoms was Srivijaya, which grew up around a river in southeast Sumatra. Srivijaya lay along the trade routes between India and China and was described as 'a great fortified city' by a Chinese Buddhist pilgrim in the seventh century AD. It has been identified as the site of modern Palembang. Although Buddhism retained a strong grip on the kingdoms of mainland Southeast Asia, it was eventually eclipsed by the rise of Islam in the islands. Brought by southern Arabian and Muslim Indian traders, Islam spread inland from the coast, and by the end of the fifteenth century AD, Java's last Hindu-Buddhist kingdom, Majapahit, went into decline. Encircled by nascent Muslim states, starved of trade, Majapahit gradually collapsed, and many of its court found refuge in neighbouring Bali. Surrounded by Muslim Indonesians, the Balinese still preserve their Hindu-Buddhist faith.

Hindu-Buddhism and Islam are associated with the court-based cultures of Southeast Asia, and Christian missionaries won few converts in these societies. Christianity, introduced by European traders and colonists, tended to become established in the areas that lay beyond the influence of local sultans and rajahs. Thus Christian enclaves are found in North Sumatra among the peoples known collectively as the Batak, and in the upland border country of Burma, notably amongst the Karens. In the non-Muslim islands of eastern Indonesia, Christianity also became the dominant faith. Some inland peoples in Borneo, such as the Iban, eventually adopted Christianity. In the Philippines, which lay on the Hindu-Buddhist periphery, the picture is somewhat different. Christianity became the majority religion there, converting the northern and central islands and competing with the Muslim sultans to dominate the south.

Southeast Asia is not only linguistically and ethnically heterogeneous, but it is also varied in terms of politics and religion. The analytical frameworks employed by anthropologists have to take into account this complexity, and consequently Southeast Asia has yielded some of the richest literature in the discipline. Anthropological research has furthermore not been confined to small-scale societies, as has largely been the case in Africa and Europe, and in Southeast Asia anthropologists have ventured into areas traditionally covered by sociologists. The distinction between the two disciplines in the Southeast Asian context is consequently blurred. The situation is further complicated by the fact that varying schools of thought and research traditions arose in the areas colonized by different European powers. Anthropology developed in several distinctive ways within the region, though the trend since decolonization has been towards extensive cross-fertilization. Because of this variety it makes sense to look at the different forms of anthropology separately before moving on to a consideration of more recent developments within the wider context of the discipline.

Early anthropology

Neither sociology nor anthropology emerged fully fledged from the reflections of their presumptive founders, Auguste Comte and Sir Edward Tylor, and the fact that the study of human society in Western thought is much older should not be overlooked (Hogden 1971: 7–8). Classical scholars such as Herodotus, Pliny and Solinus discussed the customs and cultures of other cultures, as did the medieval encyclopaedists. During the sixteenth and seventeenth centuries curiosity concerning the exotic practices of peoples in faraway places sharpened, and this laid the foundations of modern anthropology, comparative religion and related subjects.

The focus on anthropology's European colonial heritage also diverts attention from the non-Western traditions, notably the writings of Arab, Chinese and Indian explorers, an especially important consideration with regard to Southeast Asia. For example, much of what we know about life in Yashodharapura (Angkor Thom) is derived from the eyewitness accounts of the thirteenth-century Chinese ethnographer, Zhou Daguan (Chou Ta-Kuan). There are also fragments in the surveys of the known world by two other Chinese scholars, Ma Tualin and Zhao Rugua, based on traders' reports. Zhou Daguan was a member of an embassy that was sent by the Yuan Emperor of China, Timur Khan (grandson of Kublai Khan) to learn about the kingdom of Zhenla or Kambuja. The emissaries lived in Yashodharapura from 1296 to 1297, with the aim of finding out how the Khmer state worked, what the people believed in, and what they grew and ate. These were practical concerns for Chinese trade and possibly for military occupation, much in the way that the Americans compiled information on Pacific societies during the Second World War (Murray 1994: 16).

The extension of Mongol power and influence not only facilitated the development of Chinese ethnography, but also provided Europeans with their first glimpses of Southeast Asia. The Vatican sent emissaries

to report on the ethnological characteristics of the Mongols, and under
the patronage of Kublai Khan the Polos made their celebrated journeys
to the East (Hogden 1971: 60). Marco Polo visited many of China's
ancient cities – Nanking, Soochow and Hang-chan – and wrote ad-
miringly of their cultural refinement. He mentions the practices of
droit du seigneur in 'Indo-China' and of couvade in Zaranda, to the
northeast of Bhamo in Burma, where the temples were decorated with
tinkling bells, and the people with gold teeth and tattoos. He is also
credited with the first European mention of the custom of betel-
chewing. Although Marco Polo retained an objectivity that was unusual
for the period, it became more difficult for him to distinguish fact
from hearsay when he ventured further afield. He also succumbed to
the medieval propensity for the fabulous when describing faraway
places and thus cannibalism is ascribed on doubtful evidence to
Sumatra, the islands off India, the Andaman islands and Japan
(Hogden 1971: 99–101).

Another two centuries elapsed before Marco Polo's accounts of
Southeast Asia were superseded in Europe by the discoveries of the
Portuguese and Spanish, and later the Dutch and English. One of the
first reports by seafarers to leave an enduring impression on the Euro-
pean consciousness was Cornelis de Houtman's record of his visit to
Bali in 1571. There is some evidence that Magellan's expedition had
sighted the island on its homeward voyage, and that the Portuguese
had contacted Bali in the mid-sixteenth century. The English under
Sir Francis Drake and Thomas Cavendish also preceded the Dutch by
a few years, so de Houtman was not the first European to visit Bali.
Western writers, however, made much of the fact that two of de
Houtman's sailors abandoned ship, allegedly because of the charms of
Balinese women (Boon 1977: 10). Jacobean Samuel Purchas, for example, produced an English version of de Houtman's report combined
with the journals of other Dutch mariners in order to highlight trade
opportunities in the East. Purchas took liberties with the Dutch sources
when describing the Hindu faith of the island, the custom of suttee
and the entourage of the king (Boon 1977: 11–12). An illustration
based on engravings from de Houtman's report was also published
with a summary of Dutch seafaring records in a German compendium
of travel literature edited by Levin Hulsius in 1598 (Boon 1977: 17).

It was not only written accounts of exotic cultures that began to
attract the attention of learned men in Europe, but also material
evidence of their existence. By the seventeenth century, examples of
human handicrafts began to find their way into collections that had
hitherto largely been concerned with classical antiquity and natural
history. The collectors and their patrons were deeply interested in the

problems associated with preserving, classifying and displaying their acquisitions, and this had implications for the development of anthropology. Larger items were often placed in halls of curiosities, and to attract the public acquisitions were often arranged on a plan copied from an apothecary's shop. For example, the walls of Tradescant's Ark in London, later to become the Ashmolean Museum in Oxford, were hung with all manner of natural and man-made curiosities (Hogden 1971: 119–21). Southeast Asian artefacts, notably three Krisses and a Moluccan sword, were included in the original Tradescant collection (MacGregor 1983: 150–7).

The British contribution

Britain can rightly lay claim to an important place in the history of anthropological research on Southeast Asia. This was largely due to its colonial past, and much has been written following Asad (1973) about the guilt of anthropologists as willing if ineffectual handmaidens of nineteenth- and twentieth-century imperialism. Colonialism brought Europeans into direct contact with alien cultures, and provided hitherto unrivalled opportunities for information gathering. However, what Talal Asad has referred to as 'the colonial encounter' was a complex process involving many different kinds of people and widely varying perspectives. The authors of accounts of Southeast Asia that could be classed as 'anthropological' ranged from the most distinguished civil servants to more humble missionaries and travellers. For example, one of the most detailed accounts of the people of Java in the English language was written by Sir Thomas Stamford Raffles (1817). From 1811 to 1816 Raffles, who later founded Singapore, administered the Dutch colonies during the Napoleonic occupation of the Netherlands, as the lieutenant governor-general in Batavia (Jakarta).

Scholar-administrators, soldiers, missionaries, travellers and others produced substantial reports on the peoples of Burma, the Malay Peninsula and northern Borneo. There was a significant concentration of anthropological research in Burma following its piecemeal absorption into British India during the nineteenth century. Sir J. G. Scott, for example, who was a remarkable linguist, gave us very detailed studies of the Burmese and the last Burmese court and the Shans, as well as accounts of other hill peoples of Burma (Scott 1910, 1921, 1932; Scott and Hardiman 1900). Systematic fieldwork by researchers informed with specifically anthropological concepts and methodologies came later, though the scholar-administrators were not working in a complete intellectual vacuum. From 1874 onwards, researchers began to organize their data in accordance with the principles laid down in *Notes and*

Queries on Anthropology, published in that year. Later, after the foundation of the Pitt Rivers Museum in Oxford in 1884, they gained the
support of the first curator, Henry Balfour (1863–1939) who kept up
an active correspondence with ethnographers in distant colonial out-
posts. Edward Tylor, officially attached to the Pitt Rivers Museum as
a lecturer, also exerted an influence, and his publications *Researches into
the Early History of Mankind* (1865) and *Primitive Culture* (1871) were
widely read.

The major sources of information became learned journals,
monographs, reports and official gazetteers. For example, under the
government of India, a remarkable series of ethnographic monographs
emerged on the Nagas and neighbouring peoples of the Assam–Burma
borderlands. These included works on the Meithei by T. C. Hodson
(1908), the Angami Nagas and the Sema Nagas by J. H. Hutton (1921a
and 1921b), the Lushei-Kuki (Mizo) by Lt. Col. J. Shakespear (1912),
the Lhota Nagas (1922), the Ao Nagas (1926) and the Rengma (1937)
by J. P. Mills, the Thado by W. Shaw (1929) and the Lakher by N. E.
Parry (1932). Hutton was the key figure here, encouraging the officers
who loved and admired the hill peoples to put their knowledge into
print. When he became involved with the 1931 Census of India he
extended the practice of publishing as appendices reports by district
officers on little-known peoples which had been a feature in earlier, less
comprehensive census reports. The well-coordinated ethnographic work
of this group was the foundation for all later work in the area by
professional anthropologists such as Tarak Chandra Das (1945) and
Christoph von Furer-Haimendorf (1939). It also provided material for
more recent pioneering work in the medium of video discs for museum
ethnography at Cambridge University (Jacobs et al. 1990).

With the appointments of Hutton to the University of Cambridge
and Mills to the University of London, the results of colonial research
were channelled into academic anthropology. As Hutton and the
younger Mills worked on the Nagas, their ideas moved away from
evolutionary anthropology towards diffusionism and eventually functionalism. By the 1930s one of the problems confronting the scholar-
administrators was how concepts derived from the West might be
utilized within the context of Asian culture and society. In *The Economics of the Central Chin*, for example, H. N. C. Stevenson discusses
how Western economic theory might be applied to a non-Western
society.

The anthropology developed in the Malay peninsula and northern
Borneo was rather different from that developed in Burma. Scholar-
administrators and others produced solid ethnographies of the peoples,
but here ethnographic museums were established very early, and

worked with anthropologists and museums in Britain as inspirations and supports for local research. In Singapore the Library and Museum was founded in 1823; in the peninsula, the Perak Museum was built in 1886 and in Borneo, the Sarawak Museum began in 1888. Thus we have solid ethnographies by administrators such as those by W. W. Skeat and Charles Blagden (1906), Charles Hose and William McDougall (1912), and Owen Rutter (1929), being backed by many books and papers by Ifor Evans, Leonard Wray, Robert Shelford, R. O. Winstedt, R. J. Wilkinson and others involved with the museums. A. C. Haddon in Cambridge was one of the important home links, and he and Laura Start published a catalogue of the Iban textiles that Haddon had brought back to Cambridge. The publication was a by-product of the Torres Straits Expedition in 1899, when Haddon also visited Sarawak.

There was a general rise in interest in anthropology during the inter-war years, and various kinds of studies were conducted in Southeast Asia. Bali, which became a mecca for the international set, attracted a number of scholars later to become famous anthropologists (Margaret Mead, Jane Belo, Claire Holt, Gregory Bateson) and others who became drawn to the subject (Katherine Mehrson, Colin McPhee, Beryl de Zoete). In Bali, the German-Russian artist, Walter Spies, was the host and guide to the visiting artists and academics. In particular, Spies was de Zoete's mentor in Balinese culture; together they wrote *Dance and Drama in Bali* (1938). De Zoete was not a trained anthropologist, but her book provided an exemplary ethnography of the Balinese dance dramas.

It was not until just before the outbreak of the Pacific War that research was undertaken in Southeast Asia by professional anthropologists using specifically anthropological approaches. Malinowski's teaching at the London School of Economics (LSE) was a vital influence in this context. One of the most distinguished of these pre-war practitioners was Edmund Leach, who undertook field research in the Kachin Hills area of highland Burma from 1939. In his *Political Systems of Highland Burma* (1954), Leach developed a theory of oscillation of political systems and demonstrated how the concept of the tribe might not be appropriate for the analysis of Southeast Asian societies. Leach showed how people over a wide area, often speaking different languages and maintaining distinct cultural identities, could participate in a single social system. Leach also demolished the idea that certain types of social organization could be linked to particular kinds of ecology.

Another researcher who figured prominently in Britain's post-war contribution to Southeast Asian anthropology was Raymond Firth. He and his wife, Rosemary Firth, conducted research among the Kelantan Malays (1939–40), which led to *Housekeeping among Malay Peasants* (1943) and *Malay Fishermen: their peasant economy* (1946). Subsequently, both Firth and Leach were given the task of undertaking socio-economic surveys in British-administered territories by the Colonial Social Science Research Council. Firth conducted a survey of Malaya (published 1948), and Leach undertook preliminary research in the Crown Colony of Sarawak (published 1950) and, more briefly, in British North Borneo. The aim of the surveys was to provide the colonial authorities with ethnographic information with reference to development and the needs of the administration (King 1989: 18). Leach's recommendations led to the completion of a series of influential anthropological studies: Freeman's work on the Iban (1970), Geddes on the Bidayuh (Land Dayak) (1954), Morris on the Coastal Melanau (1953) and Ti'en Ju-K'ang on Chinese social structure (1953). Firth's proposals also led to Maurice Freedman (with his wife Judith Djamour) carrying out research in Singapore, mainly because the Malayan Emergency made fieldwork in Malaya impossible. Leach and Firth went on to teach at the LSE after the war, Leach up until 1953 when he moved to Cambridge, and Firth more permanently.

The British-sponsored research in Southeast Asia not only yielded ethnographic information, but also reflected the theoretical changes that were taking place within the discipline. With the publication of Meyer Fortes and Evans-Pritchard's co-edited *African Political Systems* (1940), anthropologists increasingly began to abandon the functionalism associated with Malinowski in favour of what came to be known as structural-functionalism. This emergent school of thought, with its emphasis on models and the idea that the structure of a group is related to the specific tasks it performs, can be detected in the Sarawak studies of Geddes, Leach and Morris. The group's functions are commonly divided into three types – task, control and expression – which may be present in varying proportions, though care needs to be taken in distinguishing explicit functions of which the participants were not necessarily aware, but which could be detected by the analyst.

During the 1950s, the LSE supported much of Britain's anthropological research on Southeast Asia and, very importantly, provided publication outlets. Freedman and Djamour became particularly influential figures there. Freedman and Djamour were later closely associated with the London–Cornell Project on South and South-East Asian Studies, which also helped the Firths to revisit Kelantan in 1963. The LSE monographs provide a list of many British-based anthropologists and sociologists specializing on Southeast Asia in the post-war years: Rosemary Firth (1943/1966), Ti'en Ju-K'ang (1953),

Alan A. J. Elliott (1955), J. M. Gullick (1958/1965/1988), Judith Djamour (1959 and 1966), L. H. Palmier (1960), M. G. Swift (1965), E. R. Leach (1954), Derek Freeman (1970) and W. E. Willmott (1970). The LSE maintained this tradition into the 1980s and beyond, with publications such as those by Wazir-Jahan Karim (1981), William Wilder (1982) and Thomas Gibson (1986). A number of anthropologists who have continued to work on Southeast Asia completed their doctorates at the LSE: Roy Ellen (Moluccas), Jeremy Kemp (Thailand), Joel Kahn (Sumatra), Maila Stivens (Malaysia), Andrew Turton (Thailand), and Monica Janowski (Sarawak) (King 1989: 19).

Another British centre that became increasingly influential from the late 1950s onwards was the Institute of Social Anthropology at Oxford. This was largely due to the energy and commitment of Rodney Needham, who had conducted research in Sarawak (on the Penan), Malaya and the island of Sumba. He wrote extensively on the societies of the region, ranging from the Assam border region and other highland areas of mainland Southeast Asia, through the Malay Peninsula, Borneo, Sumatra and East Indonesia. In accordance with Lévi-Strauss and the Dutch structuralists, Needham emphasized the need to analyse societies in terms of their structures. Needham has been an influential theorist, particularly on the study of prescriptive marriage systems and symbolic classification.

Needham supervised many doctoral theses at Oxford on the peoples of Southeast Asia, and the Institute's work on the region was considerably strengthened with the appointment of R. H. Barnes. Recent Oxford students of Southeast Asian anthropology have included: Kirk Endicott (Malays and Batek), Clark Cunningham (Atoni), James Fox (Rote), Erik Jensen (Iban), Andrew Duff-Cooper (Lombok Balinese), Gregory and Christine Forth (Rindi, Sumba), Signe Howell (Chewong, Malaysia), David Hicks (Tetum, Timor), David Napier (Balinese), Robert Parkin (Austro-Asiatic kinship and marriage), Andrew Beatty (Nias and Java) and Sian Jay (Ngaju Dayak). Alongside this mainstream social anthropology, material culture studies continued at the Pitt Rivers Museum. Ruth Barnes (Lamalera, Lembata) and Michael Hitchcock (Bima, Sumbawa) both completed their theses at the Department of Ethnology and Prehistory there (King 1989: 20).

With Leach's appointment, it might have been expected that Cambridge would develop additional research strength on Southeast Asia, but the university's regional anthropological foci lay elsewhere. Thus while the appointments of Stanley Tambiah (1966) and Barbara Ward (early 1970s) produced some excellent studies, they did not result in a Southeast Asian focus for the department, though a number of postgraduate students – including Roxana Waterson (Toraja, Sulawesi) and C. W. Watson (Kerinci, Sumatra) – completed their theses at Cambridge. Nevertheless, Leach's interest in political systems and Kachin marriage may be linked to the structuralism of Lévi-Strauss, as can Tambiah's structural treatment of Thai Buddhism (1970, 1976, 1984). The Southeast Asian interest at Cambridge is currently maintained by Leo Howe, who wrote his thesis at Edinburgh, and anthropological research on the region is sponsored by the Evans Fund. Apart from the LSE, Oxford and Cambridge, other British universities have established expertise on Southeast Asian anthropology. Two London colleges, the School of Oriental and African Studies and University College, London, have an active record of research on the region and recent postgraduate theses on Southeast Asia have included work by Brian Durrans, Nicholas Tapp, Felicia Hughes-Freeland, Angela Hobart and Mark Hobart. The universities of Kent at Canterbury and Hull also have substantial expertise on Southeast Asia. Doctoral theses on Southeast Asian anthropology completed at Hull include those by Zainal bin Kling (Malays of Sarawak), V. T. King (Maloh/Embaloh), Robert Cooper (Hmong), Martin Barber (Lao), Mark Turner (Ilocano), Wathana Wongsekiartirat (Thai), Jean Morrison (Bajau Laut), Carol Davis (Minangkabau) and Daniel Arghiros (Thai).

Dutch anthropology

We are fortunate in having available two detailed works on the development of anthropology in Indonesia by Koentjaraningrat (1967: 1–29, and 1975). The reader is referred to these excellent studies rather than an attempt being made to summarize them here, for they cover, among other subjects, the early explorers who contributed to anthropology, the great expeditions, prominent early Dutch theorists such as George Wilken, the works by linguists and missionaries such as N. Adriani and A. C. Kruyt (1912–14, Central Sulawesi), outstanding scholar administrators such as C. Snouck Hurgronje (1893–1906 Achehnese) and the enormous amount of work done on *adatrecht* (customary law).

The history of anthropology in the Netherlands is closely associated with the Dutch colonial experience and, in particular, with the rapid rise in Indonesian studies at the end of the nineteenth and beginning of the twentieth centuries. These developments were combined with a higher standard of training offered to civil servants and missionaries prior to their departure to the Netherlands East Indies and, to a certain extent, this improved the quality of reportage on the indigenous peoples and customs. The Dutch developed their own systematic methods of recording, but also gradually adapted the British publication, *Notes and Queries on Anthropology* (1874), to their own needs. Expeditions made specifically for the purpose of exploring tropical areas scientifically and for collecting data on the peoples living there had begun some time before the turn of the century. Most notable was the 23-member *Sumatra-Expeditie* organized by P. J. Veth in 1877–79 (Veth 1881–92), which included David Daniel Verth, who used photographs to brighten up his travelogue of the Padang Highlands (*Toekang Potret* 1989: 23). Among the expeditions carried out at a slightly later date were those organized by the German geographer, Kükenthal, in 1893, and by the two Swiss doctors P. and F. Sarasin (1893–96, 1902–3). Maas, another German explorer, surveyed Central Sumatra, beginning at Padang and venturing as far as Indrapura (Koentjaraningrat 1975: 44). In 1910, Dr Johanner Elbert, the German naturalist, explored the islands of East Indonesia, Southwest Sulawesi and several areas in Java and Sumatra. His two volume report, *Die Sunda Expedition* (1911–12) contains scattered but detailed accounts of the peoples inhabiting the areas visited.

Indonesians as well as Europeans were active as explorer-ethnographers at the turn of the century. J. E. Tehupeiorij, for example, an Ambonese medical doctor, accompanied the Central Borneo expedition of 1903–4, and wrote an account of his travels entitled *Onder de Dajaks in Centraal-Borneo* (1906). The Dutch surgeon-explorer A. W. Nieuwenhuis was also assisted by an Indonesian, a Javanese sergeant, Jean Demmeni, who acted as the expedition's photographer. Nieuwenhuis commenced research in Borneo in 1894, undertaking expeditions from Pontianak to Samarinda through the unexplored reaches of the Mahakan River (1896–97). Their journey ended in 1899, but late that year the two men returned to Central Borneo as part of an official expedition which lasted until 1900 (*Toekang Potret* 1989: 37–9). In 1904 Nieuwenhuis was appointed to a chair in 'The history, literature, antiquities, institutions and the manners and customs of the peoples of the Indies archipelago etc.' at the University of Leiden, and his inaugural address indicates his interest in the relationship between the environment and culture. He later developed these ideas in his book *Die Wurzeln de Animismus* (1917), especially with regard to the early stages of the development of cultures and, in particular, religion. Nieuwenhuis subsequently became interested in theories of totemism, particularly those he referred to as *Geschlechts-* or *Sexual-totemismus* (Koentjaraningrat 1975: 47).

Under the broad heading of Dutch anthropology special mention needs to be made of the Austrian anthropologist, Robert von Heine-Geldern. Surveying the information available at the time, von Heine-Geldern (1932) drew conclusions about the links between the Asian mainland and Southeast Asia. Although his work on migrations and diffusion has limited contemporary applicability, the scope of his research remains impressive.

The link between Leiden and Indonesia eventually gave rise to Dutch structural anthropology and to what is sometimes erroneously referred to as the 'Leiden school' (P. E. de Josselin de Jong 1977: 9). Leiden was not, however, the only 'school' in Holland: social or cultural anthropology at the University of Amsterdam has an equally distinctive character and history. Anthropology also became established at other Dutch universities, but this happened at a later date and therefore need not concern us at this juncture. It is, however, helpful to compare the Amsterdam and Leiden traditions in order to appreciate the development of Dutch anthropology in Southeast Asia.

In Amsterdam, anthropology was historically associated with the other social sciences (especially Wertheim's non-Western sociology) and tended to be comparativist rather than regionally specialized. By way of contrast, Leiden was more specifically linked with Indonesian studies.

Cultural anthropology – as the subject is referred to in Holland – was also strongly influenced by the Netherlands' relationship with Indonesia. Cultural anthropology in the Netherlands, despite its American-sounding designation, follows the European tradition of relative narrowness of scope and thus resembles social anthropology. Subjects such as physical anthropology, prehistory, archaeology and linguistics are regarded as independent disciplines in the Netherlands and are thus set apart from cultural anthropology (P. E. de Josselin de Jong 1977: 1–2).

A similar situation prevails in Britain, although the tendency in both countries since the 1980s has been towards a less pronounced demarcation of disciplinary boundaries. What is noteworthy, however, is that several topics in Leiden, which are currently regarded as properly anthropological, were once separated from the mainstream of social and cultural anthropology. There was, for example, the tendency to link the study of the more complex Asian societies with language and literature studies, rather than with anthropology. If, for example, a scholar was interested in modern Indian society, they would study Sanskrit as an Indologist before taking up the sociology of India as a sideline. A person interested in customary law was not considered to belong to a sub-discipline within anthropology, but to be a different kind of scholar altogether, a specialist in *adatrecht* (customary law). It was not until 1963 that the Chair of Customary Law, in the Faculty of Law, and the Chair of Cultural Anthropology, in the Faculty of Arts, found a common meeting ground in the Faculty of Social Sciences (P. E. de Josselin de Jong 1977: 2–3).

The Dutch structural anthropologists were particularly concerned with symbolism, and devoted attention to the analysis of the thoughts and actions of Southeast Asian peoples within the contexts of their own cultures. This thematic specialization was derived from the application of insights taken from sociological theory to the study of the indigenous peoples of the Dutch East Indies (Teljeur 1990: 1). The theoretical origins of this branch of anthropology can be detected in the work of Durkheim and Mauss and their publication entitled *De quelques formes primitives de classification* (1903). This theoretical perspective was not, however, given an institutional base until the appointment of J. P. B. de Josselin de Jong to the Chair of Indonesian and General Anthropology at Leiden in 1935. That year also witnessed F. A. E. van Wouden's defence of his influential thesis entitled 'Types of Social Structure in Eastern Indonesia' (de Josselin de Jong 1984: 1).

Dutch structural anthropology developed into a separate school within the wider fields of social and cultural anthropology, and is most accurately referred to as the 'Dutch School', to acknowledge scholars such as H. G. Schulte Nordholt (Utrecht) who were not based at Leiden. The school reached a watershed in 1949 when J. P. B. de Josselin de Jong introduced Lévi-Strauss to the English-speaking world, and from that point on the 'Dutch School' became associated with structuralism. P. E. de Josselin de Jong, nephew of J. P. B. de Josselin de Jong, refers to this school as 'structural anthropology', though this is not completely accurate: some anthropologists prefer the thematic term 'symbolic anthropology' (Teljeur 1990: 4). As the school's theoretical basis became more clearly defined, some of the unnecessary colonial baggage, such as social determinism, was dispensed with. The school attracted attention from outside the Netherlands, most notably in Oxford, and continued to be admired for its work on symbolic classification. It was closely associated in this respect with an approach known as the Field of Anthropological Study (FAS or, in Dutch, *ethnologisch studieveld*), which was launched by J. P. B. de Josselin de Jong in 1935 (Niessen 1985: 1).

From the 1930s onwards the Dutch came to regard the cultures of maritime Southeast Asia as varieties of a general type (P. E. de Josselin de Jong 1984: 2). Although the peoples of the archipelago were divided into numerous distinct ethnic groups, J. P. B. de Josselin de Jong argued that they were united by a common cultural sub-stratum, which he labelled the 'structural core'. The initial assumptions of the Dutch anthropologists were based partly on the ethnographic studies available at the time and the knowledge that the languages of the Indonesian archipelago were closely related to one another. From the start the boundaries of the FAS were difficult to define, since it was known that the Indonesian languages were also related to the Melanesian and Polynesian branches of the Austronesian field. It therefore remained unclear whether the limits of the field of study were marked by the Indonesian, Austronesian or even Austric languages (P. E. de Josselin de Jong 1984: 5).

From the beginning, the FAS concept was a flexible one that was tied neither to specific cultural phenomena nor to particular geographical or linguistic groupings (P. E. de Josselin de Jong 1984: 257). This flexibility raised problems, not least because it obscured the boundaries between comparative linguistics and cultural anthropology. What J. P. B. de Josselin de Jong may have had in mind, though he never made it explicit, was the comparative study of societies that appeared to be 'genetically linked' with one another. This assumption was based on the proven links between the languages of the Indonesian archipelago, and as the body of knowledge grew, the linguistic term 'Austronesian' began to be applied more generally to cultural phenomena. Customs that appeared to have survived from the pre-Indic era could thus be described as 'Austronesian', as could whole societies that lay beyond the spheres of Islamic and Indic influence.

Having adopted concepts from comparative linguistics, the exponents of FAS began to realize that research in the vast region encompassed by the Austronesian languages would prove unwieldy. They therefore devised practical guidelines for conducting more manageable research, and P. E. de Josselin de Jong eventually recommended dividing the archipelago into two research fields delineated by sub-branches of the Austronesian family. The boundary between the two fields was to be drawn between the Western Austronesian and Central-Eastern Austronesian areas 'beginning, at its southern extremity, in Sumbawa' (P. E. de Josselin de Jong 1984: 257). Thus the island of Sumbawa came to be regarded as occupying an intermediate point between western and eastern Indonesia. The people of the west of the island, the Tau Semawa, are culturally and linguistically affiliated with the western archipelago, especially with the Sasak of Lombok. In contrast, the Bimanese of the east are oriented to eastern Indonesia, the so-called 'Groote Ooost' region denoted by van Wouden in 1935.

In keeping with the proposal outlined by van Wouden, a great deal of attention was later devoted by anthropologists to the peoples of Flores, Sumba and Timor, and the smaller islands of eastern Indonesia. The last few decades have seen an active programme of ethnography and comparative research by Dutch, British, French and American anthropologists (Fox 1980; P. E. de Josselin de Jong 1984). Much of this research has been concerned with the systems of prescriptive and preferential marriage alliance that van Wouden regarded as prototypic

for the region (Just 1986: 21). However, Sumbawa, the meeting point
of the two sub-regions, remained comparatively neglected, and anthropological research was mainly confined to the west of the island
until the late 1970s. There may have been a tendency to overlook the
island because it was not only transitional but was also complicated by
a long history of Islam. Sumbawa was too marginal to engage the
attention of scholars interested in the major cultures of the western
archipelago, and yet too influenced by Islam to attract scholars working
on the eastern Indonesian FAS.

Scholars working on large-scale cultures such as Java also found de
Josselin de Jong's analytical frameworks helpful. For example, Rassers
relied heavily on de Josselin de Jong's concept of the divine trickster
in his studies on the symbolic meaning of ornaments and the sacred
Javanese dagger, the *keris* (Koentjaraningrat 1975: 145). Many of de
Josselin de Jong's students likewise tried to reconstruct similarities
between the social structures of non-European cultures by searching
for ancient structural principles in kinship systems and by examining
myths for examples of totemic symbols, dualism and initiation rites,
etc. Thus the influence of de Josselin de Jong can be detected in the
work of G. J. Held (the Mahabharata epic, 1935), J. Ph. Duyvendak
(West Seram, 1926), H. J. Friedericy (Bugis, Makasars, 1933), F. A. E.
van Wouden (Nusa Tenggara, 1935, 1968), C. Nooteboom (East
Sumba, 1940), M. M. Nicolspeyer (Alorese, 1940), H. Schärer (Ngaju,
1946, 1963), Koes Sardjono (Java, 1947), P. E. de Josselin de Jong
(Minangkabau, Negri Sembilan, 1951), N. J. C. Geise (Badui, Java,
1952), R. E. Downs (Toraja, 1956) and P. O. L. Tobing (Toba Batak,
1963).

French perspectives

As was the case elsewhere in Europe, the French anthropological
tradition owes much to the work of travellers and traders, missionaries
and colonial officials. French anthropology has been mainly, but not
exclusively, concerned with the countries that comprised French Indochina: Laos, Vietnam and Cambodia. The French tradition is well
established and there is a substantial body of literature written in
French pertaining to Southeast Asia, although much of it is concerned
with the languages, literature, history, archaeology and geography of
the region. The work of G. Coedès, for example, is recognizably part
of this tradition. The continuity of French anthropology has, however,
been disrupted by the wars that engulfed their former possessions
during the period of decolonization. But despite these problems,
American anthropologists such as Gerald Hickey (1964, 1982a, 1982b)

were beneficiaries of work conducted earlier by the French, especially
the colonial ethnology on the 'Montagnards'.

Had it not been for the sheer diversity of the colonial experience,
certain ethnological discoveries would probably not have been made as
early as they were. For example, the fact that the French had colonial
possessions in both Madagascar and Southeast Asia doubtless facilitated
research on the link between the two regions, though it was not until
the early twentieth century that the connection was firmly established.
Alfred Grandidier and his son Guillaume were the first to propound
the view that the ancestors of the Malagasy came from South Asia, a
perspective that was later modified by other scholars (Mutibwa 1974:
3). The Grandidiers paved the way for research on the material culture,
social organization, linguistics and ethnobotany of Madagascar, leading
to the conclusion that the ancestors of the Malagasy originated in the
Indonesian Archipelago. The theme was taken up by Hubert Deschamps, who charted the distribution of outrigger canoes around the
Indian Ocean and speculated that the proto-Malagasy had lived for
several generations in East Africa before moving on to Madagascar
(Deschamps 1961: 15; Mutibwa 1974: 3). There was also the important
Mekong expedition of Doudart de Lagrée and François Garnier in
1873, and work by Henri Mouhot on Siam and Laos.

French anthropology is also widely associated with the structuralist
tradition of Lévi-Strauss, and his antecedents and followers, and thus
cannot readily be separated from French sociology and philosophy. In
terms of field research, Lévi-Strauss was concerned primarily with
South America and therefore his Southeast Asian connections have
been somewhat overlooked. Lévi-Strauss did, however, briefly conduct
research in the Chittagong Hill Tracts, leading to some short reports
(e.g. Lévi-Strauss 1952). This was followed by another brief account
of the Chittagong area, which was written by P. Bessaignet to encourage his students. Lévi-Strauss has also been involved in Southeast
Asian research in other ways, notably in the support and encouragement he provided for researchers such as George Condominas. In 1948
Condominas undertook a study of the Mnong Gar, a Montagnard
people in a remote highland village in Vietnam. The outcome was *We
Have Eaten the Forest* (1957, 1977), an example of 'stream of consciousness' reportage, written in a recognizably literary style with little
of the jargon and theorizing associated with more conventional
ethnographies. Jacques Dournes' work on the 'Montagnards' (e.g. 1972)
also grew out of an extended study, although, generally speaking, the
French conducted less fieldwork than the British and Dutch.

The French also produced a series of substantial studies that were
designed to provide baseline data on the peoples of Southeast Asia.

For example, J. Delvert's book, *Le Paysan cambodgien* (1961), is based on research carried out in the 1940s and 1950s, and is full of detailed information on many aspects of Khmer rural society. S. Thierry's *Les Khmers* (1964) offers a brief but finely written account of the early history and traditional culture of the Khmers. Thierry's work also extended to folk culture as embodied in Cambodian oral traditions, in *Etude d'un corpus de contes cambodgiens* (1978). E. Porée-Maspero's major study of Khmer traditional culture and its origins, which appeared in three volumes entitled *Etude sur les rites agraires des cambodgiens* (1962–69), is often overlooked. Fascinating insights into Khmer beliefs regarding the supernatural world are provided by Ang Chouléan's *Les Etres surnaturels dans la religion populaire khmère* (1986). P. Mus's *India Seen From the East: Indian and indigenous cults in Champa* (1975) is still a significant interpretation of the influence of Indian culture on mainland Southeast Asia.

American perspectives

The Americans maintained a colonial presence in Southeast Asia (in the Philippines), but for a much shorter period than the British, Dutch and French. Although the Americans developed considerable expertise on the Philippines, their research coverage was broader, with notable foci on Indonesia and Thailand. Thus although it is misleading to link the development of American anthropology too closely to the colonial experience, there are parallels with the European traditions, especially with regard to the role played by missionaries and explorers. Like the Europeans, the Americans made use of surveys, particularly in the Philippines in the 1920s and 1930s. There were also early studies on religion and the customary laws of the Philippine peoples, such as Laura Benedict's work on the Bagobo religion (1916) and R. F. Barton's on the Ifugao and Kalinga (1919, 1946, 1949). With Barton, legal systems became a favourite theme, later taken up by Edward Dozier (1966), Stuart Schlegel (1970), Thomas Kiefer (1972) and others. Also important were the Chicago programmes on the Philippines of Fred Eggan and H. Otley Beyer. A distinctive, but not unique, feature of American anthropology has been its practitioners' sometimes uneasy relationship with the United States government. This was particularly the case during the Vietnam War, when anthropological research was sometimes used as a cover for more clandestine activities, especially espionage (Wakin 1992). This has made American anthropologists particularly sensitive to issues such as academic freedom and the rights of indigenous peoples.

Generally speaking, American anthropology reflects the debates taking place within the discipline as a whole, though certain distinctive features can be associated with the Southeast Asian experience. Between 1936 and 1939, for example, Gregory Bateson and Margaret Mead collaborated in the study of a Balinese village. Bateson, a British citizen, had just completed work on *Naven* (1936), his acclaimed monograph on New Guinea, whereas Mead was already renowned as the author of *Coming of Age in Samoa* (1928). As a student of Franz Boas, Mead subscribed to the view that social rather than genetic factors shaped human behaviour, the so-called 'nature versus nurture' debate. The Balinese project investigated these issues and made several important contributions to anthropology, with Mead and Bateson's integration of film, photography and ethnographic research being particularly important. The outcome was *Balinese Character* (1942), which included a chapter by Bateson on Balinese camera-consciousness and the factors that diminish this problem. This chapter is widely regarded as formative within the development of what was later known as visual anthropology.

Knowledge of Burma was enhanced by F. K. Lehman's work on the Chin and how they have adapted to Burmese civilization (1963). A number of scholars worked on Burmese Buddhism and popular religion, notably Manning Nash (1965) with his village studies of Buddhism and development, and Melford Spiro using a psychological approach (1967, 1971). These became key works in the vigorous debates about the nature of Buddhism as practised in Southeast Asia (see Keyes 1979: 109–10 for a bibliography).

Americans have conducted important research on Indonesia, especially the Massachusetts Institute of Technology (MIT) studies on Java. Robert Jay, for example, produced the first solid study of a Javanese community in the English language (1963), whereas Alice Dewey provided the first account of 'peasant marketing' on that island (1963). Clifford Geertz's *The Religion of Java* (1960) and Hildred Geertz's work on Javanese kinship (1961) occupy a special place within anthropology as a whole and not just Southeast Asian research. Such is the quality of Clifford Geertz's writing that he has attracted attention outside anthropology from disciplines such as theology and English. Geertz's division of Javanese society into three broad categories – the aristocracy-bureaucracy of the state as bearers of Javanese high culture with mystical and Hindu–Buddhist roots, the Javanese merchant class of the urban markets as bearers of orthodox Islam, and the peasantry of the countryside as bearers of the ancient 'animist' traditions – was adopted as a model by many other scholars for its elegant simplicity, often with only minor amendments. Yet the study was soon criticized by Koentjaraningrat (1963) for misconstruing the roles of Islam and education in Javanese religion, views later expanded in his comprehensive study of Javanese culture (1985). Other scholars familiar with Islam and Dutch texts have questioned Geertz's analysis, suggesting that if one considers Javanese Islam from the perspective of the wide Muslim tradition, it does not differ markedly from the Islam of the Middle East and India (Hodgson 1974: 551). Taking a different perspective, others point to the changes taking place in modern Indonesia and simply question the contemporary applicability of Geertz's model. Struck by the vitality of religious life in 1980 as compared with earlier decades, Mulder has argued that the ongoing Islamization is not a sign of fundamentalism, but a response to changing times in which religious association remains one of the few vehicles for moral self-expression (Mulder 1992: 9).

It is no exaggeration to say that American anthropologists have dominated Thai studies. American interest in Thailand stems from the Cornell University Thailand Project, set up in 1947 by Lauriston Sharp. This gave rise to a vast body of research (e.g. Sharp et al. 1953; Philips 1965; Hanks 1972; Sharp and Hanks 1978), much of which came from the study of one central Thai village, Ban Chan, now engulfed by Bangkok. Data were collected on almost all aspects of social life over a decade. The Cornell Thailand Project also produced what are now considered classic studies of the Chinese in Thailand (Skinner 1957, 1958) and stimulated village studies in other regions of Thailand.

As well as conducting the bulk of early ethnographic research in Thailand, American anthropologists have generated a succession of influential models of Thai society. Early accounts took their cue from an article that asserted, rather ambiguously, that Thai society is characterized by 'loose structure' (Embree 1950). This has been variously interpreted as implying an absence of social structure (Potter 1976) and a behavioural characteristic of 'loose' adherence to existing structural norms (Phillips 1965). Thoroughly criticized on a number of grounds, the central place this concept once held in Thai studies was occupied in turn by the idea of 'patron–clientage'.

Patron–client relations were, for several years, seen as the cornerstone of Thai social structure (Hanks 1975, Van Roy 1971). Hanks asserted that society consists of a multitude of interlocking asymmetrical, dyadic relationships. The patron of several clients, together comprising an 'entourage', is in turn the client of a superordinate. Society is thus composed of a pyramid where entourages are linked vertically with one another. This framework has until relatively recently informed many studies, but has been strongly criticized (Keyes 1978) on at least two counts. First, over-attention to hierarchical linkages has tended to obscure horizontal cleavages. That is, a clientelist approach tends to obscure the existence and significance of economic classes. Second, in the process of giving the concept universal relevance, the notion of patron–clientage has been rendered analytically sterile. In the light of the first criticism, Brummelhuis and Kemp (1984) recommended an approach combining class and clientelist analysis and encompassing both 'structures' and 'strategies'. The debate continues. Reflecting trends in anthropology generally, no new paradigmatic theories of Thai society have become dominant. Contemporary Thai studies in America cover a wide range of interests, with many focusing on aspects of social change. Probably the most authoritative commentator on contemporary Thailand is Charles Keyes, whose publications touch on most debates that have arisen in Thai studies, and include a country study (1987) of the kind normally written by political scientists or sociologists.

Southeast Asian anthropologists

In 1953 the Dutch anthropologist, G. J. Held, observed that virtually all scientific research in Indonesia was being conducted by Europeans (Koentjaraningrat 1975: 28 n.19). At the time, despite Indonesia's recent and hard-won independence, the teaching and research staff at the University of Indonesia and its various institutes were still predominantly Dutch. But as early as 1950 the situation had begun to change with the appointment of T. S. G. Moelia, an Indonesian professor, to the Chair of Sociology. The situation in Gadjah Mada University was somewhat different because of its association with the revolutionary government in Yogyakarta. The staff at Gadjah Mada were predominantly Indonesian during the early years after the revolution, though this did not stop the university appointing a foreign anthropologist, M. A. Jaspan, to its staff. Jaspan later moved on to Bandung, and then to ANU and Perth in Australia, eventually taking up the Chair in South-East Asian Sociology at the University of Hull. Anthropology in Yogyakarta was taught by a philologist, Prijohutomo, and sociology by a lawyer, M. M. Djojodiguno, the latter having conducted research on the *adat* personal law of Central Java. Djojodiguno's previous experience proved invaluable and he was able to stimulate interest in research on the part of the staff and students at the Faculty of Law and the Faculty of Political Science. Arrangements were also made for cooperation between MIT and Gadjah Mada, though the collaborative effort eventually foundered (Koentjaraningrat 1975: 223).

The results of research projects conducted by Gadjah Mada staff were published in journals such as *Hukum, Madjalah Gama* and

Sosiografi Indonesia. There were publications by Soedjito Sosrodihardjo on Javanese rural religion and leadership, Pandam Guritno on social pathology and child health in rural Java, and Masri Singarimbum on the Karo Batak. Soedjito Sosrodihardjo later studied at the University of London, where he wrote an MA thesis on the sociology of religion in Java (1959). Masri Singarimbum also studied abroad, taking up a graduate fellowship at the Australian National University (ANU) in 1962.

There was little opportunity to conduct research at the University of Indonesia during the early independence years, though Koentjaraningrat collected data in South Central Java in 1958 and 1959. Another staff member, J. B. Avé, also published a report (1964) based on his research among the Ngaju of Kalimantan, while Ina Slamet-Velsinck wrote a book on a Central Javanese community (1963). In the years that followed, anthropologists and sociologists returned from abroad, almost all having received either MA or Ph.D. degrees from Cornell University. The strong focus on Java in the United States is shown by the titles of dissertations by Samiati Alisjahbana (1954), Hasan M. Shadily (1955), Kusmuljo Sedjati (1959), Soelaeman Soemardi (1961), Sunardi Sudarmadi (1964) and Pandam Guritno (1964) (Koentjaraningrat 1975: 225–6). The Indonesian scholars who published monographs in this period include Selosoemardjan (*Social Changes in Jogyakarta*, 1962, Cornell University Press) and Tan Giok-Lan (*The Chinese of Sukabumi*, 1963, Modern Indonesia Project). Despite the Javanese orientation, Indonesian scholars did conduct research elsewhere, such as Harsja W. Bachtiar who worked on the Minangkabau. Anwas Iskandar and Koentjaraningrat were also among the Indonesians who carried out research in New Guinea following the transfer of West Irian to Indonesia in 1963. The University of Indonesia also sponsored the development of a sister institute, Hasanudin University, in Ujung Pandang (Sulawesi). Anthropology and sociology were taught by *dosen terbang* (flying lecturers) from Jakarta, and between 1954 and 1957 the lectures were given by H. J. Heeren (Koentjaraningrat 1975: 227).

Malaysia also has an established anthropological tradition. Syed Husin Ali, for example, who was trained by Firth, conducted research on social stratification in *Kampong Bagun*. Much of the Malaysian research, especially that conducted at Universiti Pertanian Malaysia (the agricultural university), has been concerned with the Malay peasantry, social change and development (see, for example, Rokiah Talis). Work on the 'Orang Asli' by Hasan Mat Nor has reflected the strength of applied anthropology in Malaysia. Wazir-Jahan Karim and Zainal Kling (Saribas Malays) have played a key role in encouraging anthropological studies in Malaysia.

Some of the closest links between Southeast Asian anthropologists and scholars outside the region have been forged in Australia. Australia's impressive commitment to Southeast Asian research lies beyond the scope of this chapter, but mention should be made of W. R. Geddes' Hmong studies in Northern Thailand and Freeman's supervision of theses by M. Heppell, Penny Graham, George Appell, M. Uchibori and J. Masing. An appreciation of the breadth and depth of Australian research can be obtained from James Fox's edited volume entitled *Indonesia: Australian perspectives* (1980).

Conclusion

Looking back over the account above, we realize that we have done scant justice to many anthropologists who have made considerable contributions to the development of the subject. The chosen framework disguises or omits many of the key debates that have been nourishing anthropology as a discipline with Southeast Asian data. So we briefly mention some of them here.

The great debate has been about social change and its consequences for the societies of the area. This has ranged over many issues, some of which have been touched on above. Anthropologists have contributed their knowledge of living cultures to the classical study of the influences of exterior civilizations on the area, and over the past century this contribution has led to considerable changes in the evaluation of the role of indigenous cultures in the process. Part of this change has been the re-emergence of studies of material culture after a long period of comparative neglect while structural anthropology was dominant, reviving and initiating museums, and spawning new journals and a plethora of studies from comparative technology to symbolism in design. More recently the social change debate has moved to the discussion of the problems of modernization and development, Westernization and globalization. In this area anthropologists have been accepted as legitimate contributors to the planning process. Applied anthropology has become important, and is now part of mainstream anthropology.

In the discipline itself, one of the most important changes has been the vigorous development of gender studies. Although there have been some female anthropologists working in Southeast Asia since early in the century whose work has been important in the development of the subject, such as Benedict (1916), Mead (1942), Firth (1943), Djamour (1959) and Ward (1963), it is only in recent years that their numbers have become sufficient to make a large impact in the subject. Feminist scholars have vigorously exposed the weaknesses in work done by male anthropologists, for not only had most anthropological studies presented societies from a purely male viewpoint, but also many had failed to include solid information about women at all. As more studies of women in Southeast Asian society become available (see Wazir-Jahan Karim 1995, and Summers and Wilder 1995 for recent work), it becomes increasingly obvious that most existing ethnography will have to be analysed anew so that the patterning dynamics of Southeast Asian society can be better understood. This task must fall on all anthropologists, regardless of sex or specialism: adopting a gender perspective at its most basic is part of the constant refining of fieldwork technique and methodology, and part of the anthropologists' enhanced awareness of the effects of their own presence on their field data and how this affects the text they produce.

From early days, anthropologists have devoted a great deal of their work to the analysis of kinship and descent. It is the classical core of their studies, and Southeast Asia has been the scene of two great debates. First, Southeast Asia has more societies with rules prescribing marriage to the matrilateral cross-cousin than anywhere else in the world. The debate has ranged over the organization of such societies, the relation of the marriage rules to other aspects of social structure and culture such as symbolic classifications, and the relation of such marriage systems to other kinds of prescriptive and preferential systems, and indeed, the very existence of such rules. More broadly, there has been some difficulty in accepting standard models of lineal systems for the understanding of the lineal societies of the area.

Second, the attempt has been made to bring the understanding of cognatic kinship systems (which are common in the societies of the great states, such as Burmese, Thai, Cambodian, Javanese, Sundanese, Madurese and Malay, and found almost everywhere in Borneo, Sulawesi and the Philippines) to a level similar to that achieved by anthropologists working on lineal systems. The debate was begun by G. P. Murdock in 1950. Some agreement on the nature of Southeast Asian cognatic systems has emerged (Husken and Kemp 1991).

We should also mention the importance of the area in pulling the anthropologist away from isolated field studies into broader studies of society. Nowhere has this been clearer than in the study of religion, where the researches have become increasingly sophisticated. Having studied the great religions at the village level, anthropologists have been able to offer new approaches to the comprehension of religion in everyday life. For example, the work of Spiro and Tambiah has been particularly influential in this field in Buddhist societies, but there have been many other studies and extensive debate (see Keyes 1979: 109–10). Similar work has been done on Islam and Christianity. Taking another tack, increasing understanding of spirit beliefs and associated practices has allowed anthropologists to contribute to the understanding of indigenous conceptions of disease and curing, and their relationship to modern medical systems.

Anthropology, then, has developed a great deal from the days when it dealt with curious practices noted by inquisitive travellers in Southeast Asia. By the late nineteenth century it could claim to be a scientific discipline, and by the 1930s it had become a profession with its own theories and a well-developed set of fieldwork techniques. By then it had built a substantial body of ethnography, despite the tiny number of trained professionals. Since then it has expanded enormously in scope as each year more people have entered the profession. Above all its influence has increased because its value as a discipline has become accepted in Southeast Asia. It can look forward to a continuing and expanding role into the next century.

Bibliography

Adriani, N. and Alb. C. Kruyt (1912–14), *De Bare'e sprekende Toradja's van Midden Celebes*, 3 vols (Batavia: Landsdrukkerij) (2nd edn 1950–51).

Asad, Talal (ed.) (1973), *Anthropology and the Colonial Encounter* (London: Ithaca Press).

Ayal, E. B. (ed.) (1978), *The Study of Thailand: analyses of knowledge, approaches, and prospects in anthropology, art history, economics, history and political science* (Athens, OH: Ohio University, Centre for International Studies).

Barnes, R. H. (1974), *The Kedang: a study of the collective thought of an Eastern Indonesian People* (Oxford: Clarendon Press).

Barth, Fredrik (1993), *Balinese Worlds* (Chicago: University of Chicago Press).

Barton, Roy Franklin (1919), 'Ifugao law', *American Archaeology and Ethnology*, 15: 1–186.

— (1946), 'The religion of the Ifugaos', *American Anthropological Association Memoir*, 65: 1–219.

— (1949), *The Kalingas: their institutions and custom law* (Chicago: University of Chicago Press).

Bateson, Gregory (1936), *Naven* (Stanford, CA: Stanford University Press) (2nd rev. edn).

— and Margaret Mead (1942), *Balinese Character. A photographic analysis* (New York: New York Academy of Sciences).

Bellwood, Peter (1985), *Prehistory of the Indo-Malaysian Archipelago* (Sydney: Academic Press).

— (1991), 'The Austronesian dispersal and the origin of languages', *Scientific American*, 265: 88–93.

Belo, Jane (1949), *Bali: Rangda and Barong*, Monographs of the American Ethnological Society, 16 (Seattle: University of Washington Press).

— (1960), *Trance in Bali* (New York: Columbia University Press).

Benedict, Laura Watson (1916), 'A Study of Bagobo ceremonial, magic and myth', *Annals of the New York Academy of Sciences*, 25: 308.

Bessaignet, Pierre (1958), *Tribesmen of the Chittagong Hill Tracts* (Dacca: Asiatic Society of Pakistan).

Blust, R. A. (1984), 'Indonesia as a "field of linguistic study"', in P. E. de Josselin de Jong (1984): 21–37.

Bois, Cora Du (1944), *The People of Alor,* (Cambridge, MA: Harvard University Press).

Boon, James A. (1977), *The Anthropological Romance of Bali 1597–1972: dynamic perspectives in marriage and caste, politics and religion* (Cambridge: Cambridge University Press).

— (1990), *Affinities and Extremes: crisscrossing the bittersweet ethnology of East Indies history, Hindu-Balinese culture, and Indo-European allure* (Chicago: Chicago University Press).

Brewer, Jeffrey Daniel (1976), 'Agricultural knowledge and practice in two Indonesian villages' (Ph.D. thesis, University of California, Los Angeles).

Brummelhuis, H. T. and J. H. Kemp (1984), 'Introduction', in H. T. Brummelhuis and J. Kemp (eds), *Strategies and Structures in Thai Society* (Amsterdam: Anthropological-Sociological Centre).

Chouléan, Ang (1986), *Les Etres surnaturels dans la religion populaire khmère* (Paris: Cedoreck).

Clifford, Hugh (1899), *In a Corner of Asia: being tales and impressions of native life in the Malay Peninsula* (London: T. Fisher Unwin).

— (1897), *In Court and Kampong: being tales and sketches of native life in the Malay Peninsula* (London: Grant Richards).

Coedès, Georges (1967), *The Making of South East Asia* (trans. by H. M. Wright of *Les Peuples de la péninsule indochinoise*; originally published 1962) (London: Routledge & Kegan Paul).

Condominas, Georges (1977), *We Have Eaten the Forest: the story of a Montagnard village in the central highlands of Vietnam* (originally published 1957) (London: Allen Lane).

Das, Tarakchandra (1945), *The Purums: an old Kuki tribe of Manipur* (Calcutta: University of Calcutta).

Delvert, J. (1961), *Le Paysan cambodgien* (Paris and The Hague: Mouton).

Deschamps, H. (1961), *Histoire de Madagascar* (Paris: Editions Berger-Levrault).

Dewey, Alice (1963), *Peasant Marketing in Java* (New York: Free Press of Glencoe).

Djamour, Judith (1959), *Malay Kinship and Marriage in Singapore*, London School of Economics Monographs on Social Anthropology, 21 (London: The Athlone Press).

— (1966), *The Muslim Matrimonial Court in Singapore*, London School of Economics Monographs on Social Anthropology, 31 (London: The Athlone Press).

Dournes, Jacques (1972), *Coordonnées: structures Jorai familiales et sociales*, Université de Paris, Travaux et memoires de l'Instituut d'Ethnologie 77 (Paris: Musée de l'Homme).

Downs, R. E. (1956), *The Religion of the Bare'e-speaking Toradja of Central Celebes*, thesis, Leiden (The Hague: Excelsior) .

Dozier, Edward P. (1966), *Mountain Arbiters: the changing life of a Philippine people*, (Tucson: University of Arizona Press).

Durkheim, Emile and Marcel Mauss (1963), *Primitive Classification* (trans. of *De quelques formes primitives de classification* by Rodney Needham; first published 1901–2) (London: Cohen and West).

Duyvendak, J. P. (1926), *Het Kakean-genootschap van Seran* (Almelo: W. Hilarius).

Elbert, J. (1911–12), *Die Sunda-expedition des Vereins für Geographie und Statistik zu Frankfurt am Main*, 2 vols (Frankfurt am Main: H. Minjon).

Elliott, Alan J. A. (1955), *Chinese Sprit-Medium Cults in Singapore*, London School of Economics Monographs on Social Anthropology, 14 (London: The Athlone Press).

Embree, J. F. (1950), 'Thailand: a loosely structured social system', *American Anthropologist*, 52: 181–93.

Evans, Ivor H. N. (1923), *Studies in Religion, Folk-lore, and Custom in British North Borneo and the Malay Peninsula* (Cambridge: Cambridge University Press).

— (1937), *The Negritos of Malaya* (Cambridge: Cambridge University Press).

— (1953), *The Religion of the Tempasuk Dusuns of North Borneo* (Cambridge: Cambridge University Press).

Firth, Raymond (1946), *Malay Fishermen: their peasant economy* (2nd edn 1966) (London: Kegan Paul).

Firth, Rosemary (1943), *Housekeeping among Malay Peasants*, London School of Economics Monographs on Social Anthropology, 7 (London: The Athlone Press).

Fortes, M. and E. E. Evans-Prichard (1940), *African Political Systems* (London: Oxford University Press for the International African Institute).

Fox, James J. (ed.) (1980), *The Flow of Life. Essays on Eastern Indonesia* (Cambridge, MA and London: Harvard University Press).

Freeman, J. D. (1970), *Report on the Iban*, London School of Economics Monographs on Social Anthropology, 41 (London: The Athlone Press).

Friedericy, H. J. (1933), 'De standen bij de Boegineezen en Makassaren', *Bijdragen tot de Taal-, Land- en Volkenkunde van Nederlandsch-Indie*, 90: 447–602.

Fürer-Haimendorf, Christoph von (1939), *The Naked Nagas* (London: Methuen).

Geddes, William R. (1954), *The Land Dayaks of Sarawak; a report on a socio-economic survey of the Land Dayaks presented to the Colonial Social Science Research Council*, Colonial Research Studies, 14 (London: Her Majesty's Stationery Office).

Geertz, Clifford (1960), *The Religion of Java* (Glencoe, IL: Free Press).

— (1963a), *Agricultural Involution. the process of ecological change in Indonesia* (Berkeley: University of California Press).

— (1963b), *Peddlars and Princes: social change and economic development in two Indonesian towns* (Chicago: University of Chicago Press).

Geertz, Hildred (1961), *The Javanese Family: a study in kinship and socialization* (New York: Free Press of Glencoe).

Geise, N. J. C. (1952), *Badujs en Moslims in Lebak Parahiang Zuid-Banten* (thesis, Leiden) (Leiden: De Jong).

Gibson, Thomas (1986), *Sacrifice and Sharing in the Philippine highlands: religion and society among the Buhid of Mindoro* (London: The Athlone Press).

Gullick, J. M. (1958). *Indigenous Political Systems of Western Malaya* (2nd and 3rd edns 1965 and 1988) (London: The Athlone Press).

Haddon, A. C. and L. E. Start (1936), *Iban or Sea Dyak Fabrics and their Patterns* (Cambridge: Cambridge University Press).

Hanks, Lucien M. Jr. (1972), *Rice and Man: agricultural ecology in Southeast Asia* (Chicago: Aldine Press).

— (1975), 'The Thai social order as entourage and circle', in Skinner and Kirsch (1975): 197–218.

Heine-Geldern, Robert von (1932), 'Urheimat und früheste Wanderungen des Austronesier', *Anthropos*, 27.

Held, G. J. (1935), *The Mahabharata: an ethnological study* (London: Kegan Paul, Trench, Trubner and Amsterdam: Holland).

Hickey, Gerald Cannon (1964), *Village in Vietnam* (New Haven, CT and London: Yale University Press).

— (1982a), *Sons of the Mountains: ethno-history of the Vietnamese Central Highlands to 1954* (New Haven, CT and London: Yale University Press).

— (1982b), *Free in the Forest: ethno-history of the Vietnamese Central Highlands 1954–1976* (New Haven, CT and London: Yale University Press).

Hitchcock, Michael (1992–93), 'Research report on Indonesian and Tanzanian maritime links', *Indonesia Circle*, 59/60: 62–7.

Hodgson, M. G. S. (1974), *The Venture of Islam: conscience and history in a world religion*, 3 vols (Chicago: University of Chicago Press).

Hodson, Thomas C. (1908), *The Meitheis* (London: David Nutt).

Hogden, Margaret T. (1971), *Early Anthropology in the Sixteenth and Seventeenth Centuries* (first published in 1964) (Philadelphia: University of Pennsylvania Press).

Hose, Charles and William McDougall (1912), *The Pagan Tribes of Borneo*, 2 vols (London: Macmillan).

Hulsius, L. (ed.) (1598), *Eerste Shiffart an die Orientalische Indien, so die Hollandisch Schiff, im Martio 1595 aussgefahren, und in Augusto 1597 wiederkommon, verzicht* (many later editions) (Nuremburg: Hulsius).

Husken, Frans and Jeremy Kemp (eds) (1991), *Cognation and Social Organization in Southeast Asia*, Verhandelingen van het Koninklijk Instituut voor Taal-, Land- en Volkenkunde 145 (Leiden: KITLV Press).

Hutton, J. H. (1921a), *The Angami Nagas* (London: Macmillan).

— (1921b), *The Sema Nagas* (London: Macmillan).

Jacobs, Julian, Alan MacFarlane, Sarah Harison and Anita Herle (1990), *Hill Peoples of Northeast India: the Nagas: society, culture and the colonial encounter* (London: Thames and Hudson).

Jay, Robert R. (1963), *Javanese Villagers: society and culture in rural Modjokuto* (New York: Free Press of Glencoe).

Josselin de Jong, J. P. B. de (1951), *Lévi-Strauss's Theory on Kinship and Marriage*, Mededelingen, 10 (Leiden: Rijksmuseum voor Volkenkunde.)

Josselin de Jong, P. E. de (1951), *Minangkabau and Negeri Sembilan: socio-political structure in Indonesia,* (Leiden: Eduard Ijdo).

— (ed.) (1977), *Structural Anthropology in the Netherlands: a reader*, KITLV Translation Series 17 (The Hague: Martinus Nijhoff).

— (ed.) (1984), *Unity in Diversity: Indonesia as a field of anthropological study*, Verhandelingen KITLV 103 (Dordrecht: Foris Publications).

Just, Peter (1986), 'Dou Donggo social organization: ideology, structure, and action in an Indonesian society' (Ph.D. thesis, University of Pennsylvania).

Kent, R. K. (1970), *Early Kingdoms in Madagascar 1500–1700* (New York: Holt, Rinehart and Winston).

Keyes, Charles F. (1978), 'Ethnography and anthropological interpretation in the study of Thailand', in Ayal (ed.) (1978).

— (1979), *The Golden Peninsula: culture and adaptation in mainland Southeast Asia* (New York: Macmillan; London: Collier-Macmillan).

— (1987), *Thailand: Buddhist Kingdom as modern nation-state* (Boulder, CO: Westview).

Kiefer, Thomas M. (1972), *The Tausug: violence and law in a Philippine Moslem society* (New York: Holt, Rinehart and Winston).

King, V. T. (1989), 'Sociology and anthropology', in V. T. King (ed.), *Research on South-East Asia in the United Kingdom: a survey* (Hull: University of Hull, Centre for South-East Asian Studies): 17–26.

— (1993), *The Peoples of Borneo* (London: Oxford University Press).

Koentjaraningrat, Raden Mas (1963), Review of Clifford Geertz's 'The religion of Java', in *Madjallah Ilmu-ilmu Sastra Indonesia*, 1: 188–91.

— (1975), *Anthropology in Indonesia: a bibliographic review*. KITLV Bibliographical Series no. 8 ('s-Gravenhage: Nijhoff).

— (1985), *Javanese Culture* (Singapore: Oxford University Press/Institute of Southeast Asian Studies).

— (ed.) (1967), *Villages in Indonesia* (Ithaca, NY: Cornell University Press).

Koes Sarjono (1947), *De Botjah-Angon (Herdersjongen) in de Javaanse Cultuur* (Leiden: mimeo).

Kroeber, Alfred L. (1943), *The Peoples of the Philippines*, Handbook Series no. 8 (rev. edn) (American Museum of Natural History).

Leach, Edmund R. (1950), *Social Science Research in Sarawak*, Colonial Research Studies no. 1 (London: His Majesty's Stationery Office).

— (1954), *Political Systems of Highland Burma* (Cambridge, MA: Harvard University Press).

LeBar, Frank M., Gerald C. Hickey and John K. Musgrave (1964), *Ethnic Groups of Mainland Southeast Asia* (New Haven, CT: Human Relations Area Files Press).

— (ed. and comp.) (1972), *Ethnic Groups of Insular Southeast Asia Volume 1: Indonesia, Andaman Islands and Madagascar* (New Haven, CT: Human Relations Area Files Press).

— (ed. and comp.) (1975), *Ethnic Groups of Insular Southeast Asia Volume 2: Philippines and Formosa* (New Haven, CT: Human Relations Area Files Press).

Lehman, F. K. (1963), *The Structure of Chin Society. A tribal people of Burma adapted to a non-western civilisation* (Urbana: University of Illinois Press).

Lévi-Strauss, C. (1949), *Les Structures Elémentaires de la Parenté* (Paris: Presses Universitaires de France).

— (1952), 'Kinship systems of three Chitagong hill tribes', *Southwest Journal of Anthropology*, 8: 40–51.

— (1962), *Le Totémisme aujourd'hui* (Paris: Presses Universitaires de France).

— (1969), *The Elementary Structures of Kinship* (rev. edn, trans. James Harle Bell, John Richard von Sturmer and Rodney Needham) (London: Eyre and Spottiswoode).

MacCannell, D. (1976), *The Tourist: a new theory of the leisure class* (New York: Schocken).

MacGregor, Arthur (ed.) (1983), *Tradescant's Rarities* (Oxford: Clarendon Press).

Mabbett, I. and Chandler, D. (1995), *The Khmers* (Oxford, and Cambridge, MA: Blackwell).

Mead, Margaret (1928), *Coming of Age in Samoa* (New York: Morrow).

— and Gregory Bateson (1942), *Balinese Character: a photographic analysis* (New York: Academy of Sciences).

Mills, J. P. (1922), *The Lhota Nagas* (London: Macmillan).

— (1926), *The Ao Nagas* (London: Macmillan).

— (1937), *The Rengma Nagas* (London: Macmillan).

Morris, H. S. (1953), *Report on a Melanau Sago-producing Community in Sarawak*, Colonial Research Studies no. 9 (London: Her Majesty's Stationery Office).

Mulder, Niels, (1992), *Inside Southeast Asia: Thai, Javanese and Filipino interpretations of everyday life* (Bangkok: Editions Duang Kamol).

Murdock, George P. (ed.) (1960), *Social Structure in Southeast Asia*, Viking Fund Publications in Anthropology, 29 (Chicago: Quadrangle Books).

Murray, S. O. (1994), 'A thirteenth century imperial ethnography', *Anthropology Today*, 10: 15–18.

Mus, P. (1975), *India Seen From the East: Indian and indigenous cults in Champa* (ed. and trans. I. W. Mabbett and D. P. Chandler; first published 1933) (Clayton, Vic: Monash University, Centre of Southeast Asian Studies).

Mutibwa, P. M. (1974), *The Malagasy and the Europeans: Madagascar's foreign relations 1861–95* (London: Longman).

Nash, Manning (1965), *The Golden Road to Modernity* (New York: John Wiley and Sons).

Needham, Rodney (1984), 'The transformation of prescriptive systems in eastern Indonesia', in P. E. de Josselin de Jong (ed.) (1984): 221–33.

— (1987), *Mamboru: history and structure in a domain of northwestern Sumba* (Oxford: Clarendon Press).

Nicolespeyer, M. M. (1940), *De sociale structuur van een Aloreesche bevolkingsgroep* (thesis, Leiden) (Rijkswijk: V. A. Kramers).

Niessen, Sandra A. (1985), *Motifs of Life in Toba Batak texts and Textiles*, Verhandelingen van het Koninklijke Instituut voor Taal-, Land- en Volkenkunde 110 (Dordrecht: Foris Publications).

Nieuwenhuis, A. W. (1917), *Die Wurzeln des Animismus* (Leiden: Internationales Archiv für Ethnographie).

Nimmo, A. H. Arlo (1972), *The Sea People of Sulu* (London: Intertext Books).

Nooteboom, C. (1940), *Oost-Soemba: een volkenkundige studie*, Verhandelingen KITLV 3 ('s-Gravenhage: Nijhoff).

Notes and Queries on Anthropology (1951) (6th edn, first published 1894) (London: Routledge, Kegan Paul).

Palmier, L. H. (1960), *Social Status and Power in Java*, London School of Economics Monographs on Social Anthropology, 20 (London: The Athlone Press).

Parry, Neville Edward (1932), *The Lakhers, with an introduction and supplementary notes by J. H. Hutton* (London: Macmillan).

Peacock, James L. (1973), *Indonesia: an anthropological perspective* (Pacific Palisades, CA: Goodyear).

Phillips, H. P. (1965), *Thai Peasant Personality: the patterning of interpersonal behaviour in the village of Bang Chan* (Berkeley, CA: University of California Press).

Porée-Maspero, E. (1962–69), *Etude sur les rites agraires des Cambodgiens*, 3 vols (Paris: Mouton).

Potter, J. M. (1976), *Thai Peasant Social Structure* (Chicago: University of Chicago Press).

Provencher, R. (1975), *Mainland Southeast Asia: an anthropological perspective* (Pacific Palisades, CA: Goodyear).

Purchas, Samuel (1625), *Hakluytus Posthumous or Purchas His Pilgrimes*, vol. 5 (repr. 1905) (Glasgow: The Hakluyt Society).

Raffles, Thomas Stamford (1817), *The History of Java*, 2 vols (London: Black, Parbury and Allen).

Rassers, W. H. (1940), 'On the Javanese kris', *Bijdragen tot de Taal-, Land- en Volkenkunde*, 99: 501–82.

Rutter, Owen (1929), *The Pagans of North Borneo* (London: Hutchinson).

Scharer, Hans (1963), *Njagu Religion: the conception of God among a South Borneo people* (first published 1946), KITLV Translation Series 6 (The Hague: M. Nijhoff).

Schlegel, Stuart A. (1970), *Tiruray Justice: traditional Tiruray law and morality* (Berkeley: University of California Press).

Scott, James George (1910), *The Burman: his life and notions* (published under pseudonym Shway Yoe) (London: Macmillan).

— (1921), *Burma: a handbook of practical information* (3rd rev. edn) (London: Alexander Moring, De La More Press).

— (1932), *Burma and Beyond* (London: Grayson and Grayson).

— and J. P. Hardiman, (1900), *Gazetteer of Upper Burma and the Shan States*, (Rangoon: Superintendent of Government Printing and Stationery).

Shakespear, J. (1912), *The Lushei-Kuki Clans* (London: Macmillan).

Sharp, L. and L. M. Hanks (1978), *Bang Chan: social history of a rural community in Thailand* (Ithaca, NY: Cornell University Press).

Sharp, L., Hazel M. Hauck, Kamol Janlekha and Robert B. Textor (1953), *Siamese Rice Village: a preliminary study of Bang Chan, 1948–1949* (Bangkok: Cornell Research Centre).

Shaw, William (1929), *Notes on the Thadou Kukis* (ed. J. H. Hutton) (Calcutta: Asiatic Society of Bengal).

Skeat, Walter William (1900), *Malay Magic, Being an Introduction to the Folklore and Popular Religion of the Malay Penisula* (London: Macmillan).

— and Charles O. Blagden (1906), *Pagan Races of the Malay Peninsula*, 2 vols (London and New York: Macmillan).

Skinner, G. W. (1957), *Chinese Society in Thailand: an analytical history* (Ithaca, NY: Cornell University Press).

— (1958), *Leadership and Power in the Chinese Community of Thailand* (Ithaca, NY: Cornell University Press).

— and A. T. Kirsch (eds) (1975), *Change and Persistence in Thai Society: essays in honor of Lauriston Sharp* (Ithaca, NY: Cornell University Press).

Snouck Hurgronje, Christiaan (1906), *The Achehnese*, 2 vols (trans. of *De Atjehers* (1893) by A. W. S. O'Sullivan) (Batavia: Landesrukkerij; Leiden: E.J. Brill)

Spiro, Melford E. (1967), *Burmese Supernaturalism* (Englewood Cliffs, NJ: Prentice-Hall).

— (1971), *Buddhism and Society. a great tradition and its Burmese vicissitudes* (London: George Allen & Unwin).

Stevenson, H. N. C. (1943), *The Economics of the Central Chin Tribes*, (Bombay: Times of India Press, published by order of the Government of Burma).

Summers, Laura and William D. Wilder (eds) (1995), 'Gender and the sexes in the Indonesian Archipelago', *Indonesia Circle*, 67.

Sutton, J. (1990), *A Thousand Years of East Africa* (Nairobi: British Institute in Eastern Africa).

Swift, M. G. (1965), *Malay Peasant Society in Jelebu*, London School of Economics Monographs on Social Anthropology, 29 (London: Athlone Press).

Tambiah, S. J. (1970), *Buddhism and the Spirit Cults in North-East Thailand* (Cambridge: Cambridge University Press).

— (1976), *World Conqueror and World Renouncer: a study of Buddhism and polity in Thailand against a historical background* (Cambridge: Cambridge University Press).

— (1984), *The Buddhist Saints of the Forest and the Cult of Amulets* (Cambridge: Cambridge University Press).

Tehupeiorij, J. E. (1906), *Onder de Dajaks in Centraal-Borneo* (Batavia).

Teljeur, Dirk (1990), *The Symbolic System of the Giman of South Halmahera*, Verhandelingen KITLV 142 (Dordrecht: Foris Publications).

Thierry, S. (1964), *Les Khmers* (Paris: Senil).

— (1978), *Etude d'un corpus de contes cambodgiens* (Paris and Lille: Libraire Honoré Champion).

Ti'en Ju-K'ang (1953), *The Chinese of Sarawak: a study of social structure*, London School of Economics Monographs on Social Anthropology, 12 (London: The Athlone Press).

Tobing, Philip O. L. (1963), *The Structure of the Toba-Batak Belief in the High God* (Macassar: South and Southeast Celebes Institute for Culture).

Toekang Potret: 100 Years of Photography in the Dutch Indies 1839–1939 (1989) (Rotterdam: Museum voor Volkenkunde).

Tylor, Edward B. (1865), *Researches into the Early History of Mankind and the Development of Civilisation* (London: J. Murray).

— (1871), *Primitive Culture: researches into the development of mythology, philosophy, religion, language, art and custom* (London: J. Murray).

Van Roy E. (1971), *Economic systems of Northern Thailand* (Ithaca, NY: Cornell University Press).

van Wouden, F. A. E. (1968), *Types of Social Structure in Eastern Indonesia* (trans. by Rodney Needham of *Sociale Structuurtypen in de Groote Oost* (1935)) (The Hague: M. Nijhoff).

Veth, P. J. (1854–56), *Borneo's Westerafdeeling*, 2 vols (Zalt-Bommel).

—(1881–92), *Midden Sumatra. Reizen en Onderzoekingen der Sumatra-expeditie Uitgerust door het Aardrijkskundig Genootschap, 1877–1879, Beschreven door de Leden der Expeditie, onder Toezicht van P. J. Veth*, 4 vols (Leiden: E. J. Brill).

Wakin, Eric (1992), *Anthropology goes to war: professional ethics and counterinsurgency in Thailand* (Madison: University of Wisconsin).

Ward, Barbara (1963), *Women in the New Asia* (Paris: UNESCO).

Wazir-Jahan Karim (1981), *Ma' Betisék Concepts of Living Things*, London School of Economics Monographs on Social Anthropology, 52 (London: The Athlone Press).

Wazir-Jahan Karim (ed.) (1995), *'Male' and 'Female' in Developing Southeast Asia* (Oxford/Washington: Berg).

Wilder, William D. (1982), *Communication, Social Structure and Development in Rural Malaysia: a study of kampung Kuala Bera*, London School of Economics Monographs on Social Anthropology, 56 (London: The Athlone Press).

Willmott, W. E. (1970), *The Political Structure of the Chinese Community in Cambodia*, London School of Economics Monographs on Social Anthropology, 42 (London: The Athlone Press).

de Zoete, Beryl and Walter Spies (1938), *Dance and Drama in Bali* (London: Faber & Faber).

2 History

Hong Lysa

What is Southeast Asian History?

Nowadays, it would obviously be foolhardy and fruitless to attempt a definitive coverage of Southeast Asian history in a chapter. Ours is the age of specialization and the monograph, and confident general surveys are the preserve of individuals at two extreme situations: the writer of school textbooks who seeks to simplify, and the veteran leading specialist scholar who has, after a lifetime of research and writing, arrived at a synthesis and distillation of Southeast Asian history. Aside from such projects, the complexity of the region that undergraduates invariably complain about – the number of societies and languages involved, and the coverage of a time-span of about a millennium – renders the task of writing a fully comprehensive chapter on the history of Southeast Asia wellnigh impossible.

However, the main reason for arguing that a chapter on the general history of Southeast Asia is not the most satisfactory of endeavours is that historians have become aware of the untenable nature of claims that history is composed of a quantifiable set of recoverable facts which of themselves would reveal the shape of the past. Thus a chapter purporting to present the most important facts that one must know about Southeast Asian history just cannot work, for it would be assuming that these facts are considered important equally by everyone, and more importantly, that they are related to one another in a particular way which is beyond dispute. In fact what they amount to is but the handiwork of the historian, who selects evidence that he or she deems significant, puts it in a certain sequence, and by so doing suggests an explanation for certain outcomes.

Hence Southeast Asian history can be understood as how the Southeast Asian past has been presented by parties who have made it their business to assert that it happened in a certain way. While some interpretations are better grounded than others, no one way is inherently superior to another – generally, the way that history is written is reflective of the concerns of the age in which it was produced, and quality should be gauged according to how successfully the historian has been able to marshal the evidence to build up his or her case, so that the evidence has more explanatory power in his or her version of the past than in an alternative or oppositional one.

However, the dominance or prevalence of a particular view of history is not necessarily always based on its scholarly merit alone. Official patronage of that view leads to the production of works which corroborate it. Means of promoting orthodoxy in history-writing include: permitting only approved personnel to write history; releasing documentary evidence that would support, and suppressing those that challenge, the sanctioned version of the past; or, even more overtly, banning and destroying history books that are deemed offensive. Such means are certainly not alien to Southeast Asia. They militate against the notion that history is or can be an objective retrieval and recounting of the past.

Traditional Southeast Asian history-writing

Indigenous Southeast Asian history was never meant to serve a purely archival function – simply for the record. It had far more vital functions: the past was captured in chronicles and other forms of narration to boost the moral and hence the political authority of the kingly sponsors of history-writing. The value in recording the past was in the provision of examples of good and bad kings, to demonstrate the effect of their conduct on the welfare of their subjects. History, by relating ethical and religious instruction to actual events, became a teaching aid for all mankind, but especially for kings (Reid and Marr 1979: 68).

The moral lessons derived from standards measured against immanent or abstract moral and religious values served to demonstrate how an existing dynasty or ruler matched a set of prescriptions. At the same time, the chronicles' assessments of past rulers and their deeds were determined by the contemporary ruler – it was he who decided which of his predecessors were to be lauded as great and good kings who ruled according to the precepts, which to be dropped from mention altogether, and which to be condemned as bad and evil rulers. Thus history was written and rewritten as authorized by its sponsors: genealogies were constructed; apocryphal biographies of the incumbent written, embellished with stories of feats which pointed to his kingly destiny;[1] countervailing forces such as defeated rivals condemned as negative examples or expunged from the records if their cause was still too much alive and powerful to be thus consigned to ignominy.[2]

History-writing in Southeast Asia was thus undoubtedly part of the royal regalia – creation and possession of it was the privilege of power.

It was a fount and symbol of legitimacy, authority and potency on the basis of possession of arcane knowledge of cosmic principles revealed through understanding of the pattern and meaning of the past.

This genre of indigenous writing has been dismissed as being of scant value as analysis of the past in its own right because it is not objective or meant to record a factual past, but is filled with myth, legend, and details about ceremonies.[3] It was not valued as history by Western, scientific, colonial agencies, who had nothing but disdain for the indigenous systems that they overwhelmed militarily and economically. The chronicle and other forms of traditional history writing became largely obsolete. Its sponsors had in effect lost power, and it concomitantly lost its raison d'être.

The colonial enterprise and history-writing

The new rulers, the colonial regimes, had a different set of modalities – the study of the colonized peoples including their history was to be encyclopaedic and classificatory. Court chronicles were replaced by agendas to gather as much information as possible to facilitate effectiveness of government. Colonial histories sought to understand pre-existing patterns of the power structure, land and judicial systems, for example, mostly to confirm that these were largely obstacles to development and should be either adapted, marginalized or demolished in order to enable the natives to be export producers. Thus, Raffles dedicated his monumental *The History of Java* to the Prince Regent, in the hope of:

> interesting your Royal Highness in favour of the amiable and ingenuous people whose country [the volume] describes. The high respect they entertain for British valour and justice, and the lively gratitude they retain for the generous system of British Legislation, will, I am sure, give them a strong claim upon your Royal Highness's good opinion (Raffles 1972: v).

Raffles instituted an inquiry into the land tenure system of the Javanese village. He concluded that all land was the property of the state, and under the superintendence of the village headman. As the critical colonial scholar-administrator J. S. Furnivall noted:

> The idea of using the village as a unit of administration must have been familiar to Raffles from his acquaintance with the system of British India, and it was also the tradition of British India that the state was the universal landlord; it is difficult therefore to resist the suggestion that in the material collected in this enquiry Raffles found what he wanted, and expected (Furnivall 1944: 70).

In a variant pattern, religion, culture, language were studied to understand the 'mentality' of the colonial subjects in order to accommodate the putative Southeast Asian natives, be they Malay, Lao, Cambodian or even Vietnamese, largely by marginalizing them from the activities of colonial society and economy. As Frank Swettenham explained:

> Just as I think the Eastern is never so well or becomingly dressed as in his national costume, so I think it should be our object to maintain or revive his interest in the best of his traditions, rather than encourage him to assume habits of life that are not really suited to his character, constitution, climate, or the circumstances in which he lives – which are in fact, unnatural to him, and will lead him to trouble and disappointment, if not to absolute disaster (Swettenham 1983: 186–7).

It is under such assumptions that colonial regimes imported 'the other' – Asian migrants from the century-old colony of India, and from China. Western knowledge of the East had it that Chinese and Indians were breeds which possessed qualities which were missing in the Southeast Asians, such as diligence and a sense of enterprise. Southeast Asia had of course dealt for centuries with both Indians and Chinese, but the relationships were now changed. The latter were no longer the purveyors of religious and political systems and of regional trade whom the Southeast Asian rulers welcomed as agents who could enhance their might. These foreigners were now part of the Southeast Asian landscape on very different terms: they were defined as, and fashioned into, the economic handmaiden of the colonial enterprise, and posited as a critique of the native. In a sense, then, we can see that the colonialist's Southeast Asian history, like the traditional indigenous depiction, served to justify and strengthen the state. While the latter called on the authority of religion for verification, the former summoned science and the scientific methodology of the day.

While the historical works of colonizers such as Raffles and Swettenham were overtly framed by their official positions, the monumental studies by scholars on ancient Southeast Asian civilizations – such as the recovery and examination of Angkor by French archaeologists and historians – were no less part of the colonial enterprise. The study of early Southeast Asian history is perhaps the most enduring aspect of the pre-independence scholarship, least tainted by the notions of colonial superiority of the day, and hence least prone to the vicissitudes of changing political fortunes. However, this does not mean that it was free from larger involvements. The colonial state 'found an interest in establishing a "noble ancestry" on the tropical spot, and in demonstrating its magnanimity and superiority by

supporting the spectacular recovery of "forgotten" local pasts. Hence
the astonishing amount of money spent on archaeological work and
museums by typically skinflint colonial regimes' (Anderson 1992: 27).
The splendour of Angkor stood in stark contrast to the contemporary
nineteenth- and twentieth-century Cambodian subjects, whom the
French saw as being like children, a weak and ineffectual people who
had lost their capacity for greatness. This early greatness was attributed
by that generation of scholars to the Indianization process – 'the
Cambodian is an Indianised Pnong', pronounced Coedès.[4] It was an
exogenous force which had transformed Cambodians into mighty
empire-builders at the turn of the millennium. Later, another external
engine – French colonialism – would guide and supervise the revital-
isation of the Cambodian kingdom.

'National' history

With the decolonization process in the post-war period came a widespread rejection of colonial historiography and its replacement by
'national' history within Southeast Asia itself. Indeed, the political
upheaval was paralleled by historiographical upheaval even in the inter-
war period. At its most hostile and least refined, the colonial period
was portrayed by the succeeding historiography as an age of darkness,
one that choked off the peoples' lifeline to their glorious past; and this
was the source of all problems confronting them. As Sukarno pre-
scribed as early as 1930:

> First: we show the people that they have a past, a glorious past; second:
> we increase the people's consciousness that they have a present, a dark
> present; third: we show the people the rays of the future, shining and
> clear, and the means to bring about that future full of promise ... What
> Indonesian's national spirit will not live when hearing the greatness of
> the kingdoms of Melayu and Sriwijaya, the greatness of the first
> Mataram, the greatness of the time of Sindok and Erlangga and Kediri
> and Singasari and Majapahit and Pajajaran – the greatness too of Bintara,
> Banten, and Mataram under Sultan Agung! ... Whose hope and faith
> will not live, that a people with *such* a great past, *must* have enough
> strength also to attain a glorious future.[5]

Drawing from colonial 'discoveries' without saying so, such regimes
employed the potency of the past in configuring the future. The
clearest illustration of this is the symbol that Angkor represents for
the Cambodians. An image of the Angkor Wat has been emblazoned
on the national flags of regimes as diverse and bitterly opposed as
Sihanouk's Kingdom of Cambodia (1953–70), Lon Nol's Khmer

Republic (1970–75), Pol Pot's Democratic Kampuchea (1975–79), the Vietnamese-backed People's Republic of Kampuchea (later the State of Cambodia) under Heng Samrin and Hun Sen (1979–93), and the current Royal Government of Cambodia. However, whereas Sihanouk made it an icon of royalism, the Khmer Rouge transformed it into the symbol of corrupt, decadent and exploitative feudalism, yet also of what the power of the people working collectively can accomplish (Keyes 1990: 56–9).

Academic history

Thus it can be seen that our understanding of Southeast Asian history has to encompass the forces that go into its construction and repro-duction. It is not simply the truth about the past that is involved in the study of history. In the three periods delineated above, it has been stressed that history was very much a political battleground. The argument can be made, however, that professional, academic historians based in universities have taken over from the colonial bureaucrats and scholars since the Second World War, and it is their works, rather than the official histories generated by the Southeast Asian states, that have the most valid claim to offering knowledge of Southeast Asia's history. In fact, it was the last generation of colonial scholars and officials who joined universities – such as Harry Benda, who was one of the first to speak for the autonomy of Southeast Asian history (Benda 1962: 106–38) and who helped set up Southeast Asian studies centres and pro-grammes in the United States – that put modern Southeast Asian history on a scholarly footing.

Arguably, it is post-colonial Western academics, concerned with carving a niche for themselves in 'area studies', who gave currency to the term 'Southeast Asia', which was after all only of Second World War vintage, and grew out of conveniences of military command rather than intrinsic commonalities and inherent coherence. (Coedès' classic, first published in 1944 and known to the English-reading world as *The Indianized States of Southeast Asia*, was actually entitled *Les Etats hindouisés d'Indochine et d'Indonesie*. The English translation was published in 1968 by the East–West Center Press, University of Hawaii. The book broke new ground in its attempt to understand the region as an entity based on the common experience of Indianization.) As a concept, 'Southeast Asia' was not particularly subscribed to by the peoples whom it purported to distinguish. In fact, the colonial states of the region had more interaction with the 'mother' countries than with their neighbours. With independence some turned inward, shutting themselves off economically and culturally, and remaining firmly neutral in world affairs (as in the case of Burma/Myanmar between the early 1960s and early 1990s). Other Southeast Asian states saw themselves as part of the world and regional community, but effectively aligned themselves with one side or the other in the Cold War: SEATO and the Bandung Conference represented newly founded common ideologically based grounds that were dividing the region (Turnbull 1992: 585–6), rather than reflecting any Southeast Asian spirit.

It was Western and Western-trained academics who set out to write the autonomous, as opposed to the colonial and anti-colonial, history of Southeast Asia, to reveal 'the authentic Indonesian beneath clothes we call the Netherlands Indies' (Smail 1961: 92). Smail's 1961 paper, presented at the First International Conference of Southeast Asian Historians, cogently argued that autonomous Indonesian history, as opposed to one dominated by the Dutch, could be found in the study of an Indonesian society strong and vital enough to adapt new cultural elements that appeared useful to it and to grow with the times (Smail 1961: 91–102).

This call made in the 1960s for an autonomous history drew inspiration from the criticisms of contemporary scholarship made by the Dutch scholar J. C. van Leur, who wrote in the 1930s: 'the Indies are observed from the deck of the ship, the ramparts of the fortress, the high gallery of the trading house'.[6] Although van Leur's words are often quoted, scholarship on Indonesia generally did not pursue his larger questions about economic history and the strength of the indigenous bedrock. Even while Smail emphasized that the study of cultural adaptation should not be confined to the more striking cases of the elites (1961: 92), that was in fact largely what ensued. Historians examined elite political history, focusing largely on the colonial and nationalist period and studying of political leaders, nationalist movements and parties. These were considered to be the most dynamic forces, which would be channelled into shaping the political future of the nation-states and hence needed to be understood in their context.

A case study: towards an autonomous history of Thailand

Such an 'indigenous perspective' is best typified by the studies of the history of Thailand. The country was, after all, never colonized; the use of indigenous sources to examine the indigenous actors would thus naturally result in an indigenous, autonomous history – at least this was the premise of a whole set of studies on King Chulalongkorn modelled on David Wyatt's *The Politics of Reform in Thailand: education in the reign of Rama V* (Wyatt 1969). D. G. E. Hall's colonial classic, first published in 1955, had considered Mongkut and Chulalongkorn as enlightened rulers on the basis of their policy of employing Europeans to reorganize the government services (Hall 1955: 578–90). The relevant primary source material cited in Hall's bibliography is the British Foreign Office's *Correspondence Affecting the Affairs of Siam* (Foreign Office 1894), as well as accounts by Western contemporaries such as H. Warington Smyth, *Five Years in Siam from 1891-1896* (Smyth 1898).

Wyatt rejected Hall's interpretation of Siam in the second half of the nineteenth century on the grounds that it 'fails to explain what happened and merely describes; and for lack of adequate historical materials, the most crucial domestic factors in this process have been left out' (Wyatt 1969: vii).

In Wyatt's narration, it was King Chulalongkorn who led and guided the reforms, not the Western advisers. Wyatt's is about the earliest historical study on modern Thailand not written by a Thai that is based on Thai primary materials. He consulted the records of the Ministry of Instruction, Ministry of Finance, Ministry of the Interior, papers from the Royal Scribes' Department, and other documents, as well as a thorough list of secondary writings in Thai. It certainly set the standard for how Western-trained historians could produce 'autonomous' Southeast Asian history.

Yet the study is in fact not as 'autonomous' as its methodology of using indigenous sources and studying indigenous Southeast Asian leaders as historical actors implies. Wyatt claimed that 'Thailand's response to the West was a creative one which flowed painfully but naturally out of Thai history, society and culture to transform the old Kingdom of Siam into a new modern Thai nation' (Wyatt 1969: vii). He stressed that this process was accomplished largely through 'action from above'. The dilemma facing the Siamese rulers in the age of colonialism was that

> Her rulers both admired and feared the West; they wanted to be both Thai and modern; they were asked to move closer to 'civilised' standards yet wished to maintain the continuity that bound them to the values and traditions of their own civilisation; and they wished to be accepted as equals, yet were reluctant to pay the high cost of such acceptance (Wyatt 1969: 380).

In the end the king realized that he could modernize without Westernizing, that Thais could recast their old society, cultural traditions and institutions in new, modern modes without destroying the values that made them uniquely Thai. In practical terms this meant, for instance, running Thai institutions – such as schools operated by the monastic order – on modern lines while maintaining their traditional nature. This theme of the cultural battles fought by Southeast Asian elites also runs through *In Search of Southeast Asia* (Steinberg 1987), one of the more recent and influential attempts to put together a history of Southeast Asia.[7]

To point out, as I am going to, that Wyatt's study can be read as a product of the 1960s – the period when it was written – in no way detracts from the worth or integrity of the scholarship. It simply reinforces the proposition that history-writing, even at its most rigorous, is not uninvolved in perceptions that emanate from the historian, and that the historian is a product of his or her age. For the implications of Wyatt's study has resonances for the Thai leadership in the 1960s. Wyatt heavily emphasized 'leadership from above' and the distinction between Westernization and modernization, with the former being linked to disruption, loss of cultural autonomy and breaking of the social fabric, whilst the latter spelt progressive change, stability, and the retention, if not the strengthening of 'Thai-ness'. This was in essence the very message that Prime Minister Sarit (1957–63), a paternal despot who ruled without a constitution, effectively transmitted – that Thai democracy could be achieved without the trappings of foreign institutions such as parliament and political parties but should instead hark back to the traditional Thai concepts of state, which he defined as the rule of a leader who has *khuntham* (moral responsibility) and ability. In Sarit's picturesque terms:

> Let us hope that our democracy is like a plant having deep roots in Thai soil ... It should produce bananas, mangoes, rambutans, mangosteens and durians; and not apples, grapes, dates, plums or horse chestnuts (Chaloemtiarana 1979: 158).

Sarit was not a reactionary. It was he who oversaw the opening of the country to foreign investment, as well as to the increasing American security presence. He coupled his despotism with these developments through the claim that political stability, which could best come about through preserving the uniqueness of Thai institutions and values, was the key to national security and economic development. This very message can be read into Wyatt's study of King Chulalongkorn.

In the case of Thai history-writing in Western scholarship, it took a political scientist, and (at that time) a non-Thai specialist (who was therefore perhaps less enamoured of the 'cultural uniqueness' and 'great man' approaches) to point out the uncritical assumptions behind the identification of king and nation, and to question the reality of Thailand's 'independence' in the face of the colonization of the rest of the region. Political scientist Benedict Anderson (1978) shook the serene world of Thai studies by challenging the axioms, which he identified thus:

1. Non-colonization was an unqualified blessing, which marked Siam as unique in nineteenth- and early twentieth-century Southeast Asian history.
2. Accordingly, Siam was in effect the first independent modern nation-state in Southeast Asia.
3. The Jakri dynasty's historical role was 'modernizing' and 'national'.
4. Siam's success was due mainly to the basic 'stability' of Thai society and to the famous 'flexibility' of its patriotic leaders.

Anderson countered each of these with what he called his 'doubtlessly scandalous hypotheses':

1. In certain important respects Siam was unfortunate, not so much in being colonized, as in being indirectly colonized.
2. In certain important respects Siam was almost the last to become an independent *national* state in Southeast Asia.
3. The role of the Jakri dynasty, if modernizing, was modernizing only in the special sense that the regimes of colonial governors were modernizing.
4. Siam's 'success/failure' is to be understood primarily as a result of the European imperialist pacification of Southeast Asia; Thai leaders have in fact been comparatively inflexible, and Thai political life has been (at least since the 1930s) an exemplary case of instability (Anderson 1978: 198–9).

Within Thailand itself, conditions set in that brought about political upheaval, and a related 'revolution' in history-writing. In the early 1970s, Thailand's involvement in the Indochina war, the anti-war protests in the US campuses where Thai academics were studying, and the rise of a middle class which was increasingly intolerant of the politically repressive regime led to a radical reassessment of the received wisdom in history, which exalted kings, prime ministers and the nation-state, and which provided the ideological underpinnings of the military regimes. The contrast between the exhilaration which followed the overthrow of the regime by popular forces in 1973, and the rapid disillusionment on the part of the student movement with the pace of reform, led many Thai intellectuals towards more radical critiques. A number reassessed Thai history in vulgar Marxist terms: there was a preoccupation with identifying slave and feudal, and with some, the Asiatic Mode of Production in Thai history (Hong 1991:

99–112). These categories were in antithesis to the hitherto dominant historiography, which was by and large either hagiographic or dealt with foreign relations (stressing, of course, Siam as an independent nation).

The cataclysmic military suppression that ended this period of 'open politics' in Thailand in 1976 included the banning and destroying of the radical literature that had proliferated. However, both the government after 1977 and the radicals realized that their extreme stands were not particularly fruitful, for they alienated those who occupied the middle ground. Where critical history writing is concerned, one trend that emerged in the post-1976 period was the study of the state and its ideological apparatus in the process of striving for hegemony, rather than simply as a tool of the dominant class. To link up with the Hall and Wyatt narratives discussed earlier, Varuni Osapharom's 1980 MA thesis, written in the Chulalongkorn University's History Department, should be mentioned. It is entitled 'Education in Thai Society 1868-1932' and examines how the Siamese kings, especially Chulalongkorn, revamped education to harmonize with the ideology of centralization and the state, which was defined as being inextricable from the monarchy. Among the primary sources consulted, school textbooks of that era were analysed for the notions and values that they were meant to inculcate; the terms in which these notions were couched, which reflected changing definitions of words and concepts; and how they were made familiar and acceptable.

The case of history-writing in Thailand is brought up in the interests of the discussion of what is meant by 'autonomous' Southeast Asian history, and how it does not mean simply taking away the non-indigenous actors, or even taking on the perspective of the indigenous leaders, or histories written by Southeast Asians themselves, or examining 'indigenous responses to the Western challenge'. The notion of an 'autonomous' Southeast Asian history is a claim for a particular version of history as being the most authentic, valid and 'politically correct', and, as with all such claims, it cannot be understood apart from the larger framework in terms of the time and perspective within which the historian operates.

Directions in Southeast Asian History

As a whole, the discipline of history has undergone fundamental democratic changes in the last generation or so. Rankean history – which claimed that 'truth can be but one' (von Ranke 1839–47: 72), asserting that the historian could reveal the past objectively, 'as it really was' based on primary archival materials and focusing largely on the doings of 'great men' – is no longer unquestioningly subscribed to. Historians have become more conscious of both the limitations and the possibilities of their discipline. Their pronouncements about the past can no longer claim to be the final word on the matter, as they become cognizant of the different perspectives that can be adopted (for example, subaltern studies, women's history, social history, economic history) and of the instrumental role of the historian in constructing that history.

Historians of Southeast Asia who have addressed the question of what history is about can be roughly divided into those who try to rescue von Ranke's definition of history, and those who reject it. In the first category are historians who concede to Ranke's critics that studies of the past have been dependent on records which are not objective because they are accounts left by elites, and that the facts cannot speak for themselves. They argue that it is historians who ultimately determine the meaning of the history they write, as they have to select and give sense to what they consider pertinent in a mass of source materials. To overcome these obstacles to revealing the past, historians influenced by the *Annales* school (see below) have attempted to produce 'scientific' history by examining the geographical, climatic, economic and social forces that shaped the past, rather than the decisions and actions of 'great men', which have been the stuff of Rankean history. Another way of attempting to correct the flawed nature of historical testimonies has been to focus on the underclass rather than the elite, and to consult primary materials ignored by traditional historians. Hence the history of the rickshaw coolies of colonial Singapore, as culled from the records of the coroner's court, is deemed to be the true history of their suffering, and they, the true heroes of Singapore (see Warren 1986).

The contrasting approach towards writing Southeast Asian history defies von Ranke's dictum that the truth can be but one. This new direction, best illustrated in the study of the mentality of the Filipino peasantry, is based on the premise that moral and religious 'truths' are constructed by the state to enforce acceptance. That acceptance, however, is never total, but is negotiated to fit in with the peasants' sense of the world. Peasant beliefs are not viewed as inherently primitive or backward; they localize 'advanced' beliefs to form a coherent ideology with a notion of justice and morality that could in certain circumstances justify revolts and, in others, submission. In other words, the peasants, no less than the elite, are historical actors whose historical roles are not simply predestined (see Ileto 1979; Rafael 1988).

Total history

The dominant critically informed historiographical approach to the writing of a comprehensive history of Southeast Asia adheres to the principles of the *Annales* school. The *Annales* historians consider history that studies only the singular (be it the individual leader, the event or the unique society) to be totally arbitrary in selection, in fact to be pure chaos. Such traditional history was not scientific, meaning that it could not delineate 'similarities, recurrences and conformities', and hence could offer only descriptions rather than explanations (Iggers 1975: 51–2). To this end, the *Annalistes* advocate the study of total history or structural history – concerned with all the major forms of collective life, economies, institutions, social structures – all aspects of reality that have all too often been regarded as a backdrop. Only then could an objective, scientific history be attained, purged of the contaminations of the individual historian.[8]

Anthony Reid's *Southeast Asia in the Age of Commerce 1450–1680* has taken up the *Annales* call for a more broadly defined and interdisciplinary study of the past, examining the physical, material, and social structures of Southeast Asia. As Reid explained:

> I have concentrated on those features and changes which most affected the population at large, rather than on the rulers and foreigners who play such a large part in the published record. These are frequently long-term changes discernible only by looking at a canvas which is broad in both space and time, with one eye always open for comparable developments in other parts of the world (Reid 1988: xv).

The book is organized in the shape of tiered concentric circles, beginning from the outermost ring and working towards the vortex: it first sets out the physical landscape, the means of livelihood that could be derived, including population figures, techniques of agriculture, and diet; the material culture that was supported, such as architectural forms and textile and clothing, is then examined; and finally the focus narrows to the social framework governing the use of the resources and expressions of the material culture (such as the difference between religious edifices, royal abodes and simple houses) and literary, dramatic and popular culture (in the final chapter on 'Festivals and Amusements'). The sources that Reid used are the accounts of the contemporary European travellers, as well as indigenous records, which pertained largely to matters relating to ideology, law, religion and ceremonial (Reid 1988: xv).

The second volume of *Southeast Asia in the Age of Commerce* continues with the *Annales* framework and situates *conjonctures* (cyclical patterns or trends, as in changes of prices, landholding, population movements) and *évenèments* – in Braudel's terms, 'the history of events: a surface disturbance, the waves stirred up by the powerful movement of tides' (Braudel 1980: 3) – within the context of the long-term structures of Southeast Asia in the period. By examining Southeast Asia through three layers of time – geographical, social and political – Reid claims to approach the total history of the region. Urbanization, the embracing of world religions, wars, the development of absolutist states, all of which occurred in Southeast Asia between the mid-fifteenth and late-seventeenth centuries, are understood as outcomes of the international maritime trade which peaked in the 'sustained boom of the "long" sixteenth century' (Reid 1993: 1).

People's history: the underclass as heroes and victims

While the *Annales* paradigm challenged the historiography that concerned itself with the specific intentions of historical figures, the school has been criticized for in effect depoliticizing history and scholarship by stressing objective social processes that operated independently of human will and transcended ideological divisions (Iggers 1975: 51–2). Those who profess to write 'People's History' or the history of 'the underside' would object to this claim to scholarly detachment and to the operation of impersonal forces. As James Warren announced in his *Rickshaw Coolie: a people's history of Singapore (1880–1940)*, to study the history of the immigrant Chinese coolie and his impact on the growth of Singapore, 'historians must commit themselves to a sustained inquiry of those Chinese who came to Singapore to labour, who were hundreds of thousands, poor, who "never made their fortunes"' (Warren 1986: 3). Drawing primarily on coroners' records of the rickshaw-pullers who died of natural, accidental or violent deaths, Warren used 'thick description' at the micro-level to rehabilitate the experience of the coolies in such passages as:

> On the 10th July 1935 at 5 p.m. I returned home after pulling my rickshaw for two hours. I went to our room. My wife was there. I found she had been paid one dollar being repayment of a loan to someone. I took twenty cents of this one dollar and bought a durian ... My wife scolded me for taking the money and threatened to throw the rest away. I went out again to a nearby teashop with my brother-in-law. I returned home again after 8 p.m. ... that evening she accused me of spending money too freely (Warren 1986: 226).

This first-person account of a domestic tiff is preserved only because of its tragic result. Ler Cho Wing, the wife of the rickshaw-puller, hanged herself over the incident, and the narration was found in the coroner's report on her death.

Another source of material, which is extremely useful especially for writing people's history – for which there is obviously scanty archival documentation – is interviews with the subjects themselves. Warren, for example, has used interviews conducted by the Oral History Department in Singapore to obtain such accounts of first-hand, intimate experience:

> Initially, when I first started to pull rickshaws, the roads were not as good then, it used to be tarred roads, and the tar used to melt under the sun, sometimes your feet ran over the burning tar, with the fierce sun shining ... the tar stuck to the feet, and you got blisters. Later on the soles of your feet were not affected in the same way because the skin became tough and hard. It was better in rainy weather because the road was harder, and it was easier to run; the hot weather was more difficult on one's feet, the road was soft, the tar got soft and melted, it stuck to rubber, stuck to the tyre, sometimes stuck to my feet, a bit tough (Warren 1986: 200).

Warren obviously wrote with commitment. He saw himself as putting right a historical wrong. To him, the coolies are Singapore's national heroes, yet they have no place in its history. 'This book has tried to bring back to Singapore's own Chinese people and society, a *singkeh* coolie culture and history, which is, finally, their own – a People's History' (Warren 1986: 326). He tried to identify himself with the coolies of 1880–1940 to the point that he pedalled a trishaw in Singapore, there being no rickshaw left: 'I wanted to know what it felt like ... I wanted to understand what it was like to be sweat soaked, haggard and tired, and to come in at the end of a shift, hand over the rickshaw and then walk into a *kongsi* house (the sleeping quarters)' (Warren 1987: xv).

In a way, Warren's approach is no less hagiographic than the elite history he challenges. Rather than giving a history back to the rickshaw coolies, he ironically ends up stereotyping them as helpless victims of circumstances, with little wherewithal to understand their own situation, let alone to negotiate with the forces that are part of their lives. In fact, they did fashion their own forms of submission, resistance or adaptation, which for some meant eventually becoming rickshaw-owners themselves; others broke out of the trade altogether. However, Warren's tendency was to romanticize the rickshaw coolies, thence to stress his empathy with them and his role in giving them a history. As a result, despite all the 'thick description', they simply end up being rather one-dimensional, singing a collective tale of woe which drowns out the individual voices and different lives that could however be understood within the same historical context, varied though the outcomes of each might be.

People's history: the underclass as historical actors

The writing of 'people's history' is problematic on another level. Even the most earnest and scrupulous of historians who seek to find out what really happened from the point of view of the underclass can be foiled by the subjects themselves. In *Contracting Colonialism: translation and Christian conversion in Tagalog society under early Spanish rule*, Vincente L. Rafael narrates an episode of a historian interviewing a peasant leader to 'set the historical record straight', 'to infuse a sense of personal depth' into the government reports, newspaper stories and court depositions that make up the main sources of his account of the 1931 peasant uprising. The historian was after a first-person account of a historical episode. The subject, however, was not interested in the narration of the past – hence his brusque reply to the question 'How did you organize the people? Did you have secret handshakes, code words, blood pacts, and *anting-anting* [amulets]' was: 'Yes, we had all those things, but we need not discuss them. You already know all about them or you wouldn't ask the question' (Rafael 1988: 8).

On the other hand, the peasant's own recollection of the past had to do with matters that historians would dismiss as imagination and hence irrelevant:

> *Historian*: When did you come home [from Hawaii]? When and why did you form your society?
>
> *Pedro Calosa* [leader in a 1931 uprising]: I was deported from Hawaii after I got out of prison [for organizing a general strike among plantation workers]. I came home late in 1927. Conditions were still bad. The personalities of Rizal, Bonifacio, and Felipe Salvador appeared before me. They told me to form an association to end the suffering of the poor. I know Rizal's personality well. When I was in chains in Corregidor after the uprising – it was in July of 1934 – his personality told me 'I will come again'. He did not say when. He helped me escape … My body stayed, but my personality escaped. I set it to haunt three people: Manuel Quezon [the president of the Commonwealth], Aurora Quezon [the president's wife], and the American secretary of war (Rafael 1988: 9–10).

Reynaldo C. Ileto, in his much-acclaimed *Pasyon and Revolution*, demonstrated that it is just such a consistent disregard for accurate description of past events that offers historians the opportunity to study the workings of the popular mind, the collective consciousness, discerned from sources 'from below' such as poems, songs, scattered autobiographies, confessions, prayers and folk sayings (Ileto 1979: 13–14). With such a perspective, early Filipino peasant revolts, which typically exhibited belief in the potency of amulets and invulnerability, and are thus usually dismissed as fanatical, irrational, or even 'feudal', can be interpreted as peasant attempts to restructure the world in terms of ideal social forms and modes of behaviour (Ileto 1979: 11). Ileto himself studies the *Pasyon Pilapil*, a verse chronicle of Christ's suffering, death and resurrection recited and dramatized in Catholic Filipino communities during Holy Week. The Spaniards, as the colonial authority, introduced Christianity as a means of control, but they were unable to control the meanings the Filipinos read into the Catholic texts, which were assimilated in ways which were not intended or foreseen. Hence, the *pobres y ignorantes* (poor and ignorant – a phrase commonly used by Spaniards and upper middle-class Filipinos to refer to the native masses) creatively evolved their own brand of folk Christianity, from which was drawn much of the language of anti-colonialism in the later nineteenth century. The *Pasyon* enactments opened the possibility of identifying the wealthy and educated elite with the Pharisees who tormented Christ; Jesus Christ himself is cast in a revolutionary role, selecting common and lowly people as his disciples 'to popularise his teachings/ to perform astonishing feats here in the universe' and proclaim a new era of mankind (Ileto 1979: 20–4). Thus was revolution tied to the *Pasyon*.

So Ileto helps us understand that peasant leader Calosa's notion of the past and that of the historian interviewing him were quite different. To the former, there is no chronological distance between the great Filipino nationalists and himself. Death did not end their existence, they haunted the living and, through their spiritual effect, in fact guided and empowered them. The historian therefore would be paralysed were he or she to work within modern (late nineteenth- and twentieth-century) notions of reason and science. Calosa's account de-centres the modern secular narrative. In *Contracting Colonialism*, which can be read as a companion volume to *Pasyon and Revolution*, Vincente L. Rafael argues that submission to the colonial authority was achieved through the dissemination of language and religion (through translation and conversion, respectively) but that in order for it to work effectively, both the Spanish and Christianity had to negotiate with the indigenous social order in a way that reshaped it to fit the colonial enterprise. Hence Christian notions of a 'beautiful death' – that is, the attainment of 'the tranquillity of heaven where they will see God, and obtain happiness, and joy, and rest forever and ever' (Rafael 1988: 171) – brought assurances not only of reward for a life lived as a good Catholic, but also of a divide between the living and the dead. This latter notion relieved those in this world from being 'shocked' by the spirits who roamed the earth in the Indio (native Filpino) eschatology, but transferred the power of the spirits to the priests and native elite confraternities who possessed the texts and the rituals that were touted as being indispensable for reaching heaven.

Ileto and Raphael both used literary forms such as native songs (*awit*), political manifestos, missionary tracts, prayers, and books concerned with translation and instruction in Spanish, intended for Filipinos. From these sources, they drew not 'facts' but an understanding of what the language – the use of particular words, idioms, imagery – denoted about the crucial cultural intercourse between the Spanish and Filipinos in the specific historical context of colonialism. Language itself becomes an area of contest in which parties jostle to imprint the particular meaning that favours them.

When Ileto published his work in 1979, this 'post-structuralist' approach drew fire from those he called the 'traditional' historians, who accused his writing of being based not on evidence, but on a 'creative imagination like that expressed by poets and fictionists'.[9] Rafael's publication almost a decade later was similarly faulted by a leading historian in the Philippines for its neglect of historical for literary analysis (Schumacher 1989: 354–5). Ileto's response was to point out the fixed ideas that such historians hold about the absolute opposition between literature (associated with the fictive, subjective) and history (aligned with truth, objectivity, reality) (Ileto 1982: 105). Post-structuralism contends that history, no less than literature, is a narrative – it has a story-telling aspect that emerges from the framework the historian constructs to give coherence to the historical evidence. The literary text, on the other hand, can be read as more than just the aesthetically appealing, imaginative work of an author. The author cannot impose his intentions irrevocably on the readers; he cannot control the meanings that can be generated from the text in different social contexts. A master text like the *Pasyon* is capable of generating multiple meanings in relation to the audience and context (Ileto 1982: 105). Ileto thus resists the search for a fixed, non-problematic reading of history along the lines that the *Pasyon* is an elite weapon to lull the Filipinos into inaction with the promise of heaven as a reward, and therefore cannot be a weapon of resistance on the part of the peasantry. Similarly, official documents seem to show that the Philippine Revolution was a matter of the traditional patron–client relations at work, with the clients (peasants) being manipulated by their elite patron to fight in the latter's interests. Ileto, however, insists that the *Pasyon* can be both a weapon against, and a weapon of, the peasantry, and that peasant participation in the Revolution was structured on both patron–client relations, and the peasants' own logic of participation predicated on their understanding of the *Pasyon* story as one of liberation. The peasants' notions were no less valid than those of the educated Filipinos or of the colonialists and missionaries.

The Construction of Southeast Asian History

As postulated in the post-structuralist enquiries, the notion of an authentic past, a dead reality awaiting discovery, cloaks the complexity of history just as it empowers those who impose their version of it over others as being truly objective. 'To deem something "authentic" is a political act and involves the mobilisation of historical knowledge in the task of nation building' (Reynolds 1992: 150) – or in the interests of other political goals. Similarly, the very notion of 'Southeast Asia', 'Southeast Asian studies', 'Southeast Asian history' can fruitfully be understood as constructions. We have already mentioned the genealogy of 'Southeast Asia' from its origins as a colonial, wartime creation. Southeast Asian studies, we have tried to show, has a parallel genealogy.

The doyen of Southeast Asian studies, Benedict Anderson, has observed that in the United States, which took over the role of centre of Southeast Asian studies in the post-colonial period, area studies has been 'gasping for air', for there are 'very few powerful intellectual–pedagogical reasons for systemizing research and teaching along area lines' (Anderson 1992: 301). Aside from the case of Vietnam in the 1960s and 1970s, 'policy studies' on the countries of Southeast Asia were not a sustainable lifeline for scholarship, given the relatively low interest that they generated for American security and economic interests.

As a result, the field of Southeast Asian studies has not been in a healthy state. It was subordinated to the disciplines within the university framework, and was caught up in its whirlpool of theory spinning. The demands of *in situ* teaching at the universities meant that Southeast Asianists were no longer able to gain an intimate and deep familiarity with their area of study, as their colonial bureaucrat–scholar predecessors could. Mastery of the classical languages declined. Anderson, in pointing to all this, called for an honest examination of the field and for creative think about invigorating, widening, and deepening Southeast Asian studies.

Anderson contends that the future of Southeast Asian studies may well rest on the substantial indigenous academic and non-academic intelligentsia. They naturally have the fluency of language that permits access to local culture, literature, religious life, folk traditions, and so on, and have received formal academic training or, if not, at least have familiarity with studies on their country by outsiders. At its best, this scholarship is unparalleled in the wealth of sources it can command, especially in terms of literature, which has been under-used by Western scholars in large part because of the relative weakness of their linguistic capability.

Anderson goes on to argue that there should be a division of labour to make Southeast Asian studies a comprehensive, intellectually vital enterprise. Southeast Asians would translate out of English into their own vernaculars, while for the non-Southeast Asians (including Americans, Europeans, Japanese and Australians), the main task is to render Southeast Asian vernacular work into English. For this task, the outsiders would need to deepen their command of Southeast Asian languages, both classical and vernacular. This international communication would be a basis on which to build the kind of region-specific comparative work that is essential as an intellectual basis for post-colonial area studies, such as comparative study of religions, colonial regimes and modern political systems (Anderson 1992: 31–6).

Anderson's concern is to give intellectual respectability to Southeast Asian studies as a field of area studies. Yet it can be argued that such an agenda is not much different from that of the colonial days, when local vernacular texts were primarily 'material' for colonial scholarship. As Anderson envisaged it, the translated works by Southeast Asians would enhance the sophistication of scholarship and provide a basis for comparative studies of the region. However, such an agenda is not necessarily on the Southeast Asian's mind.

Anderson cited Nidhi Aeusrivongse, who examined the cultural life of early Bangkok through dissecting the poetry of the period, as an exemplar of the new breed of the indigenous academic intelligentsia that he has discerned (Anderson 1992: 36). Nidhi is certainly a fine example of an indigenous Southeast Asianist. After obtaining his MA in history from Chulalongkorn University (the title of the thesis was translated as 'The Suppression of the Haw Uprisings and the loss of Thai Territories in 1888'), he received his Ph.D. from Michigan University in 1976 for his dissertation 'Fiction as history: A study of pre-war Indonesian novels and novelists, 1920–1942', which of course demonstrated his skills in the Indonesian language. Nidhi is hence one of the very few Southeast Asian Southeast Asianists whose scholarship goes beyond that of his own society. Yet since then, he has consistently turned to writing only Thai history, and, consciously, only in the Thai language. In the last few years, he has increasingly disseminated his writings not in the form of academic publications but in popular journals on culture, and even in newspaper columns, where his barbed historical references have been put to the service of political commentary. Narrowly speaking, Nidhi is a nationalist; his premise is that his scholarship should be addressed to Thai society and provide a critique of the authoritarian, capitalist regimes. His priority is not that of a Southeast Asianist, concerned with furthering the intellectual basis of the field, although he is most eminently qualified for such a role.

As the case of Nidhi shows, Southeast Asian studies as a concept is a product of Western academic interests. In the countries of the region itself, indigenous scholars have no need to justify their national focus, and in fact have a compelling sense of mission in pursuing their work, which often simply cannot be divorced from their responsibility as members of that society. The study of history in Southeast Asia itself is therefore similarly entangled in the web of national politics within which historians unavoidably are positioned. They are engaged scholars, and their engagement just does not encompass a supra-national entity or audience. Southeast Asian studies and Southeast Asian history do not really exist where they are concerned.

However, this state of affairs is of course not permanent. In the present multi-polar world – and in particular with the questioning of the Western system as a political model and economic powerhouse – rhetoric about neighbourliness, economic cooperation and complementarity, regional security and stability has intensified. 'Southeast Asia' will be redefined. A shift has occurred, from 'region of revolt' (as defined by Western scholars in the 1960s and 1970s based on fear of the communist threat, and on separatism), to being part of the exploited Third World (a view held by radical scholars, including Southeast Asian ones), to a dynamic economic growth area of the twenty-first century.

The states of Southeast Asia are forging a system that places economic growth and political stability at a premium, ostensibly following Southeast Asian values and traditions. Such is the portrayal put forth by the governments of Singapore (though here the stress is more on the Asian, or more specifically Chinese rather than Southeast Asian, bedrock), Indonesia, Malaysia, Thailand and even Vietnam. The official catch-phrases today are economic complementarity, regional growth and stability. Southeast Asians may well find impetus, and indeed sponsorship, to master a second Southeast Asian language and to research the history of their neighbours – for the same reasons that the Japanese, the region's leading investors, have done so.

Notes

1. Such activities were for instance undertaken by Alaung-hpaya, founder of the Kon-baung dynasty (1752–1885). See Koenig (1990): 76–7.

2. For example, the chronicle written by the court of Rama I, founder of the Chakri dynasty, portrayed his predecessor as king, Taksin, whom he had executed, as an enemy of Buddhism whose practice of Buddhism was unorthodox, who created schisms in the *sangha* (monastic order), and who demanded unreasonable exactions from the people. See Reynolds (1979): 92, 97.

3. For the perceived differences between the traditional and the 'modern, international tradition of historical enquiry', see Legge (1992): 2–3.

4. Pnong being a people who have remained in a stage of tribal organization. Coedès (1968): xvii.

5. Sukarno (1960) cited in Reid (1979): 290.

6. van Leur (1955): 261. For a discussion of van Leur, see Smail (1961): 83–6.

7. The authors of the Thai and Indonesian sections of this volume were Wyatt and Smail respectively.

8. For an exposition, see Braudel (1980): 3–5.

9. Ileto (1982): 104–5. Ileto was responding to a review article on *Pasyon and Revolution* by Guerrero (1981): 240–56.

Bibliography

Anderson, Benedict R. (1978), 'Studies of the Thai State: the state of Thai studies', in Ayal (ed.) (1978): 193–247.

— (1992), 'The changing ecology of Southeast Asian Studies in the United States', in C. Hirschman et al. (eds), *Southeast Asian Studies in the Balance: reflections from America* (Ann Arbor, MI: Association of Asian Studies): 25–40.

Ayal, Eliezer B. (ed.) (1978), *The Study of Thailand: analyses of knowledge, approaches, and prospects*, Papers in International Studies, Southeast Asia series, 54 (Athens, OH: Ohio University, Center for International Studies).

Benda, Harry (1962), 'The structure of Southeast Asian history: some preliminary observations', *Journal of Southeast Asian History*, 3: 106–38.

Braudel, Fernand (1980), *On History* (Chicago: University of Chicago Press).

Chaloemtiarana, Thak (1979), *Thailand: the politics of despotic paternalism* (Bangkok: Social Science Association of Thailand and Thai Kadi Institute).

Chitkasem, Manas and Andrew Turton (eds) (1991), *Thai Constructions of Knowledge* (London: School of Oriental and African Studies).

Coedès, G. (1968), *The Indianized States of Southeast Asia* (originally published in 1944) (Honolulu: East–West Center Press).

Foreign Office (1894), *Correspondence Affecting the Affairs of Siam* (London: Foreign Office, 1894).

Furnivall, J. S. (1944), *Netherlands India: a study of plural economy* (Cambridge: Cambridge University Press).

Guerrero, Milagros C. (1981), 'Understanding Philippine revolutionary mentality', *Philippine Studies*, 29: 240–56.

Hall, D. G. E. (1955), *A History of Southeast Asia* (London: Macmillan).

Hong Lysa (1991), 'Warasan setthasat kanmu'ang: critical scholarship in post-1976 Thailand', in Chitkasem and Turton (eds) (1991): 99–112.

Iggers, Georg G. (1975), *New Directions in European Historiography* (Middletown, CT: Wesleyan University Press).

Ileto, Reynaldo C. (1979), *Pasyon and Revolution: popular movements in the Philippines, 1840–1910* (Qezon City: Ateneo de Manila Press).

— (1982), 'Critical Issues in "Understanding Philippine revolutionary mentality"', *Philippine Studies*, 30: 104–5.

Keyes, Charles (1990), 'The Legacy of Angkor', *Cultural Survival Quarterly*, 14: 56–9.

Koenig, William J. (1990), *The Burmese Polity 1752–1819: politics, administration and social organisation in the early Kon-baung period*, Michigan Papers on South and Southeast Asia, 34 (University of Michigan Press).

Legge, J. D. (1992), 'The writing of southeast Asian history', in Tarling (1992): 1–50.

van Leur, J. C. (1955), *Indonesian Trade and Society* (The Hague: van Hoeve).

Rafael, Vincente L. (1988), *Contracting Colonialism: translation and Christian conversion in Tagalog society under early Spanish rule* (Quezon City: Ateneo de Manila University Press).

von Ranke, Leopold (1839–47), 'Introduction to the *History of the Reformation in Germany*', in Wines (1981): 68–72.

Raffles, Thomas Stamford (1972), *The History of Java*, 2 vols (originally published in 1817) (Singapore: Oxford University Press).

Reid, Anthony (1979), 'The nationalist quest for an Indonesian past', in Reid and Marr (eds) (1979: 281–95).

— (1988), *Southeast Asia in the Age of Commerce 1450–1680, Volume One: The Lands below the Winds* (New Haven, CT: Yale University Press).

— (1993), *Southeast Asia in the Age of Commerce 1450–1680, Volume Two: Expansion and Crisis* (New Haven, CT: Yale University Press).

— and David Marr (eds) (1979), *Perceptions of the Past in Southeast Asia* (Singapore: Heinemann Educational Books for the Asian Studies Association of Australia).

Reynolds, Craig J. (1979), 'Religious historical writing and the legitimation of the first Bangkok reign', in Reid and Marr (eds) (1979): 90–107.

— (1992), 'Authenticating Southeast Asia in the absence of colonialism: Burma', *Asian Studies Review*, 15: 141–51.

Schumacher, John N. (1989), Review of *Contracting Colonialism: translation and Christian conversion in Tagalog society under early Spanish rule* by Vicente L. Rafael, *Journal of Southeast Asian Studies*, 20: 354–5.

Smail, John R. W. (1961), 'On the possibility of an autonomous history of modern Southeast Asia', *Journal of Southeast Asian History*, 2: 72–102.

Smyth, H. Warington (1898), *Five Years in Siam from 1891 to 1896*, 2 vols (London: Murray).

Steinberg, David Joel (ed.) (1987), *In Search of Southeast Asia*, rev. edn (Honolulu: University of Hawaii Press).

Sukarno (1960), *Indonesia menggugat: pidato pembelaan Bung Karno di muka Lakim kolonial* (Djakarta: Teragung).

Swettenham, F. A. (1983), 'British Rule in Malaya', in Paul Kratoska (ed.), *Honourable Intentions: talks on the British Empire in South-East Asia delivered at the Royal Colonial Institute, 1874–1928* (Singapore: Oxford University Press): 170–211.

Tarling, Nicholas (1992), *The Cambridge History of Southeast Asia*, 2 vols (Cambridge: Cambridge University Press).

Turnbull, C. M. (1992), 'Regionalism and nationalism', in Tarling (1990): 585–645.

Warren, James Francis (1986), *Rickshaw Coolie: a people's history of Singapore (1880–1940)* (Singapore: Oxford University Press).

Warren, J. F. (1987), *On the Edge of Southeast Asian History* (Quezon City: New Day Publishers).

Wines, Roger (1981), *Leopold von Ranke: the secret of world history. Selected writings in the art and science of history* (New York: Fordham University Press).

Wyatt, David K. (1969), *The Politics of Reform in Thailand: education in the reign of King Chulalongkorn* (New Haven, CT: Yale University Press).

3 Literature

Geoffrey E. Marrison

It is not difficult to define Southeast Asia geographically, but when we come to consider its peoples and their cultures, the diversity is so great that it becomes difficult to make general statements about them. Even if only the national languages are taken into account, four or perhaps five language families are represented: Tibeto-Burman (Burma), Tai-Chinese (Thailand, Laos), Mon-Khmer (Kampuchea), Vietnamese (Vietnam – sometimes, but doubtfully, grouped with Mon-Khmer), and Indonesian (Malaysia, Singapore, Indonesia, Brunei and the Philippines). This fact, reflected in extreme differences of vocabulary and sentence structure, also accounts for some of the diversity of literary expression. Another major influence is that of religion, which affects not only scriptural texts, but also the sentiments apparent in historical and imaginative writings. In Burma, Thailand, Laos and Cambodia, Theravada Buddhism is the traditional faith; in Vietnam, Chinese religions and Catholicism have both played their part; in Malaysia and Indonesia, Islam is the religion of the majority, while in the Philippines, Catholicism holds sway.

Status of languages

Each of the present states of Southeast Asia has its national language, used by the majority of speakers, and essential for political, economic and educational purposes, as well as for general communication through the media. There are also non-national literary languages, which represent the survival of formerly dominant groups. Such are the Mon in Burma and Thailand, the Cham in Vietnam and Cambodia, and the Javanese, as well as several other languages of the principal islands of Indonesia; while in the Philippines, in addition to Pilipino (deriving chiefly from Tagalog), some of the regional languages have a recorded literature, both past and present. Third, throughout Southeast Asia, many tribes and island peoples have oral literatures, reflecting their diverse cultures.

In addition to these, some of the languages of mainland Asia and of Europe have had a major place in the life of the region. From the beginning of the Christian era, Indians brought Hinduism, with its classical language, Sanskrit, as well as Buddhism, with scriptures both in Pali and in Sanskrit. Chinese became the classical language for Vietnam, but also had influence in other parts of the region. Islam brought Arabic, as well as some knowledge of Persian. From the beginning of the sixteenth century, European languages, at first Portuguese and Spanish, and later Dutch, English and French, were all used by traders, and by colonial administrators, educators and missionaries. The Japanese presence in recent times not only reshaped the political scene, but also had its influence on a generation of Southeast Asian writers.

Phases of literature

Four phases of literary tradition and development may be recognized.

Indigenous The indigenous phase began in prehistoric times and continues to the present day. It is reflected chiefly in oral literature, but also underlies much of the sentiment and expression in the major modern languages, and is determined by local geography, flora, fauna, social structures, agricultural and other occupations, animistic ideas and ceremonies. Swellengrebel summarized the early indigenous elements in Balinese culture as including wet rice cultivation, involving irrigation; cockfighting; wooden constructions, especially small pavilions; working in iron and bronze; dyeing and weaving; some aspects of music and dance; family, village and regional temples, and the offerings made in them; a large part of the folk-tales handed down orally; and the language itself, which, he said 'with its structure, must be considered an autochthonous cultural possession'. All these he contrasted with another list of cultural features of Hindu or Hindu–Javanese origin. Many of the items Swellengrebel cites as being indigenous might be attributed to Indonesian life more generally, and are paralleled in other parts of Southeast Asia. From the point of view of literature, they represent characteristics widespread in Southeast Asia, which also to some degree distinguish them from the literary character of other regions (Swellengrebel 1960: 29).

Period of influence of the major civilizations of Asia From about the beginning of the Christian era until the end of the fifteenth century, Indian traders, colonists and missionaries brought Hinduism and Buddhism to Southeast Asia, together with the Sanskrit and Pali languages, artistic traditions, social ideas and items of material culture.

Some of these things may be studied from the numerous inscriptions
in Sanskrit and indigenous languages, and in the literatures themselves,
particularly Old Javanese, whose writings have survived to modern
times. The Chinese dominated Vietnamese culture: the Vietnamese
wrote in Chinese for many centuries, and only later used their own
language as a literary medium. The Chinese also penetrated to other
parts of Southeast Asia, where they traded and settled and, besides
bringing items of material culture and political ideas, had some
influence on literary developments: some favourite Southeast Asian
stories were adapted from Chinese originals. Arab, Persian and Indian
Muslim traders crossed the Indian Ocean. Islamic kingdoms were
founded in North Sumatra at the end of the thirteenth century, and at
Malacca in the fifteenth, profoundly influencing the development of
Malay literature.

Period of European trade and colonization, and of Islamic penetration
This lasted from the beginning of the sixteenth century until the
Japanese occupation of Southeast Asia in 1942. European languages
were introduced, and in some parts, especially for official purposes,
became dominant, such as Spanish in the Philippines and, to some
degree, Dutch in the East Indies. Christian missions were established,
translated scriptures, and provided Western-style education, in which
colonial governments generally followed much later. During the same
period, Islam spread eastward from Malacca to become the major
religion in the islands of Indonesia. The Muslim influence on literature
was much more direct than the European; Arabic was studied in
Qur'anic schools. During this period too, Sri Lanka was instrumental
in reforming Buddhism in Burma, Thailand, Laos and Cambodia.
Meanwhile the older influences from India and China continued
throughout the region.

Period of national movements and independence From the earliest presence of Europeans, indigenous reaction and resistance were known:
but it was in the nineteenth and especially in the twentieth centuries
that these movements were effectively articulated. Colonial administration, Western education, Christian missions, general contact with the
outside world, new political ideologies and the advances of science and
technology all had their effects on Southeast Asian societies. These
influences have been reflected in the languages of the region: imported
or translated terminology for new ideas, and the promotion of
indigenous languages for patriotic and nationalistic purposes. Literature
was often used for political ends. This sometimes resulted in a break
with past traditional literature, in content, style and attitude, or sometimes in the continuance of traditional and modern literary activity

side by side. The Japanese occupation of Southeast Asia between 1942 and 1945 was the penultimate and one of the most potent influences in this process, and was rapidly followed by independence for the former colonies of Britain, France and the Netherlands, and for the Philippines. Promotion of national languages became a major feature in the development of nationhood. This was reinforced by national educational programmes and by attempts by some of the states to encourage and to control literature, the arts and the media.

Critical approaches to Southeast Asian literatures

The earliest approaches to the languages and literatures of Southeast Asia from the European side were practical, determined by the needs of commerce, the aspirations of missionaries and the requirements of colonial administration. Attention was given to indigenous legal codes and to the study of Asian religions, since while there was a determination to control local populations, efforts were made to avoid offending social and religious susceptibilities through ignorance of the regional cultural backgrounds. Christian missionaries were active in parts of the region, and were especially prominent in language studies. Scholar-administrators collected manuscripts or had them copied, and began to list, describe and analyse them and, with the collaboration of indigenous scholars, to produce critical editions of important texts. However, much of the traditional literature has never been printed, so the scholar must often go to the originals for research.

Another important field is that of the oral literatures of the region. Even where literacy, publication and urbanization are well advanced, oral traditions persist, and probably count for more than is the case in the West. Folk-tales, folk-songs, lyric and erotic verse, legal maxims, proverbs and riddles are widely current in the national societies, while in the pre-literate, tribal societies these categories comprehend most of their literary activity. In many parts of the region, sophisticated and extensive performance of epics, dramas and religious ceremonies are determined at least as much by oral tradition as by published laws or written texts.

In the modern literatures of Southeast Asia, some additional significant considerations apply. Printing and publication, and presentation through radio, cinema and television, cassettes and videos, all have to be taken into account. Moreover, since these modern literatures are, at least in part, influenced by European models, they are more readily susceptible to modern Western literary-critical approaches. These have been attempted, not only by Western scholars, but also by indigenous writers, for whom literary criticism is a comparatively new genre, but one which is well understood and widely practised. In all the main languages of Southeast Asia, the novel, the short story, Western-style poetry, social drama, essays on social and political themes and journalistic practice are widespread, while academic textbooks and technical handbooks on every aspect of modern life bulk large in local publication output. Journals, magazines and newspapers are the carriers of much of these classes of material. Writers are often schoolteachers, journalists and broadcasters.

General sources for the study of Southeast Asian literatures

The *Penguin Companion to Literature*, Volume 4 (Dudley and Lang 1969), has an Oriental section, which includes brief general articles, with bibliographies, on the various national literatures of Southeast Asia, as well as bio-bibliographical entries for individual authors and descriptions of important anonymous works. Herbert and Milner (1989) has general introductions for each country, together with extensive bibliographies up to the 1980s. Jenner (1973) is a bibliography with 3,690 entries arranged by countries, and for each literature has sub-sections according to genres. Tham Seong Chee (1981), and Davidson and Cordell (1986) have edited collections of papers dealing with different aspects of the literatures of the region.

The literatures of Southeast Asian countries

Burma

The Burmese empire of Pagan was founded by Anawrahta, who ruled from 1044 to 1077. According to their tradition, the Burmese adopted the Theravada Buddhist faith and acquired the Pali scriptures when they defeated the Mons to their south in 1057. In later times, the Burmese monks became famous for their scholarship. Pali terms were introduced into the Burmese language and, in time, Burmese commentaries were written on Pali texts. This can best be studied in Bode (1909). The Myazedi Inscription of Rajakumara of 1113 is reckoned to be the earliest surviving use of literary Burmese. Texts were generally written on palm leaves in the rounded Burmese script, which was inherited from the Mon. A few early manuscripts from the fifteenth century survive, but most are much later, originating long after the disintegration of the Pagan kingdom at the beginning of the fourteenth century.

In the earliest or classical period, down to the end of the Toungoo dynasty in 1752, Burmese poetry was written in lines of four syllables, with internal rhymes. Religious poems with exhortations to virtuous conduct were called *pyo*; panegyrics to glorify the ruler were *mawgun* and *egyin*; and the poets wrote lyrics on personal themes of sadness, love and longing. In this period, the earliest *yazawin* or royal chronicles were composed; they were adapted and added to in later times. The earliest was the *Yazawin-gyaw* of Thilawuntha, the 'Celebrated Chronicle', based upon the Pali chronicle, the Mahavamsa of Sri Lanka, but also including notes on Burmese kings. These works were in prose and were continued in later times: the *Maha-yazawin-gyi* of U Kala, 1714–33, the *Hmannan Yazawin* or 'Glass Palace Chronicle', 1832, and the *Konbaungzet Yazawin* of 1886. During the early period, the *Jatakas*, accounts of the former lives of the Buddha, were translated from Pali into Burmese prose: these stories have been influential in much of the later Burmese writing.

The Konbaung dynasty, which ruled from 1752 to 1885, heralded a new period in Burmese literature. A new type of verse, *yagan*, freer in structure than the classical poetry, drew on the legends of the Jatakas, as well as stories from Hindu and other sources. The Burmese conquered the Thai of Ayuthia in 1767. It was from them that they received the *Ramayana*, rendered into Burmese *yagan* verse at the end of the eighteenth century. The Burmese theatre developed in this period, also influenced in the late eighteenth century by Thai models. In the nineteenth century, stage plays called *pyazat* became popular.

The modern Burmese period began with the British annexation of Mandalay in 1886, and the increased use of printing from then on. Literature no longer depended on court patronage, but became a public activity. The older types of poetry died out, and more use was made of prose; plays, novels and short stories were written. In the 1930s, the *Khitsan* movement sought to develop modern literature, while preserving the best features of traditional writing. With Burmese independence in 1948, Burmese displaced English as the official language.

The Mon language, which has an older history than Burmese, and has had some influence over it, now survives as the speech of minorities in Burma and Thailand. There are early inscriptions, and some literary works. These may be followed up from the bibliography in Bauer (1984) and the work of Halliday (1917). The Shan language of North-East Burma also has an established literature. It is closely related to Thai, but written in the Burmese script. The literature consists chiefly in renderings of Buddhist works and local histories. These have not been published, but there is an important manuscript collection, the Scott Collection, in the Cambridge University Library. There is an account by Cochrane (1910: 208–20).

Around the hilly perimeter of Burma are many tribal peoples. Most of these speak Tibeto-Burmese languages, so are related to the Burmese. However, for the most part they remain animist. They include the Chins in the west, the Kachins and Lisu in the north and the Karens in the east; among the last, there are many Christians. Descriptions of their oral literature must be sought among the anthropological monographs devoted to the various minority groups.

An introduction to Burmese literature, including bio-bibliographical notes on individual writers and works, is given by Allott (1971). Bibliographical information, chiefly about general works on Burmese literature, is to be found in Herbert (1991). The Burmese scholar, Hla Pe, produced *Burma: literature, historiography, scholarship, language, life and Buddhism* (1985) and other more specialized works and articles (1962, 1971). Lustig (1986) selected Burmese poems and provided texts and English translations. Among the many works of Htin Aung, we may mention *Burmese Drama* (1937) and *Burmese Folk Tales* (1954). He also provided a forward to Myint Thein's *Burmese Folk Songs* (1987). A section on Mon literature is included in Halliday (1917) and there is a bibliography in Bauer (1984). There is a chapter on the Shan language and literature, including translations of folk-tales and proverbs, in Milne (1910). Simmonds (1965) gives references to Shan Buddhist literature, histories and folk-tales.

Thailand

In early times, the Tai people lived in south China, but the Mongol invasions in the thirteenth century put pressure on the population and Tais and others moved southward. In 1238, Thai chiefs captured Sukhothai, then the northern capital of the Cambodians. This marks the beginning of the principal establishment of the Thai in their present homeland, and is significant in relationship to their language, literature and culture. The inscription of the ruler, Rama Kamheng, of 1292 tells how he invented an alphabet for Thai. This was in fact a modification of the existing Cambodian alphabet. From the Cambodians too, the Thai received the Buddhist faith, and many influences on their art and culture as well as in their literature, which began at this time.

It was, however, in the kingdom of Ayuthia (1350–1767) that traditional Thai literature was developed. From the fifteenth century, a form of drama called the *Lakhon chatri* became popular, performed by itinerant actors and musicians, with stories from the *Paññasa-jataka*, an unorthodox collection of fifty *Jatakas*. Among these was the *Manohara*, the story of love and romance between a bird-woman and a human prince, which has survived in south Thailand in the *Nora* performances. At the same time, stories from the *Ramayana* were performed as dance-dramas at court, and in various forms of shadow-play. The high point in Ayuthia's literature was reached in the reign of King Narai (1657–88), when many narrative historical poems and secular verse romances were composed, in which the love theme was often accompanied by mystery and magic. Popular tales included *Phra Law* (the Magic Lotus) and *Khung Chan Khung Phan*, a love triangle of Chinese origin. At this time, the poet Si Prat wrote of exile from court in *Kamsuan Si Prat* ('The mourning of Si Prat'). This established a genre known as *Nirat*, in which a traveller addresses his lady-love about his separation from her on a journey. Two forms of verse, called *khlong* and *kap*, are used, with intricate internal rhymes.

When the Burmese sacked Ayuthia in 1767, much of the old litera-ture was lost. However, a revival took place after the foundation of Bangkok as a new capital by a new dynasty. During the reign of King Rama I (1782–1809) a new full version of the *Ramayana* was composed, and the poet Sunthorn Phu wrote his masterpiece, the epic poem *Phra Abhaimani*, the romance of a prince with a beautiful maiden, his adventures at sea, and his confrontations with Malays and Europeans. In later times poetry declined, and gave way to prose works from 1850 onwards, though lyric and folk poetry did survive. During the reign of King Rama VI (1910–25), Western literary genres were adopted, and there were some women novelists. Si Burapha, born in 1905, led the way with his novel *Luc Phuchai*, the story of a poor man who trans-cends his social class to achieve a high position. Other novelists also wrote on social themes, and the short story and drama were promoted not only through the press, but also by radio and television.

Phya Anuman Rajadhon (1961) describes 'seven great works of Thai literature, selected as representative of Thai culture in its homogeneity'. He was judging his own literature; the choice he made shows how Thai culture was derived from a number of sources and harmonized into a new synthesis. His selection includes *Khun Chang Khun Phan*, the reworking of a Chinese romance; the *Mahachat* or 'Great Jataka', the story of the sacrifice of Prince Vessantara, from a Pali source; *Ramakien*, the Thai version of the Ramayana; *Inao*, a rendering of the Indonesian Panji story; *Sam Kok*, 'The three King-doms', an historical novel of Chinese origin; *Rajadhirat*, from Mon history, and the *Phra Abhaimani*, a romance by Sunthorn Phu. In quite another sphere, Thai folk-stories are well represented in Le May (1930), a volume of translations.

For the study of Thai literature, a first resource is Simmonds (1965). In addition to Thai, this bibliography also contains information about

Lao, Shan and other related languages. An old but useful general introduction is included in Graham (1912) which deals with music, dance and drama, as well as the language and literature. Extensive general treatments are provided by Schweisguth (1951), Mendiones (1970) and Jumsai (1973).

Prince Damrong Rajunabhab (1915) discussed *The Story of the Records of Siamese History*. On the Thai theatre, there are books by Nicholas (1924), Yupho (1952) and Rutnin (1975). On Thai poetry, see Mosel (1961), Chitakasem (1972), and Cooke (1980). For modern developments, reference may be made to Poolthupya (1979).

Laos

The state of Laos, bordered by the middle course of the River Mekong, possesses a long frontier with Thailand, to which it is akin in race, language and culture. All the Tai languages are fairly close one to another, but Lao has its own script and significant differences of speech, and shows both similarities with and divergences from Thai literature. A great part of Laotian literature is unpublished, and remains in the form of palm-leaf manuscripts. French scholars have carefully catalogued and described materials in the Buddhist monasteries and in library collections. Laotian literature is characterized by long prose works, and poetic stories derived from the *Paññasa-jataka*; there are also verse romances, based on the *Ramayana* and parts of the *Mahabharata*. The *Thep-malai* (like the *Phra-malai* in Thailand) is the story of a monk who visited heaven and hell, and returned to earth to report his experiences. The *Maha-jataka*, the ten great *Jatakas* at the end of the Pali collection, are rendered in Lao, while the Indian *Pancatantra* stories are provided in Lao as *Tantai Mahathewi*, with a princess as narrator of the various moralizing animal fables.

Laos, being landlocked and until recent times remote from modern influences, has been conservative in its literature. A favourite romance is the *Sang Sin Sai* from the *Paññasa-jataka* (or *Ha sip sat*), with a hero prince and a princess, magic, mystery and adventures in the forest and in the air. A modern literature has been slow to come into being, but there are some short-story writers now. For bibliographical references on Laotian literature, see Simmonds (1965). For general background, de Berval (1959) is a definitive survey, including lists of manuscripts, summaries of the romances and synopses of folk-tales. Lafont (1962a, 1962b, 1965) also published some useful articles on Laotian literature. Coedès (1966) contains extensive descriptions, especially of tales from the *Paññasa-jataka*. On folk-tales, there are Fleeson (1899) and Brengues (1905). For the romantic poems, see Peltier (1988).

Cambodia

The classic period of Khmer civilization was that of the dynasties who ruled from 802 to 1432. For the greater part of that time Hinduism was dominant. From the monuments, especially some of the reliefs at Angkor and elsewhere, and from the inscriptions, it is clear that there was a knowledge of Sanskrit, and probably also a literature written in Khmer, though nothing has survived directly of these. After the downfall of the Cambodian kingdom, Theravada Buddhism was adopted under the influence of neighbouring Thailand, and this has been a shaping force in later Cambodian literature. It has been said that:

> Cambodian literature is largely made up of romances in verse and scholarly poems, based on the *Ramayana* and on Indian legends of the Buddha. Almost all the romances and poems have a moral purpose, and the merit of a particular composition lies not so much in its aesthetic beauty or emotional power, as in its depth of learning and scholarship. Alliteration and internal rhyme are characteristic features of the prosody. Prose works also form a considerable part of the literature; they include expositions of the tenets of the Buddhist faith and technical treatises on astrology, medicine and ceremonial etiquette (Darby 1943: 142).

The most important and best-loved work of Khmer literature is the *Reamker*, the Cambodian version of the *Ramayana*. This has been extensively studied by Pou (1977a, 1977b, 1979, 1982). There is an excellent English translation by Jacob and Haksrea (1986). In her introduction, Dr Jacob draws attention to the relationship of the poem to other art forms, including bas-reliefs at Angkor Wat, the shadow-play, the masked dance and the Cambodian Royal Ballet. The purpose of the text was to provide 'a dramatic recitative intended to accompany a performance of the mimed ballet' (Jacob and Haksrea 1986: ix). It is much shorter than the Sanskrit epic, differing also in its introduction of many Cambodian features of scenery, birds, flowers, trees, customs and so on. The Hindu background remains, but it has been given a Buddhist veneer by representing Rama as an incarnation of the Buddha. However, in the second part of the text, which was composed later and deals with events after Sita had been rescued from Sri Lanka, Rama is criticized for his ignoble treatment of Sita, and this part of the work almost bears the character of female protest.

Some of the classes of Khmer literature can be recognized by the initial word describing them. Thus *cpap* are poems of moral advice, especially to young men and young women; *kbuon* are manuals on a variety of subjects; *neang* in a title signifies a story about a woman; *reach* (Raja) introduces royal chronicles; and *preah* (noble, holy) often indicates a work of Buddhist teaching. In the eighteenth and nineteenth centuries many verse romances were written, such as the *Preah Cina-vong*, the story of how a prince lost a magic sword to a mischievous monkey, and regained it from the ogre king who had obtained it, by enlisting the help of a lady-in-waiting from the palace. Another favourite is *Vorvong Saurivong*, the story of two princes, of whom the former was a Bodhisattva. There are also Khmer versions of the *Vessantara-jataka* and the *Enau*, the latter from the Javanese *Panji* stories.

Some of the texts preserved on palm-leaves have been edited and published by the Buddhist Institute at Phnom Penh, which has also undertaken the issue of the whole Pali Buddhist *Tripitaka* in the recension of Cambodia. Dr Jacob notes that modern Cambodian authors have either imitated Western detective and romantic novels, or else have written more serious works, such as nationalistic poems and religious treatises (Jacob 1969: 268–9). Writing appeared to come to a halt under Pol Pot's Khmer Rouge regime between 1975 and 1979. It is too soon to assess literary developments under the subsequent regimes.

In addition to the works already mentioned, the following should be noted. For manuscripts, see Au Chhieng (1953). For the Royal Chronicles, there are works by Garnier (1871–2), Khin Sok (1977) and Mak Phoeun (1981). On the didactic poetry, refer to Pou (1981), and for folk tales, Leclère (1895), Monod (1944), Chandler (1976) and Thierry (1978). For modern literature, see Piat (1975).

Vietnam

Vietnam differs from the countries so far considered in several ways. It has a language which is unique, unlike those of its neighbours. Its relationships with Mon-Khmer have been debated, but the matter is not settled. What is certain is that even if an original connection is proved, the divergence between Vietnamese and, say, Cambodian is so great as to show few signs of affinity now. A second feature of Vietnam is that whereas most of the other Southeast Asian countries were profoundly affected by Indian culture, Vietnam was for many centuries under the direct rule of China, and received much of its civilization from that source. A third factor is that the country was profoundly affected by French colonialism and by Catholic missions. Then, after the Japanese war, the attempt by the French to reestablish themselves led to the partition of the country, a war which later embroiled the Americans in what amounted to a crusade against communism, and the reunification of Vietnam in 1975 under a communist government.

All these three aspects – a unique language, long links with China, and the turmoil of recent years – have had a profound influence on Vietnamese literature, which has had a long and varied past, and a vigorous life in the present.

The history of Vietnamese literature reflects changes in the political fortunes of the country, which in their turn were signalled by changes in the script used for the language, and in the conventions which came to dominate literary expression. From 111 BC to AD 939, Tongking, the heartland of the Vietnamese in the Red River valley and delta, was incorporated into China, and the Chinese script and Chinese literature were current in Vietnam with all that that conveyed for social and political organization and in the realms of ideas and culture. However, even after this time Chinese language and culture continued to have a dominating influence. By the thirteenth century Vietnamese was being written with Chinese characters, which were adapted and modified to suit the language, and were not used according to Chinese conventions. This system of writing was called *Chu nom*, persisted in use up to the nineteenth century, and was used for important Vietnamese literary works in the eighteenth and nineteenth centuries. Meanwhile, the seventeenth-century French missionary, Alexandre de Rhodes, produced a romanization for Vietnamese, with two sets of diacritics – one to represent vowel quality and the other to indicate the six tones of the language – which enabled preachers to achieve an accurate pronunciation. For a long time, this *quoc ngu* system was only used among Christians, but with the coming of the French it became more widespread, and today has superseded the old Chinese characters. One consequence of this was to reduce the Chinese element in the language and literature, and to help Vietnamese to achieve a more truly national expression.

There is an important historical and legendary literature in Vietnamese. Stories abound of supernatural events, and usually portray the triumph of good over evil. Much of this legendary material, though, was not recorded, but handed on orally from generation to generation. Vietnamese proverbs are characterized by their ironic sense of humour, alluding to agricultural experiences, social affairs and to astrology (Darby 1943: 142). Eighteenth- and nineteenth-century stories in verse, written in *Chu nom*, have held a special place in Vietnamese esteem. These include *Chinh phu ngam* (the Lament of a Soldier's wife), *Cung oan ngam khuc* (the Concubine's complaint), and especially *Kim van Kieu*, this last by Nguyen Du (1765–1820) being received as the national epic. In the story of Kieu, the heroine suffers many ordeals as expiation for faults in a former existence, which come to be expressed in unhappy relationships with men, but in the end vindicate the triumph of self-sacrificing love over the forces of evil. There is an exemplary edition, with text rendered in *quoc ngu* and English translation by Huynh Sanh Thong, with an extensive analytic discussion both of the work, and of the society in which it was produced (Huynh 1983).

In the latter part of the nineteenth century, the wider use of *quoc ngu* was signalled by the first daily newspaper, *Gia Dinh Bao*, by the introduction of Western ideas into Vietnamese writing, and by the beginnings of a patriotic and nationalistic literature. In the 1930s, a literary group, *Tu-luc Van-doan* ('Self-strength'), headed by the novelist Nguyen Tuong Tam, was influenced by modern prose writing; its lively narrative style and the use of everyday language, with passages of dialogue and soliloquy, gave a new character to the Vietnamese novel. However, it was the struggle of the Vietnamese communists, first against the French from 1945, and then with the Americans, which produced the liveliest change. A North Vietnamese view of this phase is given in the book *Vietnam Today*, published in Hanoi in 1965, which stresses that 'literature was used as a weapon in the service of the political struggle' (Foreign Languages Publishing House 1965: 121) and cites the *Prison Diary* of Ho Chi Minh, poems written when he was detained by the Kuomintang in 1942 and 1943. *Vietnam Today* goes on to speak of the literature of the Resistance, 1948–54, saying: 'The versatile socialist life of the North, and the lofty spirit of sacrifice and heroism of the South Vietnamese people have been powerfully depicted in many collections of poems' (Foreign Languages Publishing House 1965: 124). The author mentions Giang Nam and Thanh Hai, poets from the South, whose *Letters from South Vietnam* 'have stirred millions of people in North Vietnam and the world' (Foreign Languages Publishing House 1965: 125). A final judgement on the revolutionary literature will require a space of time and some detachment. The important thing is that literature became an instrument, passionately employed, to forward the movement and to arouse and encourage its followers.

There is a great deal of writing about Vietnamese literature, both in the old spirit of literary history and criticism and in the engaged manner of those for whom literature is a tool for and an expression of a heartfelt political cause. A few only of such works, some in French, others in English, are mentioned here. For a bibliographical survey of the older literature, reference should be made to Cordier (1967). For introductions to Vietnamese literature, see the works by Baruch (1963), Duong Dinh Khue (1976), Nguyen Khac Vien and Huu Ngoc (1982), and Duran and Nguyen Tran Huan (1985).

For folk-tales, there are Chivas-Baron (1920) and a survey of Vietnamese folklore, with an introduction and a bibliography, published under the title *Nha-trang cong-huyen-ton-nu* (1970).

For the history of Vietnam, there is a French translation by des Michels (1889 and 1892) of the Imperial Annals of Annam, while Pozner (1980) deals with the problems of origins and foreign influences that affect them. Poetry is discussed by Ly Chanh Trung (1961) and by Huynh Sanh Thong (1979). More recent literature is surveyed by Sluimers (1962), in a series of articles edited by Lafont and Lombard (1974) and by Vo Phien (1987), while Banerian (1986) has written an introduction to Vietnamese short stories.

There are a number of minority groups in Vietnam, among whom the most important historically are the Cham. They are a people of Indonesian origin, who ruled a medieval Indianized kingdom in Central Annam from AD 192 to 1471. Their monuments and inscriptions compare with those of Cambodia, but they were less successful as a nation, being pressed for most of their time by the Vietnamese advancing from the north. Their remnants are now to be found in Southern Vietnam and along the Mekong in Cambodia, where many adopted Islam. For a survey, see Marrison (1985), which includes a bibliography, and Lafont, Po Dharma and Naravija (1977). The collection *Kerajaan Campa*, published by the Balai Pustaka in Indonesian, contains a survey of Cham literature by Po Dharma and an essay on *Pram Dit Pram Lak*, the Cham version of the Ramayana, by G. Moussay (*Kerajaan Campa* 1981).

Some of the mountain peoples are closely related to the Chams: for a sample of their literature, see Lafont (1963). Some general indications about the Mon-Khmer and Indonesian tribes of Vietnam are given by Mole (1970) and in various numbers of the *Mon-Khmer Studies* series issued by the Linguistic Circle of Saigon (*Mon-Khmer Studies* 1964–79).

Malaysia

Malaysia is the literary heir of Malacca, which in the fifteenth century was the great emporium of Southeast Asia, with trade from India, the islands which now make up Indonesia, and China, and cultural influences from all these sources. Most important were the establishment of Islam and the development of Malay literature, both of which had developed earlier in North Sumatra, from the end of the thirteenth century. Malacca in its turn was to be instrumental in bringing Islam to Java and other parts of Indonesia, especially from the sixteenth century. That there was an early use of Malay for literary purposes is suggested by the survival of seventh-century Srivijaya inscriptions from the neighbourhood of Palembang in South Sumatra and of indigenous writings from that region recorded in a local script, the *rèncong*, which is free for the most part of Islamic influence or the later developments of Classical Malay. For the literary history of the Malay Peninsula, we may think of three periods: the classical, from the fifteenth century in Malacca and the later coastal states including Johore, until the end of the eighteenth century; a second comprising the nineteenth and first half of the twentieth centuries, when the main external influence was British colonialism and when many Chinese and Indians were brought to the country, especially to work in the tin mines and on rubber estates, and when European education was introduced; and, third the period of independence, with the development of Malay as a national language, the extension of political control to the northern parts of Borneo, and more significant interaction with Indonesia. In the second period, English, Chinese and Tamil were used in addition to Malay for educational and some official purposes, and there were some original writings and publications in these languages. We note these here as important, but outside the scope of the present survey.

Malay has a threefold tradition in poetry. First, there is the *pantun*, a quatrain in which the first half is a picture or a simile, and the second carries the tag or resolution. In form, it probably derives from the Sanskrit *sloka*. It is important because of its seeming spontaneity, a good vehicle for indigenous Malay ideas, in contrast to the more formal artificial verse; and because it has become influential in many of the other languages of Indonesia. It is a genre that deserves more critical study than it has received. Second, there is the poetry in *bahasa irama* – rhythmic verse, unrhymed, with lines of varying length, often used for descriptive passages, or for incantations, in the course of a text mainly in prose. This style is also traditional, sometimes pre-Islamic in its reference and sentiment. Third, there is the *syair*, in quatrains with all four lines rhyming, which is used for narrative, including artificial romances and Islamic works. These types of poetry may be studied from the examples in Winstedt and Blagden (1917) and in Alisjahbana (1954).

The main body of classical Malay literature, however, is in prose (though it may include short verse passages), and the principal genre is the *hikayat*, a story or account. More than half of Winstedt's 'A history of Malay literature' (1939) is devoted to this genre, which he divides into a number of categories by period, source and subject-matter. In folk literature he includes works of indigenous Malay–Indonesian origin, such as the mouse-deer tales, *Hikayat pelandok jenaka*, and local romances such as *Awang Sulong* and *Raja Muda*; and versions of the Hindu epics like the *Hikayat Seri Rama* and of

Malayanized *Panji* tales, especially the romance of old Malacca, *Hikayat Hang Tuah*. Then there are fairy-tale romances of Indian background, like the *Hikayat Inderaputera*, Muslim legends of the Prophet Muhammad and of early Islamic heroes like *Amir Hamzah*, and romances and cycles of tales of Islamic background.

Most important in classical Malay literature are the historical works. The earliest, the *Hikayat Raja-raja Pasai*, is of interest as it relates legends of the coming of Islam to northern Sumatra at the end of the thirteenth century. The *Sejarah Melayu* (the Malay Annals) is rated by Winstedt as 'the most famous, disintictive and best of all Malay literary works' (Winstedt 1939: 106). It tells of the origins of Malacca by quoting legends of rulers in Sumatra and Singapore, the founding of Malacca at the beginning of the fifteenth century and the establishment of Islam there, and of the Sultans of Malacca, the glory of their city and its eventual fall to the Portuguese in 1511. It is characterized by originality, vigour of narrative and a subtle understanding of human nature (Brown 1952). There are many other local histories of the states in the Peninsula, as well as throughout Indonesia, also composed in Malay, but generally at a later time. Complementing these histories are local law codes in which traditional *adat* elements and Islamic juris-prudence are both to be seen (see Liaw 1976).

Malay was an important medium for the propagation of Islam in Indonesia. Malacca was involved in this, but after its fall to the Portu-guese, North Sumatra resumed its leading role, with the seventeenth-century Hamzah of Barus composing mystic poems like the *Syair perahu*, comparing life with a voyage at sea, and the theologian Nuruddin of Raniri, whose *Bustan as-Salatin* and other works covered many aspects of Muslim history and doctrine.

In the nineteenth century, Abdullah bin Abdul Kadir broke new ground. His autobiography, *Hikayat Abdullah*, gives his observations on Singapore and Malacca, his impressions of Raffles, Crawfurd and others and ideas on many matters which Malay literature had not previously dealt with, which he discussed in a realistic manner, and with a strong tendency to moralize (Hill 1955). He was without an immediate successor but, in the latter part of the nineteenth century, many Malay writers composed books of an informative kind on all sorts of modern subjects, as well as translations. In the twentieth century a number of journals were started, and training colleges for teachers were influential, because many schoolmasters became Malay authors. The modern Islamic movement in Egypt had its influence in Malaya; Arabic schools taught the Qur'an, and popular works on Islam were written. Winstedt also notes the work done by the Malay Translation Bureau, and materials, largely of an Islamic background, published by the Asasiyyah Press in Kelantan from 1929 (Winstedt 1939: 156–62).

After the Second World War, the *Asas 50* (the Generation of the 1950s) was an influential group of writers, who especially concentrated on the social novel. The *Dewan Bahasa dan Pustaka*, the government publishing agency, was founded in 1956 and has greatly developed its work since Malaysia was formed in 1963. *Sajak*, or free verse, has become popular and displaced the traditional forms of poetry, and government agencies and the universities have concerned themselves with language study and language development in response to modern needs.

The aboriginal groups in Malaya are now a dwindling minority. Their life, including their folklore, is described by Skeat and Blagden (1906). In Sarawak and Sabah there are many groups with languages more or less akin to Malay, and their own oral literature is recorded in anthropological monographs and in the *Sarawak Museum Journal*. One aspect of interest here is that ideas and themes of non-Muslim origin may be identified which are widely distributed in the Indonesian region, and may prove of help in analysing some aspects of traditional Malay literature.

For recent bibliographical material on Malaysia, including Malay literature, reference should be made to the volume by Brown and Ampelevanar (1986), to Baharuddin Zainal (1985) and to work by Ding Choo Ming, including his *Bibliography of Malay Creative Writings* (1980). The *Journal of the Malaysian Branch, Royal Asiatic Society* (Kuala Lumpur), *Indonesia Circle* (School of Oriental and African Studies, London), and *Archipel* (Paris), all carry articles on Malaysian and Indonesian literature. Especially important on manuscripts are Ricklefs and Voorhoeve (1977), and Kratz (1981).

Articles and books by Amin Sweeney, including *The Ramayana and the Malay Shadow Play* (1972), 'Professional Malay story-telling' (1973), *The Literary Study of Malay-Indonesian Literature* (1983), and *Authors and Audiences in Traditional Malay Literature* (1987a) make a special study of the relationship between oral and written literature. For the *pantun*, or allusive quatrain, see especially the anthology compiled by Wilkinson and Winstedt (1923) and the literary analysis by Overbeck (1922). On the *syair*, used for Malay narrative verse, see the articles by Teeuw (1966) and Sweeney (1971). For the *hikayat*, the Malay prose story, see the discussions by Bausani (1979) and Brakel (1979). Finally, for a survey of modern Malay writing, reference should be made to Mohd. Taib bin Osman (1964).

Singapore

As an independent city-state with a cosmopolitan population, Singapore makes its own contribution to literature in many languages. From the foundation of the city in 1819 by Raffles, it attracted commercial enterprise, which was followed by the establishment of cultural institutions. English education was promoted, the Raffles Museum was founded and in 1878 a branch of the Royal Asiatic Society was established – this was active, among other things, in Malay studies. Singapore became an important publishing centre for English, Chinese and Malay works. Since the independence of Singapore in 1965, these activities have been transformed and enlarged, and the National University, the National Library and the Institute of Southeast Asian Studies have all played their part. In relation to Southeast Asian literature, the role of Singapore has been not so much in original writing as in servicing education and research, and in its active publishing industry.

Indonesia

Indonesia shares with Malaysia the heritage of classical Malay literature. Here we shall be concerned with Javanese as the major language of Indonesian culture over a thousand years, certain regional literary languages, oral literature throughout the region, and the development of Indonesian as the national language, based upon Malay but incorporating other linguistic elements and a new spirit in its literature.

Javanese is now spoken by some 60 million people in Central and East Java. The earliest literary works go back to the ninth century AD, and are written in Old Javanese. This is an Indonesian language, strongly influenced by Sanskrit. The prose works, of which the most important are renderings of books of the *Mahabharata*, include Sanskrit *sloka* verses in their texts. The most important is the *Adiparwa*, which contains Hindu origin stories and the genealogy of Pandavas and Kauravas, whose fratricidal war is the central subject of the Mahabharata. The poetry is known as *kakawin*, and likewise deals mostly with Indian themes. Sanskrit metres are used, together with much Sanskrit vocabulary, including many proper names. Most of the stories are of Hindu origin, although a few are Buddhist. The *Sang Hyang Kamahayanikan* is the only purely doctrinal text in Old Javanese of any length. In its description of the orientation of various Mahayana divinities, and in its instructions for attaining contemplation, it reflects the character of the great Buddhist monument of Central Java, the Borobudur.

The first, longest and most loved of the *kakawin* is the Old Javanese *Ramayana*, which was believed to have been composed in the ninth century. The earlier part closely follows the *Bhattikavya*, a Sanskrit *kavya* later than Valmiki's *Ramayana*. In the Javanese poem, all the main elements of the story are present: Rama's exile from the court of Ayodhya with his wife Sita and brother Laksmana; Sita's abduction by Ravana, the demon king of Sri Lanka; and Rama's subsequent campaign to rescue his wife with the help of Hanuman and his monkey army. More than half of this version is devoted to the fighting in Sri Lanka of the sixth book of Valmiki, the *Yuddha-kanda*, the reunion of Rama and Sita and their return to Ayodhya. The *Ramayana* has a prominent place in many of the literatures of Indonesia, is represented on temple reliefs at Prambanan and elsewhere, and is one of the main subjects of the *wayang-purwa*, the Javanese classical shadow-play, and the dance-drama.

Another major early *kakawin* is the *Arjuna-wiwaha*, ultimately based on an episode of the *Mahabharata*. Arjuna, one of the Pandava brothers, was meditating on a mountain to gain spiritual strength to pursue the war. Indra sent heavenly nymphs to distract him, but he resisted the temptation. Later he saw a great boar at the same time as Siva, who had come disguised as a hunter, and the two shot the boar together. Siva presented Arjuna with a magic arrow; later he was sent to kill a demon who was disturbing the gods, and in heaven married the chief of the nymphs, Suprabha. This poem, written in the early eleventh century, became widely popular, and its elements of adventure, asceticism, eroticism and mystic power characterize much of the Hindu-Javanese and later Balinese literature. The *Bharata-yuddha* is an Old Javanese poetic version of the central part of the *Mahabharata*, covering *parwas* 4–11, that is those parts which deal with the war itself. This work, together with the *Adi-parwa*, also provides much of the repertoire of the Javanese shadow-play. The *Nagarakertagama* of Prapanca is a later work, describing a royal journey in 1359 in the last of the Hindu kingdoms of Java, Majapahit. A later prose work on the history of the period is the *Pararaton*, the 'Book of Kings'.

The middle period in Javanese literature is difficult to define, but was marked by changes in language, in verse forms, and a more indigenous rather than Indian background to literary works. It is typified by such works as the *Tantri Kamandaka*, a prose version of the Pancatantra tales, and by the poems *Sudamala* and *Sri Tanjung*, which are romances with elements of mysticism and exorcism. Modern Javanese, from the sixteenth century onwards, is characterized by new types of metre, *macapat*, with fixed numbers of syllables and a fixed vowel ending each line. Long narrative poems, with cantos in different metres, were written on many themes – religious, romantic and historical – and range over the kind of topics treated in Malay in the prose *hikayat*. These developments came at the time that Islam was first being extended in Java. Among the Muslim texts, there are many stories concerning the Prophet Muhammad; others recounting the lives of the earlier Prophets, including *Yusup* (the story of Joseph); and a cycle of tales, the *Menak Amir Hamzah*, concerning an early hero of Islam about whom many adventures are told, which provided the repertoire for certain kinds of shadow-play in Java and in Lombok. Also important is the *suluk* literature, consisting of mystical devotional poems.

The writings in Java during this and the subsequent period were, however, by no means confined to Muslim themes, and there was a revival of literature in the court of Surakarta at the end of the eighteenth century. The old stories were rewritten in the new metres, and compendiums of Javanese traditions were composed. Attention was also given to historical writing in verse (the *babad*), an established genre in which the local histories were brought up to date and new ones written. By the end of the nineteenth century, modern themes were being written, many in prose, and were printed. Javanese texts were transliterated into the Roman script, at first in scholarly editions, but later more generally used in education and publication, so that the old script for Javanese is no longer generally current. Moreover, with the adoption of Indonesian as the national language, new Javanese writing has declined, though the language continues a vigorous life as the natural medium of communication among the Javanese people.

A concise introduction to traditional Javanese literature is provided in Poerbatjaraka (1952). Pigeaud (1967) and Zoetmulder (1974) are both comprehensive and indispensable.

In West Java, Sundanese is spoken, and in Madura and parts of East Java, Madurese. Both these have their own literatures, strongly influenced by Javanese. For an introduction to all three, with extensive bibliographies, see Uhlenbeck (1964). The Hindu Balinese have maintained a living involvement with Old Javanese literature, but have also developed a lively and original one in their own language. Reference may be made to Hooykaas (1979), and to Marrison (1987). In Lombok, the Muslim Sasak also cultivated Javanese, but later wrote in their own language. See the selections and descriptions given by the Tim Penyusun ('Editorial team') (1991) and Marrison (1996).

Sumatra has a number of literary languages. In the north is Achehnese: see Snouck Hurgronje (1906: 66–189) for an exemplary description of a literature, mostly in verse, deriving from both traditional and Islamic sources. Achehnese literature has many points of similarity with Malay, and includes many examples of versions of Malay stories. By contrast, the Batak of North Sumatra wrote in their own script on folding books made of the inner bark of the *alim* or *gaharu* tree, but used writing only for the texts used by their *datu* for medicine or magic. They also have folk-tales, which have been transmitted orally. For the study of all of these, the best sources are the many works of P. Voorhoeve, including useful introductions in his *Catalogue of Batak Manuscripts* (1961) of the Chester Beatty Library in Dublin, and 'Batak bark books' (1951), in which he describes the collection in the John Rylands Library, Manchester.

The Minangkabau language of Central Sumatra is close to Malay. The distinguishing characteristics of the local tradition include a matriarchal society, the custom of *merantau*, by which men leave their homeland to seek work elsewhere, and also a body of *adat*, or customary law, preserved in collections of rhythmic verses. Another tradition is embodied in their orally transmitted epics, as described by Phillips (1981). Materials in these languages, as well as in Rejang, Lampung and South Sumatran Malay, are discussed by Voorhoeve (1955).

A similar service for Borneo (Kalimantan) is provided by Cense and Uhlenbeck (1958). In this island, in addition to Malay, used in the coastal sultanates, there are many related tribal languages with oral literatures. An example is that of the folk tales in Ngaju Dayak, edited by Klokke-Coster and others (1976). In Sulawesi, the Muslim Bugis and Macassarese both have recorded literatures. These include translations from the Malay, original local histories and the heroic poetry in Bugis *La-Galigo*; and there is a local tradition of keeping diaries. For these languages, many works in Dutch by B. F. Matthes (1818–1908) and G. K. Niemann (1823–1905) are of great importance, together with Kern (1939).

Although Javanese is the language of the largest community in Indonesia, it was not adopted as the national language, a role that was accorded to Malay. A number of reasons can be adduced for this. Javanese was influential in the lands bordering the Java Sea: the whole of Java, beyond its own homeland, southern Sumatra, southern Borneo, together with Madura, Bali and Lombok. To some degree, this reflected the power of Majapahit radiating from its East Javanese bases, especially in the fourteenth and fifteenth centuries. By that time, however, the seafaring Malay traders had ventured even further, from the north of Sumatra to the Moluccas and Timor in the east. It was Malay that became the lingua franca of the Archipelago, and it was Malay in the first instance that became the bearer of Islam. It was Malay also that the Dutch adopted for administration and education. This language, which was already in use throughout the East Indies, and is of a relatively simple structure, was at hand as an instrument for the Indonesian patriots and nationalists at the end of the nineteenth century. Malay in its new guise as *Bahasa Indonesia* was adopted by the nationalist movement in 1927, with the slogan: 'One nation, one country, one language'. A further reason why Malay prevailed was that Javanese is structurally a more complex language, with differentiated terminology according to the relative social status of the speakers. This feature did not accord with the democratic ideals of the patriots; Malay accorded more readily with their requirements.

In its basic vocabulary, and in its grammar, *Bahasa Indonesia* continues as a form of the Malay language. It has, however, developed new features – some of them artificially nurtured – to enable it to fulfil its expanded role. Western terminology for the technology and ideas of modern life was introduced into the vocabulary, while many words were taken from other Indonesian languages, in particular Javanese. The Roman script was universally used, and in recent times, a new spelling has been agreed between Indonesian and the Malay of Malaysia. It is, however, in its literary function that *Bahasa Indonesia* has its most distinctive character. In the bookshops of Indonesia, the majority of the materials displayed are textbooks for schools and universities, practical manuals on improving the techniques of agriculture and other employments, and popular books on Islam, or in Bali on Hinduism. All these represent a huge activity and output to respond to the needs and interests of the Indonesian people, and distinguish modern Indonesian from traditional Malay, with its old-world themes and literary conventions.

However, it is in the imaginative literature in Indonesian that the contrast is greatest. Western forms have been generally adopted. The essay and the short story are widely cultivated, usually first appearing in newspapers and journals, and then reissued in anthologies by individual authors. The social novel became popular, and free verse replaced the conventional forms used in Javanese and Malay. The adoption of Indonesian in the 1920s gave a special opportunity to writers from Minangkabau in central Sumatra, who were experiencing a traumatic social transformation of their own and, in their struggles for new ideals, caught and sometimes led the new mood. The *Balai Pustaka* as a government agency was concerned with publishing improving materials, including translations, but developed into a means for furthering the national language. The journal *Pujangga Baru* was a medium for new writing from 1933, and novelists such as Marah Rusli (1889–1968) with *Siti Nurbaya* (1922), and Abdul Muis (1890–1959) with *Salah Asuahan* (1928), paved the way for many more writers. Among the new poets, Amir Hamzah (1911–41) was the most noteworthy. The Japanese occupation of 1942–45 had a stimulating influence on writers, which came to full fruition only when they were gone. There were literary movements in the wake of political developments: *Angkatan '45* (the first post-war group of Indonesian writers); *Lekra* (the institution of the communist writers, 1950–65), and then, after the fall of Sukarno, the *Angkatan '66* and the influential journal *Horison*.

For a bibliography of the field, reference may be made to Deakin et al. (1978). Teeuw and Emanuels (1961) is more specific to the language aspects. In a short space, it is not possible to do justice to the extent, variety and vitality of the literature, but fortunately there is a definitive work by Teeuw (1967, 1979), reflecting two stages of development. For the early development of Modern Indonesian poetry, with bio-bibliographical introductions to the writers, there is a good anthology by Alisjahbana (1946). Literary history and criticism are widely practised by Indonesians: we may cite as an example Rosidi (1965). For the role of Indonesian literature in the formation of the nation, see Alisjahbana (1983), Foulcher (1980, 1986), and Watson (1972).

The Philippines

The Philippines, like Indonesia, is an archipelago with many different Indonesian languages, some of which had an early literary tradition. The Philippine languages form a sub-group, with some of those of northern Sulawesi, within the Indonesian language family, which differ from Malay and the other languages of the south. The main cultural contrast with Indonesia followed from the Spanish conquest of 1565 and the Christianization of the people. Spanish dominance continued till 1898, when the Americans took over and left their own impress. The Philippines became one of the cockpits of the war with Japan. After Japan's defeat, and Philippine independence in 1946, one act of the new nation was to establish Pilipino, based chiefly on Tagalog, the main language of Luzon, as the new national language.

The major languages of Luzon are Tagalog and Ilocano, and in the islands of Cebu, Negros and Panay, various forms of Bisayan. Before the Spanish conquest there were written literatures in local scripts, of which little has survived. There was a rich oral poetic literature, with epics in various languages: the *Hudhod* and the *Alim* of the Ifugao of North Luzon, the *Biag ni Lam-ang* of the Ilocano, the *Ibalon* of the Bicolano of South Luzon, and the *Darangan* of the Maranao in Mindanao, which were recited or sung; proverbs (*sabi, sawikain*), sea-shanties (*soliranin*), love songs (*kumdiman*), odes (*kumintang*), and ballads (*awit*). At an early stage the Roman Catholic liturgy was translated into Ilocano, and a tradition grew up of choral chanting in Holy Week, of the *Lamentations of Jeremiah*, and the story of the Fall and the Redemption. In Tagalog, Aquino de Belen's *Pasion* was published in 1703. The Jesuits encouraged drama for religious purposes: works called *Moro-moro*, by Filipino playwrights, celebrated the conflicts between Christians and Muslims. Spanish tales of chivalry, called *corridos*, were adapted in Tagalog, of which the most famous was *Florante at Laura* (1838) by Francisco Balagtas. These were written in the *awit* metre in quatrains of assonanced lines of twelve syllables. In the nineteenth century there was an indigenous prose literature, such as *Urbana at Felisa* by Modesto de Castro, consisting of moral essays in the form of letters. Also at this time, national consciousness was expressed in Spanish, as in the novels of José Rizal (1861–96), and in the poetry of Apostol and Guerrero, who wrote in the style of the French symbolists.

Following the American occupation of 1898, English was also used. Short stories were written by José Garcia Villa and Manuel Arguilla, novels by Steven Javellana and others, and poetry by various authors was gathered in the anthology *Signatures*. There was a decline of Spanish writing after 1930 with the passing away of the Spanish-educated classes and the greater use of English, and with the rise of Tagalog as a literary medium and as the basis for the Pilipino national language.

There is a considerable literature describing and assessing the Philippine writings in indigenous languages, as well as those in Spanish and English. For Tagalog, there are descriptions by de los Santos (1909) and Eugenio (1976), and of its poetry by Lumbera (1968). For the Tagalog novel, there is a study by Reyes (1982). For literature in other Philippine languages, reference may be made to the works of Castro (1983) and Yabes (1936).

For general surveys of Philippine literature, including writings in English, there are several guides and anthologies, all published in the 1960s or later, including those by Yabes (1961), Ramos and Valeros (1964), Manuud (1967), San Juan (1974), and Lumbera (1982). There are also monographs on particular literary genres, including short stories, which were discussed by Sta. Romana (1935) and Casper (1962). Novels have been assessed by A. Majid b. Nabi Baksh (1970) and by Mojares (1983), poetry by Dato (1976), and modern drama by Hernandez (1976).

Finally, a specially useful work is Agoncillo's *A Short History of the Philippines* (1969). The author makes frequent reference to the development of Philippine literature in Spanish, English and the indigenous languages, including Tagalog in its development into the national language, Pilipino. He briefly discusses many authors, and places them in their historical and political contexts.

Conclusion

This rapid survey of the literatures of Southeast Asia indicates the extent to which unity in the directions of literary development may be perceived across the region, but much more clearly the diversity in expression, reflecting racial temperament and experience, reactions to incoming cultures, and the character and constraints of the very different languages themselves. In such a short compass it has been impossible to mention, let alone do any justice to, many significant literary movements, genres of writing or individual authors and their works, but it is hoped that the bibliographical indications provided will be sufficient to facilitate a useful entry into the leading literary fields of the region. Of all the books that I have consulted, the two covering the whole field that I have found most consistently useful have been Herbert and Milner (1989), which provides detailed information compiled by a number of the best-known specialists in the field, and Jenner (1973). The latter is a comprehensive and systematic bibliography, generally useful, but perhaps of special interest to students of Southeast Asia who need to know the literary background, but are not themselves in a position to consult the texts in the original languages. A good way to begin would be to use the translations of selected classics from the region, such as Judith Jacob's rendering of the Cambodian *Ramayana* (Jacob and Haksrea 1986), and Nguyen Du's *Tale of Kieu* with Vietnamese text and English translation by Huynh Sanh Thong (Huynh 1983), mentioned above, or C. C. Brown's English translation of the *Sejarah Melayu*, the *Malay Annals* (Brown 1952). Such reading would provide the best way of getting the feel of the region, before consulting the more specialized historical and critical works.

Bibliography

Agoncillo, T. A. (1969), *A Short History of the Philippines* (New York: Mentor).

Alisjahbana, S. T. (1946), *Poeisi Baroe* (Jakarta: Poestaka Rakjat).

— (1954), *Poeisi lama* (Jakarta: Pustaka Rakjhat).

— (1983), 'Literature's role in the emergence of a new culture', *Prisma: The Indonesian Indicator*, 29 September: 11–23.

Allott, A. (1971), 'Burmese literature', in Lang (1971): 387–401.

Au Chhieng (1953), *Catalogue des fonds khmers* (Paris: Bibliothèque Nationale).

Banerian, J. (1986), *Vietnamese Short Stories: an introduction* (Phoenix: Sphinx Publishing).

Baruch, J. (1963), *Essai sur le littérature du Vietnam* (Costeau: Thanh-long).

Bauer, C. (1984), *A Guide to Mon studies*, Working Paper 32 (Clayton, Vic: Monash University, Centre of Southeast Asian Studies).

Bausani, A. (1979), *Notes on the Structure of the Classical Malay Hikayat* (Clayton, Vic: Monash University).

de Berval, R. (ed.) (1959), *Kingdom of Laos* (Saigon: France-Asie).

Bode, M. H. (1909), *The Pali Literature of Burma* (London: Luzac).

Brakel, L. F. (1979), 'On the origins of the Malay hikayat', *Review of Indonesian and Malaysian Affairs*, 13, 2: 1–33.

Brengues, J. (1905), *Contes et legendes du pays laotien* (Saigon: Condurier et Montegout).

Brown, C. C. (1952), 'The Malay Annals', *JMBRAS*, 25: 2–3.

Brown, I. and L. Ampelevanar (1986), *Malaysia*, World Bibliography Series, 12 (Oxford: Clio Press).

Casper, L. (1962), *Modern Philippine Short Stories* (Albuquerque, NM).

Castro, J. V. (1983), *Epics of the Philippines* (Quezon City: ASEAN Committee on Culture and Information).

Cense, A. A. and E. M. Uhlenbeck (1958), *Critical Survey of Studies on the Languages of Borneo*, Bibliographical Series, 2 (The Hague: KITLV).

Chandler, D. P. (1976), *The Friends who Tried to Empty the Sea: eleven Cambodian folk tales* (Clayton, Vic: Monash University).

Chitakasem, M. (1972), 'The emergence and development of the Nirat genre in Thai poetry', *Journal of the Siam Society*, 60: 135–68.

Chivas-Baron, C. (1920), *Stories and Legends of Annam* (London and New York: Andrew Melrose).

Cochrane, The Rev. W. W. (1910), 'Language and literature', in Milne (1910): 208–20.

Coedès, G. (1966), *Catalogue des manuscrits en pali et laotien et siamois, provenant de la Thailande*, Catalogues of Oriental Manuscripts in Danish Collections, vol. 2, part 2 (Copenhagen: Bibliothèque Royale).

Cooke, J. R. (1980), 'The Thai Khlong poem', *Journal of the American Oriental Society*, 100: 421–38.

Cordier, H. (1967), *Bibliotheca Indosinica*, 4 vols (Paris: Leroux, 1912–1915; repr. New York: Burt Franklin Bibliographic and Reference Sources).

Darby, H. C. (ed.) (1943), *Indochina* (n.p.: Naval Intelligence Division).

Dato, R. (ed.) (1976), *The Emergence of Modern Drama in the Philippines*, Philippine Studies Working Paper 1 (Honolulu: University of Hawaii).

Davidson, J. H. C. S. and H. Cordell (1986), *The Short Story in Southeast Asia* (London: School of Oriental and African Studies).

Deakin, C. et al. (1978), *Indonesian Reading List*, 3rd edn (London: Indonesia Circle).

Ding Choo Ming (1980), *A Bibliography of Malay Creative Writings, Vol. 1: Brunei, Malaysia, Singapore, 1920–1980* (Bangi: Universiti Kebangsaan Malaysia).

Dudley, D. R. and D. M. Lang (1969), *The Penguin Companion to Literature, Vol. 4: Classical and Byzantine, Oriental and African* (Harmondsworth: Penguin).

Duong Dinh Khue (1976), *La Littérature populaire vietnamienne* (Brussels: Thanhlong).

Duran, M. M. and Nguyen Tran Huan (1985), *An Introduction to Vietnamese Literature* (New York: Columbia University Press).

Eugenio, D. L. (1976), 'Tagalog literature', in R.J. Bresnahan, *Literature and Society: cross-cultural perspectives* (Los Banos).

Finot, L. (1917), 'Recherches sur la littérature laotienne', *BEFEO*, 17, 5: 84–113.

Fleeson, K. N. (1899), *Laos Folklore of Farther India* (New York: Revell).

Foreign Languages Publishing House (1965), *Vietnam Today* (Hanoi).

Foulcher, K. (1980), *Pujangga Baru: literature and nationalism in Indonesia, 1933–1942*, Asian Studies Monograph 2 (Bedford Park, SA: Flinders University).

— (1986), *Social Commitment in Literature and the Arts: the Indonesian 'Institute of People's Culture', 1950–1965* (Clayton, Vic: Monash University Southeast Asian Studies Centre).

Garnier, F. (1871–2), 'Chronique royale du Cambodge', *Journal Asiatique*, 6, 18: 336–85 and 6, 20: 112–44.

Geddes, W. R. (1961), *Nine Dayak Nights* (London: Oxford University Press).

Graham, A. W. (1912), *Siam, a Handbook of Practical, Commercial and Political Information* (London: Alexander Moring).

Halliday, R. (1917), *The Talaings* (Rangoon: Government Printing Office).

Herbert, P. and A. Milner (1989), *Southeast Asia: languages and literature: a select guide* (Whiting Bay, Arran: Kiscadale for the South-East Asia Library Group).

Herbert, P. M. (1991), *Burma*, World Bibliographical Series, 132 (Oxford: Clio Press).

Hernandez, T. C. (1976), *The Emergence of Modern Drama in the Philippines*, Philippine Studies Working Paper 1 (Honolulu: University of Hawaii).

Hill, A. H. (1955), 'The Hikayat Abdullah', *Journal of the Malayan Branch of the Royal Asiatic Society*, 28, 3.

Hla Pe (1962), *Burmese Proverbs* (London: John Murray).

— (1971), 'Burmese poetry, 1300–1971', *Journal of the Burma Research Society*, 54, 1–2: 59–114.

— (1985), *Burma: literature, historiography, scholarship, language, life and Buddhism* (Singapore: Institute of Southeast Asian Studies).

Hooykaas, C. (1979), *Introduction à la littérature balinaise* (Paris: Cahier de l'Archipel).

Htin Aung (1937), *Burmese Drama: a study, with translations of Burmese plays* (Calcutta: Oxford University Press).

— (1954), *Burmese Folk Tales* (Calcutta: Oxford University Press).

Huynh Sanh Thong (1979), *The Heritage of Vietnamese Poetry* (New Haven, CT: Yale University Press).

— (1983), *The Tale of Kieu* (New Haven, CT: Yale University Press).

Jacob, J. M. (1969), 'Khmer literature', in Dudley and Lang (1969).

— and Kuoch Haksrea (eds) (1986), *Reamker (Ramakarti): the Cambodian version of the Ramayana*, trans. Oriental Translation Fund, NS vol. 45 (London: Royal Asiatic Society).

Jenner, P. N. (1973), *Southeast Asian Literatures in Translation: a preliminary bibliography*, Asian Studies at Hawaii, 9 (Honolulu: Hawaii University Press).

Jones, R. (1980), 'Problems of editing Malay texts', *Archipel*, 20: 121–7.

Jumsai, M. (1973), *History of Thai Literature* (Bangkok: Chalermnit Press).

Kerajaan Campa (1981), (Jakarta: Balai Pustaka).

Kern, R. A. (1939), *I La Galigo: catalogus der Boegineesche tot den I La Galigo cyclus behoorende handschriften* (Leiden: Brill).

Khin Sok (1977), 'Chroniques royales khmeres', *Mon-Khmer Studies*, 6 (Saigon: Linguistic Circle).

Klokke-Coster, A., A. H. Klokke and M. Saha (1976), *De slimme en de domme: Ngadju-Dajaksche volksverhalen*, Verhandelingen KITLV, 79 (The Hague: Nijhoff).

Knappert, J. (1977), *Myths and Legends of Indonesia* (Singapore: Heinemann).

Kratz, E. U. (1981), 'The editing of Malay manuscripts and textual criticism', *Bijdragen tot de taal-, land- en volkenkunde*, 137: 229–43.

Lafont, P.-B. (1962a), 'Les ecritures 'tay du Laos', *BEFEO*, 1, 2: 367–93.

— (1962b), 'Les ecritures du Pali au Laos', *BEFEO*, 1, 2: 395–405.

— (1963), *Prières Jarai* (Paris, EFEO).

— (1965), 'Inventaire des manuscrits des pagodes du Laos', *BEFEO*, 52, 2: 429–545.

— and D. Lombard (eds) (1974), *Littératures contemporaines* (Paris: Colloque du XXIXe Congrès Internationale des Orientalistes) (articles by G. Boudarel, A. Dauphin and Nguyen Tran Huyen).

— Po Dharma and Naravija (1977), *Catalogue des manuscrits Cam des Bibliothèques françaises* (Paris: EFEO).

Lang, D. M. (ed) (1971), *A Guide to Eastern Literatures* (London: Weidenfeld and Nicolson).

Leclère, A. (1895), *Cambodge: contes et legendes recueillis et publiés en Français* (Paris: E. Bouillon).

Le May, R. (1930), *Siamese Tales, Old and New* (London: Noel Douglas).

Liaw Yock Fang (1976), *Undang-undang Melaka* (The Hague: Nederlandsche Boek en Steendrukkerij).

Lumbera, B. L. (1968), 'Assimilation and synthesis, 1701–1800: Tagalog poetry in the eighteenth century', *Philippine Studies*, 16: 622–62.

— (1969), 'Consolidation of tradition in nineteenth century Tagalog poetry', *Philippine Studies*, 17: 377–411.

— (1982), *Philippine Literature: a history and anthology* (Manila: National Book Store).

Lustig, F. V. (1986), *Burmese Poems through the Ages: a selection* (Rangoon: Sabe-U).

Ly Chanh Trung (1961), *Introduction to Vietnamese poetry*, Vietnam Culture Series, 3 (Saigon: Department of National Education).

Mak Phoeun (1981), *Chroniques Royales du Cambodge (de 1594 à 1677)* (Paris: EFEO).

Manuud, A. G. (1967), *Brown Heritage: essays on Philippine cultural tradition and literature* (Quezon City: Ateneo de Manila University Press).

Marrison, G. E. (1985), 'The Chams and their literature', *JMBRAS*, 58, 2: 45–70.

— (1987), 'Modern Balinese: a regional literature of Indonesia', *Bijdragen tot de taal-, land- en volkenkunde*, 143: 468–98.

— (1996), *The Literature of the Sasaks of Lombok*, 2 vols (Leiden: KITLV).

Mendiones, F. C. (1970), *Introduction to Thai Literature* (Ithaca, NY: Cornell University, Southeast Asia Program).

des Michels, A. (1889 and 1892), *Les Annales Impériales de l'Annam*, 2 vols (Paris).

Milne, M. L. (1910), *The Shans at Home* (London: Murray).

Mojares, R. B. (1983), *The Origins and Rise of the Filipino Novel: a general study of the novel until 1940* (Quezon City: Ateneo de Manila University Press).

Mole, R. L. (1970), *The Montagnards of South Vietnam* (Tokyo: Tuttle).

Mon-Khmer Studies (1964–1979), vols 1–8 (Saigon: Linguistic Circle of Saigon).

Monod, G. H. (1944), *Contes khmers, traduits du Cambodgien* (Mouan-Sartoux).

Mosel, J. N. (1961), *Trends and Structure in Contemporary Thai Poetry* (Ithaca, NY: Cornell University).

Myint Thein (1987), *Burmese Folk Songs* (Calcutta: P.L. Writers' Workshop).

Nabi Baksh, A. Majid b. (1970), 'The Philippine novel in English: a critical history', *Philippine Social Sciences and Humanities Review*, 35: 1–2.

Nguyen Khac Vien and Huu Ngoc (1982), *Vietnamese Literature* (Hanoi: Foreign Languages Publishing House).

Nha-trang cong-huyen-ton-nu: *Vietnamese folklore: an introductory and annotated bibliography* (1970), Occasional Paper 7 (Berkeley: University of California, Center for South and Southeast Asia Studies).

Nicholas, R. (1924), 'Le Lakhon Nora, ou Chatri, et les origines du theatre traditionel siamois', *Journal of the Siam Society*, 18, 2: 85–110.

Noorduyn, J. (1991a), *Critical Survey of Studies on the Languages of Sulawesi*, KITLV Bibliographical Series, 18 (Leiden: KITLV).

— (1991b), 'The manuscripts of the Makasarese chronicle of Goa and Talloq: an evaluation', *Bijdragen tot de taal-, land- en volkenkunde*, 147: 454–84.

Osman, Mohd. Taib bin (1964), *Modern Malay Literature* (Kuala Lumpur: Dewan Bahasa dan Pustaka).

Overbeck, H. (1922), 'The Malay pantun', *Journal of the Singapore Branch of the Royal Asiatic Society*, 86: 4–28.

Peltier, A.-R. (1988), *Le Roman classique lao* (Paris: Publications de l'EFEO).

Philipps, H. P. (1987), *Modern Thai Literature* (Honolulu: University of Hawaii).

Phillips, N. (1981), *Sijobang: sung narrative poetry of West Sumatra* (Cambridge: Cambridge University Press, 1981).

Piat, M. (1975), 'Contemporary Cambodian literature', *Journal of the Siam Society*, 63, 2: 251–9.

Pigeaud, Th.G.Th. (1967), *Literature of Java*, Vol. 1 (Leiden: University Press).

Poerbatjaraka, R.M.Ng. (1952), *Kepustakaan Djawa* (Jakarta and Amsterdam: Djambatan).

Poolthupya, S. (1979), *Thai Intellectual and Literary World* (Bangkok: Thammasat University).

Pou, S. (1977a), *Ramakerti (XVIᵉ–XVIIᵉ siècles)*, traduit et comment (Paris: Publications d'EFEO).

— (1977b), *Etudes sur le Ramakerti (XVIᵉ–XVIIᵉ siècles)* (Paris: Publications de l'EFEO).

— (1979), *Ramakerti (XVIᵉ–XVIIᵉ siècles): texte khmer publie* (Paris: Publications de l'EFEO).

— (1981), 'La littérature didactique khmere: les cpap', *Journal Asiatique*, 269, 3–4: 453–66.

— (1982), *Ramakerti II (Deuxième version du Ramayana khmer)* (Paris: Publications de l'EFEO).

Pozner, P. (1980), 'Le problème des chroniques vietnamiennes: origines et influences etrangères', *BEFEO*, 67.

Rajadhon, Phya Anuman (1961), *Thai Literature in Relation to the Diffusion of her Cultures*, Thai Culture, NS no. 9 (Bangkok: Fine Arts Department).

Rajunabhab, Prince Damrong (1915), 'The story of the records of Siamese history', *Journal of the Siam Society*, 9, 2: 1–20.

Ramos, M. and F. B. Valeros (eds) (1964), *Philippine Harvest: an anthology of Filipino writing in English* (Quezon City: Phoenix Publishing House).

Reyes, S. S. (1982), *Nobelang Tagalog, 1905–1975* (Manila: Ateneo de Manila University Press).

Ricklefs, M. C. and P. Voorhoeve (1977), *Indonesian Manuscripts in Great Britain*, London Oriental Bibliographies 5 (London: Oxford University Press).

Rosidi, A. (1965), *Ikhtisar sejarah sastra Indonesia* (Bandung: Binacipta).

Rubinstein, C. (1973), *Poems of the Indigenous Peoples of Sarawak: some of the songs and chants*, 2 vols, Sarawak Museum Journal, Special Monograph 2 (Kuching: Sarawak Museum).

Rutnin, M. (1975), *The Siamese Theatre* (Bangkok: Siam Society).

San Juan, E. (ed.) (1974), *Introduction to Modern Pilipino Literature* (New York: Twayne).

Sta. Romana, O. O. (1935), *The Best Filipino Short Stories* (Manila).

de los Santos, E. (1909), *Literatura Tagala* (Madrid).

Schweisguth, P. (1950), 'Les Nirat, ou poèmes d'adieu', *Journal of the Siam Society*, 38, 1: 67–78.

— (1951), *Etude sur la littérature siamoise* (Paris: Imprimerie Nationale).

Simmonds, E. H. S. (1965), 'Tai literatures: a bibliography of works in foreign languages', *Bulletin of the Association of British Orientalists*, NS vol. 3, 1–2.

Skeat, W. W. and C. O. Blagden (1906), *Pagan Races of the Malay Peninsula*, 2 vols (London: Macmillan).

Sluimers, L. (1962), *A Bibliography of North Vietnamese Publications in the Cornell University Library* (Ithaca, NY: Cornell University).

Snouck Hurgronje, C. (1906), *The Achehnese*, 2 vols (Leiden/London: Brill/Luzac).

Sweeney, A. (1971), 'Some observations on the Malay Shair', *Journal of the Malayan Branch of the Royal Asiatic Society*, 44, 1: 52–71.

— (1972), *The Ramayana and the Malay Shadow Play* (Kuala Lumpur: Penerbit Universiti Kebangsaan Malaysia).

— (1973), 'Professional Malay story-telling: some questions of style and presentation', *JMBRAS*, 46, 2: 1–53.

— (1983), 'The literary study of Malay-Indonesian literature', *Journal of the Malayan Branch of the Royal Asiatic Society*, 56, 1: 33–46.

— (1987a), *Authors and Audiences in Traditional Malay Literature* (Berkeley: University of California Centre for South and Southeast Asian Studies).

— (1987b), *A Full Hearing: orality and literacy in the Malay world* (Berkeley: University of California Centre for South and Southeast Asian Studies).

Swellengrebel, J. L. (1960), Introduction to Wertheim (1960): 1–66.

Teeuw, A. (1966), 'The Malay Sha'er: problems of origin and tradition', *Bijdragen tot de taal-, land- en volkenkunde*, 124: 429–47.

— (1967), *Modern Indonesian Literature*, KITLV Translation Series, 10 (2nd edn 1986) (The Hague: Nijhoff).

— (1979), *Modern Indonesian Literature*, KITLV Translation Series, 11 (The Hague: Nijhoff).

— and H. W. Emanuels (1961), *A Critical Survey of Studies on Malay and Bahasa Indonesia*, KITLV Bibliographical Series, 5 (The Hague: Nijhoff).

Tham Seong Chee (ed.) (1981), *Essays on Literature and Society in Southeast Asia* (Singapore: University Press).

Thierry, S. (1978), *Etude d'un corpus de contes cambodgiens traditionels* (Paris: Lille University).

Tim Penyusun (1991), *Bunga rampai kutipan naskah lama dan aspek pengetahuannya* (Mataram, Lombok: Museum Negeri Nusa Tenggara Barat).

Uhlenbeck, E. M. (1958), *Critical Survey of Studies on the Languages of Borneo*, KITLV Bibliographical Series, 2 (The Hague: Nijhoff).

— (1964), *A Critical Survey of Studies on the Languages of Java and Madura*, KITLV Bibliographical Series, 7 (The Hague: Nijhoff).

Vietnam Today (1965), (Hanoi: Foreign Languages Publishing House).

Vo Phien (1987), *Literature in South Vietnam, 1954–1975* (New Haven, CT: Yale University Press).

Voorhoeve, P. (1951), 'Batak bark books', *Bulletin of the John Rylands Library* (Manchester), 33, 2: 281–98.

— (1955), *Critical survey of studies on the languages of Sumatra*, KITLV Bibliographical Series, 1 (The Hague: Nijhoff).

— (1961), *Catalogue of Batak Manuscripts*, (Dublin: Chester Beatty Library).

Watson, C. W. (1972), 'The sociology of the Indonesian novel' (University of Hull MA thesis).

Wertheim, W. F. et al. (eds) (1960), *Bali: studies in life, thought and ritual*, Selected Studies on Indonesia by Dutch Scholars, vol. 5 (The Hague and Bandung: W. van Hoeve).

Wilkinson, R. J. and R. O. Winstedt (1923), *Pantun Melayu*, Malay Literature Series, 12, 2nd edn (Singapore: Methodist Publishing House).

Winstedt, R. O. (1939), 'A history of Malay literature', *JMBRAS*, 17, 3.

— and C. O. Blagden (1917), *A Malay Reader* (Oxford: Clarendon Press).

Yabes, L. Y. (1936), *A Brief Survey of the Iloko Literature* (Manila).

— (1961), *The Literature of the Filipino People* (Manila: UNESCO).

Yupho, Danit (1952), *Classical Siamese Theatre* (Bangkok: Hatha Dhip).

Zainal, Baharuddin (1985), *A Bibliography of Malaysian Writers* (Kuala Lumpur: Dewan Bahasa).

Zoetmulder, P. J. (1974), *Kalwangan: a survey of Old Javanese literature* KITLV Translation Series, 16 (The Hague: Nijhoff).

4 Geography

Michael J. G. Parnwell

This chapter seeks to examine how the approach adopted by geographers towards Southeast Asia has evolved over time in broad accordance with changes that have taken place within the discipline as a whole during the post-war period. In particular it aims to identify how, if at all, Southeast Asian geography has been affected by the fluctuating fortunes of regional geography that initially lay at the heart of geographical enquiry, before being relegated rather shamefully to the margins during the discipline's positivist era (Sayer 1989), and then more recently enjoying a renaissance in the reconstituted form of the 'new regional geography' (Gilbert 1988; Pudup 1988; Thrift 1990, 1991, 1993). The central argument presented here is that the complex fusion of 'regional geography' and 'area studies' that has tended to characterize Southeast Asian geography has, in turn, created a particular type of geographer and a particular form of geography which has remained remarkably durable and consistent throughout the mother discipline's metamorphoses.

In order to achieve the above, it is necessary to make certain assumptions and generalizations about Southeast Asian geography[1] and geography as a whole which, if subjected to closer scrutiny, may not prove entirely justifiable. Since the Second World War – broadly the period under review here – geography has broadened and deepened massively in its scope and scale, giving birth to countless sub-disciplinary fields of specialization. As geography has moved further and further from its 'traditional' disciplinary core, so there has been increasing debate and decreasing levels of agreement as to 'what geography is'. In such circumstances it is both difficult and dangerous to generalize about the nature of geography and the trends occurring within the discipline.

The same applies, although less strongly, to Southeast Asian geography. In order to identify a distinct field of study for the purposes of our enquiry, there is a need to claim a certain degree of homogeneity within this sub-disciplinary field. The reality, however, is that there is considerable variation in terms of emphasis, approach and degrees of regional 'dedication' (Farmer 1973: 9–10). The field includes not only specialist Southeast Asian geographers from inside and outside the region (there are subtle differences in approach even here), but also geographers into whose work (for instance on urbanization, environmental change or the 'new international division of labour') Southeast Asia protrudes, to a greater or lesser extent, and others who have occasionally 'dabbled' with the region. Ultimately, such variations in the degree of areal specialization underpin the differences in scholarly approach with which this chapter is principally concerned.

The following discourse may also give the impression that Southeast Asian geographers exist as a breed apart from the run-of-the-mill regional geographers who were much maligned by the positivist sophisticates who deposed them from guardianship of the discipline. However, I will suggest that, had they been better informed about the work of such icons as Fisher, Pelzer, Gourou, Jackson and McGee, among many others, they may have been less dismissive of regional geography and the regional geographer. We use the sub-discipline's 'second coming' as evidence of their own shortsightedness.

Before proceeding to map the evolution of geographical approaches to the study of Southeast Asia, it is necessary first to familiarize the lay reader with developments that have taken place within the discipline of geography since the Second World War.

Changing geographies

Human geography can be seen as the study of the spatial differentiation and organization of human activity and the relationship between people and their environments. The focus on location, space and human–environment interaction constitute the principal criteria that differentiate geography from other academic disciplines – e.g. make the difference between a social geographer and a sociologist. While such criteria have remained more or less constant throughout the modern history of geography, their relative importance, and especially the method of their interpretation and application, have varied considerably over time. In simple terms, the discipline has first engaged, then disengaged and then re-engaged, a close association with place, locale and areal entities. Disengagement saw geography's quite rapid metamorphosis into a sophisticated systematic spatial science which, to many people's tastes, took the discipline too far from its areal roots, and from its 'ground-truthed' reality. The reaction to this led, much more gingerly, to the emergence of a new form of regional geography which is simultaneously sophisticated, theoretically informed, useful and grounded in reality.

Through these sea-changes, geographers dedicated to area have endured changing fortunes and occasional crises of identity. As the positivist cuckoo cleared its nest of twittering chorologists, so regional specialists grimly clung on for survival. With the emergence of a new regional geography, the survivors have bashfully emerged into a new dawn only, in some cases, to be labelled 'reconstituted old regional geographers' by the new guardians of the genre (Sayer 1989). Others, including a whole new generation, have managed more assertively to hone their art to the needs and expectations of the 1990s.

Early geography and areal differentiation The central focus of the discipline of geography before and immediately after the Second World War was with areal differentiation, with the globe divided into major regions or areal units wherein various forms of physical structure and human activity were identified and described: a process referred to as 'chorology'. This gave geography its own distinctive subject matter, and at the time was regarded as the core of the discipline. Geography claimed academic importance as the meeting ground of several academic disciplines, and in particular the natural and social sciences, whose information was systematically collated by geographers and set out uniquely in a spatial array.

Regional geography was also seen as the highest form of the geographer's art, a sentiment which must have hurried its fall from grace in the late 1950s and early 1960s. The approach was highly unsophisticated, naïve, descriptive and empirical, and became bogged down in what Sayer (1989) refers to as a 'debilitating parochialism'. Regional geography was strongly criticized for its emphasis on exceptionalism – drawing boundaries around phenomena and focusing enquiry on the unique and particular – when it was increasingly becoming apparent that the world was made up of complex processes and linkages that cross or transcend arbitrarily created areal units. The need was for a geography of generalization, not exceptionalization. It is at this stage that geography started to shift away from its focus on regional synthesis and to pursue a stronger theoretical tradition and more scientific methodologies. However, a point to which we shall return shortly was that, in the process of change, the baby of place, location and context was thrown out with the bath-water of regional description. It would be a good two decades before anyone noticed she was missing.

Movements away from the areal focus The emergence of geography as a spatial science involved movement in an entirely opposite direction, leaving committed regional geographers (including those specializing on Southeast Asia) somewhat high and dry. Several changes occurred more or less simultaneously. The more the discipline moved away from its traditional core, the more new niches and fields of study emerged. A process of internal specialization took place which saw geographers increasingly establishing links with practitioners of neighbouring disciplines, in the process becoming 'social geographers', 'economic geographers' etc., and subsequently even more specialized as 'urban geographers', 'medical geographers', and so on. As they moved away from the core, so their identity as 'mainstream' geographers became less clear: there was no longer a clearly identifiable mainstream. At the same time, they replaced their unsophisticated and descriptive methodologies with paradigms and models and with quantitative analysis, in the process moving away from the realist grounding of regional geography into the realms of the abstract and positivist. Spatial patterns and processes took on much greater prominence, and in turn became the new cornerstone of geographical analysis. Geographers became preoccupied with the spatial arrangement of phenomena, and less concerned with the phenomena themselves.

Re-engagement with the region The pendulum swinging away from pure regional geography, and into the realms of spatial science, positivism and quantification caused increasing disillusionment in certain quarters within geography because it relegated the importance of context and human values in geographical analysis. It was at this stage that the baby's absence became noticed and started to cause consternation: the skill, insight and understanding that the area specialist had been able to contribute to geographical analysis, and which had so crudely been brushed aside, was now back in demand – or fashion.

What emerged from the late 1980s onwards was a new regional geography, which was far more sensitive to the specificities and influence of place and context than positivist spatial science could ever be, and which recognized the importance of area, space, place and locale in the understanding of problems and processes in contemporary society. In essence, the basic ingredients of life are not universal, but vary in many subtle ways on the basis of, *inter alia*, environment, culture, social and economic organization, history, politics, and so on. Because the social realms of life are characterized by variability rather than uniformity, there is an important need for research which is sensitive to this variability and differentiation, and which can draw a link between variability and the specificities of place. It is here that the reconstituted regional geographer has an important role to play.

What has emerged, then, is a new approach to the study of regions which is much more broadly based in the social sciences and in social theory, whereas the old regional geography had been centred almost entirely on empiricism, with little in the way of theory to guide it. Thus, in simple terms, while the old regional geography may have represented empiricism detached from theory, and positivism theory detached from empiricism, so the new regional geography is empiricism attached to theory, or vice versa.

Not everyone has been so convinced about the 'newness' of this approach:

> Foreign-area specialists will not be impressed by the blanket dismissal of traditional regional work by the new converts who have just 'discovered' the significance of the region (Bradshaw 1990: 317).

This view is consistent with the line of argument adopted in this chapter. If one looks carefully at the work of Southeast Asia specialists before geography's positivist revolution, one can find much that would be admired even by those who have been so disparaging in their generalized criticism of the regional geographer's work. One will find in the work of the true regional specialist, even in the early years of this century, a true appreciation of the role of culture and other forms of context in shaping human activity. There are also some wonderfully informative and insightful studies of processes and problems, many of which are written in a style and with a sense of purpose that few of the modern generation could hope to match. Many pre-positivist regional geographers were 'professional amateurs', drawn to the subject as much by a spirit of discovery and adventure as by anything else.

Approaches to Southeast Asian geography

The following enquiry is somewhat arbitrarily divided into two sections, which broadly overlap with the pre- and post-positivist eras in geography. Our enquiry commences just before the Second World War,[2] and spans the golden era of traditional regional geography until the quantitative revolution of the mid-1960s. Whilst we might have divided the period 1965–1995 into two further eras – positivist and post-positivist – a perusal of the literature suggests that there would be little value in such an exercise. For reasons that will be discussed later, the effect of the positivist revolution on regional geographers and area specialists was to bring about a gradual and incremental, although far from universal, change in approach, rather than an abrupt paradigm shift. Some of the more flexible regional specialists incorporated the new methodologies and techniques, engaged theory, and specialized more in various emerging sub-disciplinary fields, whereas others steadfastly refused to change their ways. Because of the gradual and variable nature of such changes, there is greater value in treating the post-1965 period as a single 'era' in Southeast Asian geography.

In tracing the evolution of Southeast Asian geography, I hope also to say something significant about the changing fortunes of regional geography: most geographical writing has tended to look at regional geography at the opposite ends of a swinging pendulum – old and new – and has neglected the arc it forms in between.

Before the 'revolution' (c.1935–65)

In seeking to analyse the approach adopted by Southeast Asian geographers since the 1930s, several factors need to be considered. In addition to identifying what Southeast Asian geographers were doing and how they plied their trade, we need to know something about the people involved, where they worked and published, and what motivated them to do what they did and in the way that they did it. In other words, the *context* of their activity may have been important in influencing its nature. The prevailing orthodoxy allows us to understand the adopted approach, and in part helps in the preparation of a defence against accusations that were to come later: descriptiveness, chorology, ideography, lack of analysis, theory and specialization, tendency towards determinism, and so on (Cloke, Philo and Sadler 1991: 6).

How did geographers come to take a specialist interest in Southeast Asia? The answer can be found principally within the realms of colonial administration and education, and the strategic imperatives of the Pacific War. A number of Dutch geographers received their first exposure to the region as colonial officers. S. van Valkenberg (like Pelzer later to become a naturalized American) used his experience as the government geographer in the Royal Topographical Survey of the Netherlands East Indies between 1921 and 1926 to provide the basis for several articles on the human geography of Java (Fisher 1973: 204). After independence, he was followed as a staff member of the Geographical Institute of the Topographical Survey of Indonesia (1949–57) by Verstappen, who became engaged in widespread exploration and geomorphological reconnaissance of the archipelago, especially Sumatra. Ormeling was also at one time head of the Geographical Institute. Verstappen and Ormeling both used their experience to provide the foundation for later geographical texts on the geomorphology and social geography of the Indonesian archipelago (Fisher 1973: 210). The maps they produced of topography, drainage and land use were also important in planning the subsequent economic development of the islands.

The French geographer Garry, later to become professor of geography at the University of Montreal, was originally a member of the Colonial Service in French Indochina. Pendleton was attached to the Philippine Bureau of Plant Industry from 1923 to 1935, during the period of US colonial administration, and was also a member of the Mindanao Exploration Commission. He later went to the Royal Department of Agriculture and Fisheries in Siam (now Thailand) as a soil technologist and agriculturalist. Joseph Spencer, after a period of employment with the Chinese government, joined the US Office of Strategic Services (a wartime intelligence organization), and was later assigned to its Far Eastern Division as assistant chief. Pelzer became part of a large US team concerned with the development of overseas territories, first as a research assistant in the Council of Foreign Affairs (1936–37), then in the Institute of Pacific Relations (1938–39), and later as an agricultural economist in the Office of Foreign Agricultural Relations (1945–47).

Some of those who were to become leading scholars of the geography of Southeast Asia first became associated with the region as staff members of local universities, including Raffles College (Singapore), and the Universities of Rangoon, Hanoi and Phnom Penh. From newly established geography departments within these institutions geographers embarked on field-work, and otherwise developed their research interests in their host territories. Much of Gourou's research was undertaken during the 1930s as a professor in Vietnam. Stamp, who originally travelled to Burma as a petroleum geologist, was appointed professor in geology and geography in Rangoon in 1923. Spate arrived at the University of Rangoon in 1938, but in contrast had only a brief time to develop a deep interest in Burma before being displaced by the Japanese occupation, after which he worked in the Inter-Services Topographical Department in Ceylon. None the less, his short acquaintance with the country contributed to a number of insightful publications, both from Rangoon and subsequent to his departure. Dobby (also to have his first sojourn in Southeast Asia cut short by the Japanese) and, later, Hodder were among a large number of British academics who were associated with Raffles College and later the University of Malaya. Dobby returned to Singapore after the war and later became the first professor of geography in the University of Malaya.

Dutch geographical scholarship on the East Indies was a little more restricted by virtue of the relatively late (post-1945) establishment of departments of geography in universities on Java. German scholarship on Southeast Asia, in contrast, dates back to the late nineteenth century. Lacking direct involvement in Southeast Asia as a colonial power,

Germany developed a leading reputation for research by, *inter alia*, Credner on Thailand and Kolb on the Philippines, in addition to the East Indies and other parts of the region (Farmer 1983: 72). German scholars of the time were also much more willing and able to transcend national boundaries in their research, principally on account of not being tied to any one particular colonial territory. Pelzer was one of the first to use the designation 'Südostasien' (Southeast Asia) in his work (1935; see Fisher 1973: 206), some time before it was used to describe Mountbatten's South-East Asia Command.

Perhaps the most unconventional source of exposure to the human and physical geography of Southeast Asia was that 'enjoyed' by one of the greatest Southeast Asian geographers, Fisher. Posted to Singapore in the Survey Service of the Royal Engineers, Fisher was interned for more than three years by the Japanese, first in Changi POW Camp (where he helped to found the Changi POW 'University'), and then on the Burma–Siam Railway. If there was ever a case of turning adversity into a virtue, this was it. Fisher has made it quite clear that his experiences as a prisoner of war and the insight into Southeast Asian life that his internment provided had a profound impact on both his philosophy and his understanding of the region.

Fisher later became professor of geography at the University of Sheffield and the first professor of geography with reference to Asia at the School of Oriental and African Studies, University of London, in 1965. Fisher's wartime experiences may have made a significant contribution to the kind of Southeast Asian geographer he became, and hence to the distinctive approach he came to adopt. In particular, it was Fisher's degree of 'dedication to area' (see Farmer 1973: 9–10) that helped make him stand out from many of his contemporaries and successors, some of whose association with the region was relatively superficial.

Driven as they were by the imperatives of colonial administration, a central preoccupation of geographers in the immediate post-war period became the gathering and presentation of information. The needs of the time determined, to a greater or lesser extent, the task of the geographer, and thus the approach that was adopted. Superimposed upon this functional task was the prevailing orthodoxy in geography, carried over from the pre-war period – the synthesis and representation of information, set within a defined regional or areal context and typically employing various cartographic techniques.

A further preoccupation was the drawing together of the physical and human realms of life. According to Farmer (1983: 75), Gourou's pre-war work on tropical environments and their influence on human activity, clearly manifested in his book *Les Pays tropicaux* (1948), was instrumental in creating a framework within which a great deal of post-war geographical analysis would take place. Thus the prevailing task became one of preparing, for a growing audience of scholars and practitioners, papers and manuscripts with detailed descriptions of physical structure and human process. The main publication outlets of the time also tell us much about the functionalism of scholarly research, and by continuation the approaches and methods that prevailed. Whereas many today – including those who criticize the simplicity, naïveté and descriptiveness of regional geographers in the past – have the relative luxury of being able, as an integral part of their academic appointments, to undertake research for research's sake, many of their predecessors were not in such a privileged position: there had to be a purpose to, and thus usually a product (information) from, their research.

In this context it is interesting to note that, in the immediate post-war era, many Southeast Asian geographers placed articles with the *Geography Review*, published by the American Geographical Society. The *Review* was unashamedly regional in its focus, with the world divided up into geographical zones about which the articles sought to inform. Articles published in this outlet tended to be somewhat descriptive, but there was a large audience of geographers (and an even larger number of non-geographers, including industrialists, engineers, politicians, physical scientists: see Fairchild 1979: 35) who wished to be informed about phenomena and process in the world around them, and thus the *Geographical Review* served an important purpose. Its motto, like that of the Society, was 'Ubique': each issue had to contain articles of general as well as of professional interest. Another popular outlet for research (and anecdotes) was the *Geographical Journal*, which included many papers based on presentations to the Royal Geographical Society. Once again the principal objective here was to inform a predominantly lay, but deeply interested, audience.

Thus, to make judgements of the nature and approach of regional specialists on the basis of such publications, and the numerous textbooks that were similarly written to inform a hungry audience, would seem a little unfair. If we strip away this superficial view, a great deal of very valuable and important research was undertaken during this era, some of which has withstood the passage of time remarkably well. However, there is little doubt that the most durable work has tended to be that undertaken by true specialists, who were willing and able to immerse themselves in the region and to apply what they observed in an original and creative manner. This should become clearer as we turn to look more specifically at some of the work undertaken by Southeast Asian geographers during the period under review.

Physical structure and human activity

As with geography more generally, Southeast Asian geography in the peri-war years was influenced strongly by earlier research on human–environment interaction, and initially continued to have quite strong overtones of the environmental determinism. The work of one man, Gourou, was claimed by contemporary scholars to have established the mould into which subsequent Southeast Asian geographers would attempt to fit (see, for example, Farmer 1983: 75). Gourou's *Les Pays tropicaux: principes d'une géographie humaine et économique* examined the extent to which the tropical environment constrained (or otherwise) the potential for human settlement and activity. His opening sentence was:

> La zone chaude et pluvieuse s'est révélée, jusqu'à présent, un milieu moins favorable à l'homme que la zone tempérée ['The hot and wet [tropical] zone presently provides an environment which is less favourable to mankind than the temperate zone'] (Gourou 1948: 1).

This indicated the tenor of the book. None the less, he was able to use his wide experience, knowledge and intellect to put together a volume that provided a focus for subsequent studies. The book examines the influence of the tropical environment on such human activities as agriculture and industry, and devotes an entire chapter to 'l'Asie chaude et pluvieuse', with a heavy focus on French Indochina. It is here that Gourou had focused his work prior to the Second World War, producing such works as *Indochine française: le Tonkin* (1931), *Les Paysans du Delta tonkinois: étude de géographie humaine* (1936a), *Esquisse d'une étude de l'habitation annamite* (1936), *L'utilisation du sol en Indochine française* (1940a), and *La terre et l'homme en Extrême-Orient* (1940b). *Les Paysans du Delta tonkinois* followed the classical structure of initially examining in detail the physical setting of Tonkin (relief, climate, drainage, and so on), before looking systematically at such human features as population, settlement, migration, agriculture, trade and village industries. An interesting feature of this and some of Gourou's other writing, which has some bearing upon both approach and level of dedication to area, is the author's obvious and abiding interest in vernacular architecture and family names. Together with the large number of photographs that appear in the above publications, this suggests a person who took much more than a superficial and Euro-centric view of this part of the world. Thus his resultant work, however descriptive, systematic and dated it may appear to the modern reader, is also insightful, informative and represents a most useful resource even today. Because of my interest in rural industrialization, I was fascinated by the long chapter in *Les Paysans du Delta tonkinois* on 'les industries villageoises', which includes details of the the origins of certain cottage industries.

Whether or not Gourou was as influential as his contemporaries claimed, his approach can be identified in many books and papers published during the period under review. One clear illustration of Gourou's direct influence is found in the work of his protégé Jean Delvert, whose *Le Paysan cambodgien* (1961) closely follows Gourou's lead, even though it was written more than two decades later, and at a time when other geographers had significantly altered their approach. Delvert pays tribute to Gourou and his colleague Charles Robequain for their help in the book's compilation: this highlights the important role that the training of later generations of geographers plays in perpetuating orthodox approaches, or at least retarding the evolution of new approaches.

The work of early German and Dutch geographers in the region also demonstrated a tendency to integrate discussion of physical structure and human activity. Credner's volume *Siam: Das Land der Tai* (1935), whilst praised as 'the most exhaustive work on Siam that has yet appeared … a landmark in geographical papers dealing with various aspects of the human, cultural and economic geography of mainland South-East Asia' (Pelzer 1949: 334), none the less adhered rigidly to the classical format of detailed description of physical structure followed by various aspects of the Siamese economy, population and culture. Much of the book consists of documentation and description, but the more crucial point is that there was a significant need at the time for a text of this nature: Siam then was not a country that many knew much about, and thus there was a need to inform a wide academic and non-academic audience. The book is painstakingly researched and, like many of its genre, contains innumerable photographs and illustrations.

In the Dutch case it appears that the tendency to adopt the conventional approach may have been attributable to the scientific training that scholars such as Verstappen, van Valkenburg and Lekkerkerker took with them to the Dutch East Indies. Most of Verstappen's work was concerned with the geomorphological mapping of the Indonesian archipelago. However, he did on at least one occasion (1956) attempt to assess the influence of physical geography on human activity, in a manner similar to Pelzer's. Van Valkenburg's simultaneous expertise in several branches of the discipline (ranging from pre-glacial landscapes and climatology to land use and economic geography) identified him as the classical 'Jack of all trades' geographer. After moving to the United States he used his wide experience of survey work in Indonesia as the basis for several articles on the economic geography of Java and the agricultural regions of Southeast Asia (Fisher 1973: 204). As a teacher, he heavily emphasized field-work and the use of maps. Lekkerkerker's hugely detailed *Land en Volk van Java* (1938), and his earlier *Land en Volk van Sumatra* (1916), also adhered very closely to the conventional approach, using a systematic description of physical structure as the foundation upon which to describe various forms of land use, settlement and other human activities.

The writing of another Dutchman, Ormeling, is very helpful in identifying some of the contemporary debates in relation to the approach and intrinsic value of the geographer. The following passage appears in his book *The Timor Problem*:

> The struggle between the supporters and opponents of environmental determinism was decided long ago in favour of the latter. Since Vidal de la Blache's time possibilism has dominated in Geography. Thus, the emphasis is on human activity, rather than on control by the physical environment. Man is considered to be an active, creative power, acting upon and changing his physical environment. This creative power depends mainly on the cultural level of society.
>
> This view, however, does not mean that the physical environment is to be ignored. The lower the state of cultural development, including technical ability and socio-economic organization, the narrower is the frame of the natural forces in which the society must operate. In tropical areas the cultural level is often so low that the restrictive influences of the environment virtually become 'controls' of the local mode of live [*sic*]. Of the three chief environmental factors – climate, topography and edaphic conditions – it is usually climate that affects an under-developed people most of all (1956: 13).

This is a sign of the times: a recognition of the limitations of physical structure as an explanation of underdevelopment, but also a demonstrable reluctance to give up on the environment entirely, and the persistence of certain undertones of 'cultural determinism'. We can begin to understand the continuing preoccupation of contemporary geographers with articulating physical structure and human process, especially in areas where social organization and technological development, supposedly, has prevented a people from exerting a more powerful controlling influence on the physical environment.

Ormeling also discusses at some length how the contemporary development problems of (West) Timor might be ameliorated, suggesting a prominent role for the geographer:

> geographers could give considerable assistance. With their training, they are often able to provide the required co-ordination and correlation. By

providing the present situation's historical background, by analyzing the methods man has used to develop his environment and giving a synthetic interpretation of all phenomena found in the area, he can supply the basic overall information necessary in the formulation of plans for future development (1956: vii).

One scholar who attempted to move away from the convention of drawing together the physical and human realms in studies of Southeast Asia was Robequain. His full and informative 1939 publication (translated in 1944, with supplementation, as *The Economic Development of French Indo-China*), although more descriptive than analytical, contains a wealth of material on the economic and social structure of the French colonial territory, written largely from an impartial perspective which attempts to identify changes wrought in the Indochinese economy by the French colonial intervention. It deals with several issues of contemporary economic significance, such as problems relating to migration and the mismatch between the principal loci of population settlement and the spatial location and demands of mining, colonial agriculture and industry. Professor of tropical geography at the Sorbonne, Robequain was seen within the French school as a pioneer in the field of underdeveloped areas. After an initial study of the cities of Laos (1925), he focused his research on Vietnam. He published a regional study of Thanh Hoa Province (1929), which, like Delvert's thirty years later, emphasized the diversity of Asian territories. Robequain showed how several stages of underdevelopment coexisted owing to social and historical differences as well as physical ones, and was proclaimed as 'one of the pioneering contributions to tropical geography' (Gottman 1964: 594).

The American (originally German) geographer Karl Pelzer demonstrates a clear concern for the ethics of external intervention in the lives and livelihoods of indigenous peoples. He also brought an extraordinarily rich degree of familiarity with the physical and human setting within which his work on pioneer settlement was undertaken. Pelzer's diverse background and training as first an agricultural economist and later a geographer, coupled with his extensive first-hand experience of several Southeast Asian countries (especially the Philippines, Indonesia and Malaya), underpinned a scholarly quality in his work which made him stand out from many of his contemporaries. Pelzer's work was also remarkably specialized and thematically focused. His book *Pioneer Settlement in the Asiatic Tropics* (1945) provides an analysis of government-sponsored and spontaneous processes of frontier settlement and land development occurring, primarily, in response to increasing population densities in longer-established loci of settlement. In addition to providing meticulous attention to detail and a body of information which is still of value today, the book is heavily critical of the simplistic assumption that areas of sparse population settlement represent an ideal location for land colonisation. The study was inspired by Gourou's earlier work on the possibilities of settlement in tropical regions, but in some senses takes an antithetical stance, at least in relation to frontier areas.

Pelzer also expresses concern about the potential impact of pioneer settlement on indigenous peoples (a theme still relevant in relation to, for example, the Indonesian transmigration programme). In his article 'Tanah Sabrang and Java's population problem' (1946) Pelzer looks at uneven population distribution between Java/Madura and the outer islands of the Indonesian archipelago (Tanah Sabrang). He recognizes the role played by human agency (especially Western colonial intervention) in creating the conditions in which population could expand – the removal of famine, warfare and pestilence, and the improvement of medicine and sanitation – but also indicates a strong distaste for the way that the colonial powers, through their self-interest, prevented the emergence of indigenous structures and capabilities which could sustain or take over control of such things in the future (Pelzer 1946: 133).

Regional synthesis

British scholars of Southeast Asia in many ways epitomized the art of the regional geographer in the post-war era. Among them, it was probably Stamp whom later critics of ideographic geography had most in mind. Beaver described Stamp as a person with 'a passion for facts and a tidy mind [and with] an amazing facility for absorbing a mass of material and re-presenting it in a clear, almost tabular form' (1966: 389). He was 'not a profound master of theory', and had a strong financial interest in producing textbooks. In 1957, after developing a research interest in land utilization, he reaffirmed his belief that the primary concern of geography should be the mapping of data (Cloke, Philo and Sadler 1991: 11). From these snippets we can deduce a person who approximates, much more closely than others thus far considered, the stereotypical regional geographer much maligned by positivists. Viewed from a different perspective, however, Stamp was credited with popularizing geography, and making the subject accessible (Beaver 1966: 390). Textbooks such as *Asia* (1929) played an important role in this regard.

A more representative view of Stamp the Southeast Asian geographer can be obtained from some of his articles published during and after the war. His presentation on 'The Irrawaddy River' to the annual meeting of the Royal Geographical Society in 1940 was praised by the chairman, D. L. Linton:

> In bringing together from his own work and other sources *all the essential known facts* about the Irrawaddy, Dr Stamp has produced a paper of a kind which is too seldom seen ... The paucity of precise knowledge about the great rivers of the globe is one of the most serious gaps in our understanding of the lands (Beaver 1966: 355; emphasis added).

It should be emphasized that the Royal Geographical Society, though the mainstream geographical institution of the time, consisted of a host of people – military, lay and academic – with a broad interest not only in geography but also in the continuing tradition of exploration and discovery. In this connection, the audience's enthusiasm was raised not only by sharp geographical enquiry but also by introductions to far-away and fascinating new parts of the world. This was the context within which much geography was placed at the time, and it conditioned the approach adopted.

Another presentation to the Royal Geographical Society, 'Siam before the war', was based on impressions gained during an extended stay in Siam in 1938. This paper contrasted sharply with the earlier one, emphasizing Stamp's diverse talents in the human as well as physical realms but it *is* debilitatingly descriptive. None the less, it served a purpose by informing an audience that was largely previously unfamiliar with the country or region. It was also a topical piece, as Siam had recently aligned itself with the Japanese. The paper contains a number of generalized statements, which may be interpreted either as insightful or myopic: 'At heart the Siamese are lovers of the land and do not take readily to city life nor to commerce and trade' (Stamp 1942: 221).

Finally, in 'Burma: an undeveloped monsoon country' (1930), published in the *Geographical Review*, other stereotypes abound. The notion of underdevelopment, and its attribution to physical conditions, isolation and underpopulation, is evidence of the kind of narrow thinking that was quite widespread at the time but came to be readily criticized after the war. This article also follows the prevailing orthodoxy by detailing Burma's physical setting as a prelude to assessing, systematically and descriptively, aspects of production, settlement and trade. Burma is identified as 'a country of immense possibilities and one in which extensive development may be expected in the near future' (ibid: 105). Reflecting Stamp's firm belief in the contribution that geography could, and should, make to the solution of the world's problems (and also, perhaps, in a somewhat romanticized vision of the Orient), he rounds off his presentation by suggesting that this

'Cinderella' province of India, 'a happy land of happy people, desires to be freed from the troubled politics of India and to develop along her own lines' (ibid: 109).

Dobby was also a regional synthesizer. Appointed to Raffles College, Singapore, in 1936, he was largely responsible for building up the Department of Geography of what was to become the University of Malaya. Like Stamp, he possessed the classical geographer's diverse talents, being equally at home within the physical and human realms, and he steadfastly refused to play a role in their ultimate separation, as geography and geographers became more specialized. In an obituary, B. W. Hodder remarked on his ' depth of knowledge about South-East Asia [and] his breadth of interests'. His energy and initiative lay behind the launching of the *Malayan Journal of Tropical Geography* in 1953.

Dobby's *Southeast Asia* (1950) was the typical systematic textbook, covering in some detail and with some verve all of the discipline's branches. The volume was significant in that, for a long time, it represented the sole and principal textbook on Southeast Asia's geography – a point reinforced by the fact that it ran to at least ten editions. However, it did little more than provide a comprehensive description of what was taking place in the region at the time, and stands in quite strong contrast to Fisher's *South-East Asia: a social, economic and political geography* (1964). The fact that almost fifteen years passed between the publication of these two books is pertinent, the discipline having evolved quite significantly in the interim. However, in many respects Dobby and Fisher both belonged to the 'old school' of regional geography, differences between them being attributable to other factors.

Southeast Asia aims to 'present a picture of environmental conditions and human adaptations in Southeast Asia', in the process providing the student with a basic text and, at the same time, a little more ambitiously, seeking to stimulate the sociologist, the administrator, the politician and the businessman to see the relation of their work to the general field. Perhaps in reaction to criticism of geography as 'regional synthesis', Dobby claimed that the volume was not:

> a dictionary, a gazetteer or an encyclopaedia. It is one of the first studies of locational perspectives in Southeast Asia, the critical importance of which became apparent during the last war when the *scarcity of information* demonstrated how little study had been given to the region as a whole (ibid: preface; emphasis added).

None the less, it follows a highly conventional format, commencing with a simple assessment of the physical structure and characteristics of the region as a whole, before looking individually at the different countries of the region, for each of which there is a systematic assessment of physical and cultural landscape. There is also some analysis of population patterns, migrations, agricultural practices, urban settlement, trade, peoples and politics. Like Stamp's work, it is highly descriptive and, while there is an attempt to discuss contemporary issues such as dualism, pluralism, nationalism, devolution, divergences and convergences, in general it lacks analysis and the direct engagement of theory. This is only to be expected in an introductory textbook. Still, Dobby does also manage to convey the sense of someone who has travelled and carried out fieldwork quite widely within the region.

While *Southeast Asia* reveals much about the man and his approach, and the prevailing orthodoxy, Dobby also produced a number of articles during and consequent to his first-hand experience of Southeast Asia. 'Some aspects of the human ecology of South-East Asia' (1946) deals at some length with the environmental conditions of Southeast Asia, especially the soils, and their general inappropriateness for many of the forms of plantation cultivation to which they had been put (particularly in Malaya and the East Indies), especially following colonial intervention in the region's economy. This was a popular theme of the time (see also Pelzer, Pendleton, Robequain), and reflected geographers' continuing preoccupation with human–environment interaction. The paper demonstrates good understanding of the way that laterized soils are affected by the removal or transformation of the natural vegetation, and this is used to explain why soils are often so rapidly exhausted where plantations replace the natural forest vegetation.

'Settlement and land utilization, Malacca' (1939) and 'Settlement patterns in Malaya' (1942) are essentially descriptive accounts of past and 'present' trends in urban development. The former deals variously with the historical origins of the city and state of Malacca, and contains a description of various activities taking place there, including rice cultivation, human settlement, and so on. The latter is similarly full and informed, and contains much settlement mapping, one of the principal methodologies of the time. However, there is no attempt to contextualize the paper within a wider discourse on urbanization processes (although he does try, unsuccessfully, to find commonalities of form with Europe); nor does Dobby discuss some of the broader issues relating to the phenomena he describes. 'Singapore: Town and Country' (1940) demonstrates Dobby's facility to deal easily with both physical and human geography, but again the impression given is of a generalist rather than a regional specialist (although at the time he would have been seen as the latter). The paper contains a full and informed description of myriad aspects of Singapore, as well as a number of maps and photographs.

Hodder was for some time a lecturer in the University of Malaya, Singapore, where he worked under and was influenced by Dobby, as he acknowledges in his preface to 'Racial groupings in Singapore' (1953). This article relies heavily upon data gathered (and cartographically presented) as a result of a land-use survey carried out under the auspices of the (British colonial) Singapore Improvement Trust, and as such is one of a very limited number of empirical studies that I have been able to uncover from the geographical literature on Southeast Asia during the period under review. Hodder's later article 'The economic development of Sarawak' (1956) returns to the more conventional and systematic structure, focusing thematically on economic planning in the state, but dealing primarily with the demographic, economic and social context within which it occurred. Meanwhile, his book *Man in Malaya* (1959) adopted a refreshing approach to the study of social and economic development by assessing the two-way interaction between peoples and places (as opposed to the more conventional environments) in Malaya. Drawing extensively upon his first-hand experiences, the volume explores some of the ways in which various cultures, or cultural groups, interact.

Areal specialization

Finally, I consider the work of scholars who, whilst integral to the regional geographical genre, stand out from those discussed so far because of their degree of aereal specialization – although, of course, the distinction is rather arbitrary and subjective.

Spate's work on Southeast Asia mostly concerned Burma, where he was attached to Rangoon University's Department of Geography. In his paper 'The Burmese village' (1945) there is little evidence of a supposed influence on Spate's work by his predecessor in the department, Stamp. The article demonstrates a very full familiarity with and understanding of the country, and presents a well-informed typology of settlement types, showing the influence of topography, population density, economic activity and accessibility. Spate draws parallels with Dobby's earlier article on Malaya, but in general presents a much fuller and more well-informed analysis. One point of interest (other than his tendency to describe most indigenous economic activities as 'primitive') is his clear delineation of the work of the geographer and anthropologist: in discussing the layout of Naga rural settlements, he implies that the geographer's interest lies in the structure and form of the rural village, whereas the anthropologist would be more interested in 'the houses set aside for the courtship of the young people among the Nagas' (1945: 527).

Spate's intimate familiarity with the country also shows through in another of his wartime articles. 'Beginnings of industrialization in Burma' (1941) provides a fascinating and critical view of the constraints and potential faced by Burma's embryonic industrial sector. Spate makes a clear attempt to engage industrial location theory, which he finds weak when applied to a context where industry is mostly small scale and widely dispersed. The article, published in the scholarly journal *Economic Geography*, which had earlier featured several papers on the subject of industrial location, contains a full and informed overview of the various types of industrial activity found in Burma in the immediate pre-war period, their geographical pattern, and the various factors that have influenced the natural and characteristics of industrialization. Initially one is given the impression of an enlightened piece of analysis which eschewed the prevailing 'large and capital-intensive is beautiful' orthodoxy. But this notion is regrettably exploded at the last (even though Spate's prognosis was remarkably prescient):

> As regards initiative, the most casual observer in Rangoon and even up-country is at once struck by lack of Burmese enterprise ... there is little sign of any resolution to tackle the problem and make best use of such Burmese resources as exist ... [In the words of one of the country's leaders] 'Business must be interpreted in the Burmese sense, of small-scale trading; not in the un-Burmese sense of enormous enterprises, which are foreign to the genius of Burmese life'. [This statement] does reflect with clarity and certainty the hopeless outlook for Burma's embryo industry (ibid: 92).

The American geographer Spencer also more comfortably fitted the mould of 'regional specialist' than that of 'regional geographer'. Trained originally as a geomorphologist, he subsequently moved into the field of cultural geography. Two scholars had a profound influence on his work and approach: Sauer was his guru and Spencer imbibed his philosophy, methodology and personality. Garst taught Spencer to view physical–human interactions in a non-determinist manner. Spencer's wide experience of Asia clearly also had a deep and profound impact on him. His principal volume, *Asia, East by South* (1954), a regional cultural geography (extending far beyond Southeast Asia as defined here), traces the evolution of cultural groups in their regional settings, incorporating a historical–geographical perspective drawing upon material from several academic disciplines. The book included material relating to health, disease, religion, law, architecture and wildlife not often found in geographical texts. According to his colleague Nelson (1985: 599):

> The book dispelled on every page the Western notion that the Orient

was full of strange people, behaving in odd ways. It was hailed as 'a
magistral work', presenting 'novel, stimulating and thoughtful insights'.
[It was also] the first American regional geography that is really cultural
geography ... Spencer had insisted that cultural geography be given equal
footing with physical geography, and it was. ... He seems to have been
the first American geographer to understand that the cultures of the
Orient and their ecological expressions must be interpreted in terms of
their own internal logic. Western models were not appropriate ... Each
culture has its own conception of 'development.' What right do we have
to assume that our culture is the one against which all others should be
measured?

Spencer's later book *The Philippine Island World* (1967), co-written
with Wernstedt, placed similar emphasis on the cultural geography of
the archipelago, albeit set within the slightly more 'conventional' context whereby physical setting and regional structure are examined
systematically.

Perhaps because of his degree of regional specialization, Spencer
had occasional crises of identity. He thought that, as a result of his
regular forays into the region, he had become more a regional specialist
and less a geographer: 'recent methodological work had held many of
his geographic concepts to be irrelevant and [he feared] he might not
be considered a "real geographer"' (Nelson 1985: 597). Later, Spencer
viewed himself 'not as an Asian specialist, but as a cultural geographer
with varied regional and topical interests' (ibid: 599).

We come, finally, to a specialist Southeast Asian geographer, Fisher,
whose work I will use to challenge the steroetyped views of the
'regional geographer' which were widely held by later critics of the
genre. Although my selection may be subjective, I base it on the degree
to which Fisher knew and understood Southeast Asia. The insight and
'feel' for the region that he demonstrated in his writing, coupled with
his deliberate engagement of concepts and processes of contemporary
relevance, underpin my description of this scholar as the 'new regional
geographer of yesteryear'. In other words, as the world of the regional
geographer has turned full circle, modern converts are rediscovering
the importance of the qualities of approach and scholarly understanding to which Charles Fisher had long adhered.

Fisher was an internationally distinguished scholar in the fields of
both Southeast Asian Studies and political geography. I have discussed
how his wartime experiences contributed to his insight into the people
and human structures of Southeast Asia. In addition, his undergraduate training in Cambridge brought him into contact with scholars
from whom he imbibed an appreciation of the importance of history
to contemporary analysis, and of the human factor in economic and

political affairs (Farmer 1983: 252–3). His experience and training helped to mould his approach to the geographical study of Southeast Asia:

> Fisher fashioned his own coherent and consistent philosophy of geography, albeit one which was not surprisingly a little eclectic. He came out strongly in favour of the centrality of regional geography as he conceived it and reformulated it ... but even more strongly in favour of the unity of geography. He deplored what he saw as centrifugal tendencies arising from the proliferation of branches of systematic geography; and never came to terms with the much-trumpeted 'New Geography' of the 1960s, whose proclaimed rigour he castigated as *rigor mortis* (Farmer 1983: 253).

This quotation complicates my argument somewhat. Fisher is presented here as a die-hard traditionalist, one of a number who were strongly resistant to the 'revolutionary' changes that were sweeping some of the discipline's dusty corridors. Yet one could suggest that Fisher was defending not regional geography *per se* but the regional geographer's fine art, of which he was one of the most outstanding practitioners. Such a view is not inconsistent with the following description of Fisher, taken from his obituary in the *Geographical Journal* (1982: 297):

> At a time when British geography was becoming ever more parochial and inward-looking, he urged his colleagues and students to adopt a world view, and he was a trenchant advocate of the need to promote geographical research in those territories that lie beyond the cultural realms of Europe and North America. Believing as he did that regional study should be the true core of geography, it gave him particular pleasure to occupy the first British Chair in geography to be designated in regional terms.

Although he wrote several articles on matters appertaining to political development and international relations in Pacific Asia, his most significant contribution was his classic text *South-East Asia: a social, economic and political geography* (1964), started while he was professor of geography and director of the Centre of Japanese Studies at the University of Sheffield, and completed after his move in 1965 to become the first professor of geography with reference to Asia at the School of Oriental and African Studies, University of London. This massive volume is remarkable for its comprehensiveness and superb attention to detail. The structure is in many respects traditional, prefacing a systematic examination of the region's countries and a thematic assessment of, *inter alia*, the indigenous peoples, political geography, and the impact of colonialism with a detailed discussion of the region's physical setting. However, it is the content and the style with which it is expressed that are the book's principal strengths. Equally important is Fisher's ability to cover in equal strength matters appertaining to history, physical geography, politics, society and economy – a talent few of his more specialized successors possess. The volume may be informational, but it also offers much insight and facilitates clear understanding of process and form. The information may now be dated, but *South-East Asia* has provided an invaluable starting point for several generations of Southeast Asian geographers.

Fisher seldom shied away from controversy; indeed, a strength of his work was the way that he engaged with, and informed, the issues of the day. Taking just one illustration, in discussing the thorny issue of the human and physical determinants of underdevelopment – 'the connexion between human vigour and terrestrial latitude' – Fisher makes the following remarks, which also provide clues as to his approach and prevailing philosophy:

> questions of this kind need to be asked, and the geographer is neglecting his duty if he refrains from posing them out of fear of being dubbed an environmentalist or – worse still – a determinist. In the writer's experience a three-year sojourn in the jungles of Thailand went far to counter the optimistic possibilism which appeared so eminently reasonable in the air-conditioned clubs of Singapore. And if the possibilists seriously maintain that the rigours of the humid tropical environment are a wholly inadequate explanation of the retarded development of these regions, does their philosophy really amount to anything other than a reformulation, however unintentional, of the old doctrine of white supremacy? (1964: 60–1).

Why should Charles Fisher be any more insightful than his peers and predecessors? I think the answer – inasmuch as the question itself is accurate – lies in the degree to which Fisher was, to use Farmer's words once again, 'dedicated to area' (1973: 10): an area specialist with a solid disciplinary foundation, as opposed to a regional geographer. The final question should therefore be whether later critics of regional geography were aware of the work of Charles Fisher (and several areal specialists of other parts of the world). Has not their subsequent reengagement of the 'region', in some respects, brought the genre back to some (but certainly not all) of the virtues of intricately informed research that were epitomized in Fisher's approach?

After the 'revolution' (c.1965–95)

In this section, I aim to articulate description of the continuing diversity of Southeast Asian geography with an assessment of how this specialist branch of the discipline has changed in response to the more fundamental metamorphoses that have taken place within mainstream geography since the mid-1960s. The discussion is unavoidably selective. The last thirty years have seen an explosion of interest in Southeast Asia from a wide variety of academic disciplines, not least geography. Thus one could without too much difficulty identify between fifty and seventy-five geographers who have made significant contributions to the field of Southeast Asian geography, and many more into whose consciousness the region has occasionally penetrated during the period under review. However, I have no wish simply to duplicate the admirable overview that has already been provided by Savage, Kong and Yeoh (1993). The main emphasis here is on how geographers have *approached* the study of Southeast Asia. As in the preceding section, my task is made difficult by the wide variety found under the banner heading of 'Southeast Asian geography': classical regional geographers (in part reinforcing the view that 1965 is a somewhat arbitrary watershed), specialist geographers who find in Southeast Asia an appropriate setting to ply their trade, area studies specialists with geographical backgrounds, and geographers who make passing reference to Southeast Asia in relation to wider processes or ideas. Within some of these various 'types' are a growing number of Southeast Asian geographers from the region itself, whose work I shall look at in the last part of this assessment.

In order to facilitate this assessment of Southeast Asian geography since the mid-1960s, it is necessary to impose a somewhat artificial structure. So I shall look at the work and approach of a small cross-section of individuals who have been drawn from a spectrum ranging between, at one extreme, the geographer who does not specialize in Southeast Asia but whose work draws upon processes taking place within the region, and, at the other, the genuine area specialist who is dedicated to the study of Southeast Asia. In between these two extremes, there is a variety of what might be loosely described as 'regional geographers' who may be differentiated into three types: those whose work identifies them as theoretically or methodologically engaged; those who are recognized by their identity as sub-disciplinary specialists; and those who take a more generalist approach to the study of the region.

Southeast Asia viewed from a wider geographical perspective

I shall briefly consider here the work of two leading geographers (Dicken and Thrift)[3] who are not seen generally as Southeast Asia specialists *per se*, but part of whose work has been concerned with global economic (and to a lesser extent social and political) processes where either the dynamism or the ideological dogmatism of certain Southeast Asian countries has given them particular significance.

Dicken has developed a leading reputation for his work on the globalization and internationalization of economic, and especially industrial, activity (see e.g. Dicken 1986, 1992). Within this context, he has become something of a specialist on Japan, so central is an understanding of the structure of the Japanese industrial and financial system to an appreciation of contemporary global economic processes. Since the early 1980s, Southeast Asia has taken on particular prominence within the emerging 'international division of labour', with foreign direct investment from Japan, other Asian countries, Europe and the United States playing a central role in this process. Accordingly, the work of Dicken, and of many others who have taken an interest in this vitally important global process, has often referred to the dynamics of change in Southeast Asia. However, Dicken is not a Southeast Asia specialist in the way that, say, Dixon is. For Dicken, Southeast Asia is seen principally as a mosaic of states, strategies and factors of production which in some way fit into a wider array of processes and patterns. Reference to the region occurs largely through the work of others, as opposed to being based on extensive first-hand experience (see Dicken 1988). Such a situation is inevitable where the focus of enquiry is broad. However, Dicken does recognize the importance of understanding the specific expression of general processes of change as they manifest themselves in particular geographical locations (Dicken 1992: xiv). Furthermore, he emphasizes strongly the need to challenge the hyperbole and sense of homogenization that have tended to accompany the notion of 'globalization' in geographical discourse (ibid: 1):

> Change does not occur everywhere in the same way and at the same rate; the processes of globalization are not geographically uniform. The particular character of individual countries, of regions and even of localities interacts with the larger-scale general processes of change to produce quite specific outcomes (ibid: 2).

This may indeed be the case, but it could be argued that it is difficult for someone lacking the specific skills of a regional or country specialist to be able to pick up the subtleties and specificities associated with, for example, the cultural, political or historical context with which global processes are fusing. None the less, the fusion between the work of such scholars as Dicken and others who specialize on Southeast Asia allows locally informed research to be set within a wider conceptual context.

Thrift has even stronger views on this, and at the same time appears to be making an oblique reference to the myopia of the country (and perhaps also regional) specialist. The internationalization of capital, he says, is:

> still the most important economic event taking place in the world at present and it is having crucial reverberations – economic, social and cultural – on many countries. Yet, still only a few human geographers seem willing to come out of their national shells and take the wider view that would enable them to understand what is going on *within their own countries*. They seem quite willing to document the national effects of international processes. This insular view of the world cannot continue, because the world is no longer like that (Thrift 1989: 72; original emphasis).

On closer examination, it appears that Dicken and Thrift are arguing in different directions: the former suggests the need for a greater degree of contextualization or 'ground-truthing' of international processes, the latter argues that a proper understanding of these wider processes is essential if we are adequately to comprehend what is taking place within countries or regions. This is a little strange because, for a short while, Thrift specialized in the process of urbanization in Vietnam (see Thrift and Forbes 1985, 1986). Indeed, he used Vietnam to validate his wider interest in urban and territorial planning in socialist developing countries (Forbes and Thrift 1987). In their work on urbanization in Vietnam, Thrift and Forbes used empirical material to explore, and ultimately challenge, the model of urbanization in socialist states that had earlier been presented by Murray and Szelenyi (1984). Were it not for the quotation above, and in the absence of any first-hand knowledge of the evolution of Thrift's thinking, it would not seem too fanciful to suggest that his brief encounter with Vietnam had in some way influenced his later writings on the New Regional Geography that were discussed earlier. In other words, someone who has long specialized in the world of the abstract and the broad suddenly has been exposed to the light of locality, context and the specific. With this enlightenment, a whole new perspective on how to study process may have been unveiled.

In essence, though, there is little difference between the views of Dicken and Thrift in this regard. Both recognize the parallel importance of the broad and the narrow, the general and the specific. The more important point to emerge from this discussion is the way in which the engagement of theory helps to identify the approach adopted by geographers whose work touches only rather tangentially on Southeast Asia. This leads us logically to enquire whether the engagement of theory, and to some extent also methodology, becomes less strong and direct the more specialized a geographer becomes in a particular geographical region or country.

Southeast Asia viewed by geographers specializing in the region

Theoretically engaged geographers

One of the criticisms levelled at 'classical' regional geography concerned its preoccupation with empiricism at the expense of theory. Since the geographical 'revolution' of the 1960s, some Southeast Asian geographers have both engaged in prevailing theoretical discourses and also contributed to these discourses by drawing upon the Southeast Asian context and experience. Whether the work of these Southeast Asian geographers reflects the more general and sweeping changes which were taking place within the discipline as a whole is difficult to ascertain. None the less, the approaches they adopted provide clues. Two scholars have been selected here to represent the theoretically engaged regional specialist: Forbes and McGee.

While Thrift appears to have lost interest in Vietnam after it ceased to be a 'hardline socialist state', Forbes has maintained his involvement, recently publishing an article (1995) on the ways in which the reform process has affected the country's urban system. This follows the wider interest that Forbes has shown in the process of *doi moi* (renovation), which got under way in Vietnam following the Sixth Communist Party Congress in 1986 (see Forbes et al. 1991). One reason for including Forbes in the category of 'Southeast Asia specialists', and thus separating his work from Thrift's, is that Forbes has developed strong credentials as a specialist on parts of the region. This is partly because his more recent work on Vietnam has allowed him the opportunity to conduct detailed local-level field research of the kind that he and Thrift earlier identified (Thrift and Forbes 1986: 4–5) as necessary for an adequate understanding of processes within specific Vietnamese cities. However, it is his earlier work on the informal sector in Indonesian cities, and particularly Ujung Pandang in South Sulawesi (the subject of his Ph.D. research), which principally identifies him as an area specialist (see Forbes 1979, 1981a, 1981b).

Two important features of Forbes' work help to determine how it should be categorized. First, his research contains much insight into the inner workings of the urban informal sector in Indonesia. Second, his work engaged directly the theoretical formulations which were prevalent at the time, including the notion of urban economic dualism and the articulation of modes of production (ibid.: 845–6). However, he is able to use his empirical information to take these theoretical debates into fresh territory. The following quotation (which might be contrasted with the profiles of Dicken and Thrift) offers some insight into Forbes' views on the approach that must be adopted in the geographical study of developing areas:

> If one is to understand the complex process of underdevelopment then one must look in depth both at the macroprocesses of integration of these countries in the world capitalist system, and at the microprocesses occurring in Third World countries, especially those involving the mass of poor ... There is little point in stressing the characteristics of petty commodity production in isolation from its external links. [Also needed is] empirical evidence of the flow of value through the constituent forms of the Indonesian social formation, and the implications this has for an understanding of the nature of underdevelopment. [Thus] it is important not to overlook the mechanisms *within* petty commodity production which help bring about the impoverishment of some within this system ... empirical research supports the notion of an interlocking hierarchy of modes and forms of production within the city (Forbes 1981a: 851–2; original emphasis).

Southeast Asia's urban system and its internal structure have provided a very important focus for the work of geographers who have specialized in the region, most particularly because it was here that some of the most rapid changes were taking place and also, as a consequence, where some interesting and diagnostic patterns of development and change were emerging.

McGee is another geographer to have specialized in this field, and has also consistently attempted to engage prevailing theoretical debates. Much of his early writing took place when geography was in turmoil. His work in the late 1960s and early 1970s evinces a certain engagement with positivist principles, but he also continued to emphasize the role that the specificities of locale and context play in determining the precise character of spatial pattern and process. Superficially at least, this appears to be paradoxical: after all, geography as spatial science took the discipline into the realms of modelling and paradigms, which de-emphasize considerably the importance of context and locale.

McGee's earliest major work, *The Southeast Asian City: a social geography of the primate cities of Southeast Asia* (1967), established his credentials as a regional specialist. The volume sought to explore the structure and form of the Southeast Asian primate city – the 'nerve centre' of the country – and to identify common elements in process which could be used to demonstrate how urbanization in Southeast

Asia had progressed in a very different way from that experienced in the West (McGee 1967: 13). This detailed study benefited greatly from a four-year sojourn at the University of Malaya, whence forays were made to other major Southeast Asian cities. His study of Petaling Jaya, a new town which has subsequently become an adjunct of Kuala Lumpur, also demonstrated his ability to engage in empirical research with practical policy-making applications, and his belief that 'the development of more sophisticated theory rests on the collection of such empirical data as this study presents' (McGee and McTaggart 1967: vi).

This latter sentiment may be seen as significant in relation to McGee's subsequent career. In the early 1970s he directly engaged in the prevailing paradigm of urban dualism, articulating his earlier work on Asian urbanization within this conceptual framework. The objective of *Dualism in the Asian City: the implications for city and regional planning* (1970) was 'to provoke a reevaluation of certain of the assumptions and conceptions which underlie the planning process in Asian cities' (McGee 1970: 34). He was particularly interested in how the persistence of the manifestations of urban poverty, such as squatter settlement and illegal hawking, could be explained by the dualistic internal structure of the Asian city. He also sought to emphasize how prevailing planning responses, such as squatter eviction and infrastructural improvement, were misguided because they left untouched a significant section of the urban population. In a later work on hawkers in Southeast Asian cities, he claimed that there was 'no need for the hawker to be replaced by the supermarket. The two can co-exist effectively and productively in the Asian cities of the future' (McGee and Yeung 1977: 118).

Unlike many of his peers, who went either in one direction or the other, McGee successfully articulated paradigms with areal specialization. He recognized the importance of theory and a certain degree of generalization in understanding the broad direction and determinants of development and change, but he could not accept that this could be done in a contextual vacuum. However, his later work suggests that his engagement in the urban dualism paradigm took him further out of his area specialist persona than might otherwise have occurred had not the discipline been moving in a particular direction at the time. A return visit to Malaysia in the late 1970s gave him a chance to reappraise his earlier ideas, in particular the notion of 'urban involution' (whereby the informal sector creates work opportunities by expanding almost limitlessly through various forms of job-splitting), which had appeared quite plausible at the time (McGee 1982). The city in Malaysia had subsequently developed in a way which may have seemed unimaginable in the late-1960s, particularly where one's imagination had been pre-programmed by a prevailing paradigm.

Sub-disciplinary specialists

Another loose category of Southeast Asian geographers consists of those who are best regarded as specialists in certain sub-branches of the discipline, but who applied their specialisms within the context of Southeast Asia (and Asia more generally). A distinguishing feature of geography over the last three decades is the way that it has spawned specialist geographers across and sometimes beyond the length and breadth of the discipline.

Although perhaps better known as a specialist on China, Dwyer has also made a valuable contribution as an urban geographer who has explored the process of urbanization, and more recently the process of development, in Southeast Asia (see e.g. Dwyer 1964a and 1964b, 1972, 1990). The following quotation tells us much about Dwyer's early reaction to the kinds of changes taking place within geography during the early 1960s (note the close parallel with Fisher's sentiments):

> In seeking to generalise about the city in the developing world ... I do not intend to adopt the attitude which is becoming increasingly prevalent in geography: that if you cannot graph it, reduce it to an equation or put it through a computer, it is rather old-fashioned and intellectually suspect because of its lack of precision (Dwyer 1967: 1).

Dwyer's long exposure to and understanding of the Asian setting of contemporary spatial processes caused him to eschew the fashion-following tendencies of his colleagues in favour of the insightful, even anecdotal perspective that he has always managed to bring to his work. With the benefit of hindsight, we now know that the latter approach has proved to be more durable, and ultimately more useful to Southeast Asian geography, than the detached abstractism that characterized the positivist episode.

Uhlig specialized within the branch of geography that is concerned principally with human–environment interaction (see Uhlig 1969, 1984). His work on spontaneous and planned agricultural settlement continued the tradition established by, amongst others, Pelzer in the earlier post-war period, and as such enables us to see whether the specialist geographer in the 'post-revolution' period approached the subject in a different manner. This quotation provides some clues:

> Agricultural landscapes represent the interaction of nature and the life and work of human groups. The complexity of these landscapes ... needs

generalization, if we are to attempt any systematic approach. The exceptions should not ... prevent us from making effective generalizations. It
may seem unwarranted to attempt any systematic approach by the selection of a few examples from such a wide range of regions. But geography
can hardly accept the challenge of explaining the wealth of problems
present in Asian cultural landscapes, if it does not use such approaches.
It needs the discovery and enunciation of prototypes, linked with the
(often misinterpreted) concept of the geographical 'landscape' – meaning
a nomothetic synthesis of the many geofactors integrated in the ecology,
structure, functional organization and genesis of the earth's surface. It
would be hopeless to try to achieve this in countless individual descriptions; thus we need 'models', which summarize the dominant features of
comparable regions. This also facilitates the recognition and further
exploration of some still obscure and exceptional examples. Painstaking
case-studies and the establishment of more generalized rules which link
extensive regional experiences with the establishment of types for a
general geography, are likewise of importance (Uhlig 1969: 1, 18).

From this we can see that Uhlig, like others at the time, was arguing
that geography should enquire as well as inform, and that scholarly
enquiry could only effectively be carried out by means of a certain
degree of generalization and abstraction. However, the significant point
is that concepts can only effectively be informed from the bottom
upwards. In other words, the area specialist plays a crucial role in
contributing to theory.

What, though, is the utility in viewing specialized Southeast Asian
geographers separately from those whom we have earlier claimed to be
'theoretically engaged'? Is it not a feature of specialization that one
inevitably engages the conceptual discourse of others within the same
specialist field? There is little doubt that this is indeed so, and in any
case the line drawn between them is entirely arbitrary. But the point I
am trying to make here is that there is a meaningful difference between
the use of over-arching theoretical constructs (seen in the way that
Forbes and McGee both deal with the penetration of Southeast Asian
societies by the forces of capitalism), which unavoidably have a high
degree of abstraction, and the incorporation of narrower conceptual
structures within a more focused analytical approach. However, the
superimposition of areal specialization confuses the issue somewhat,
and overlapping identities tend then to emerge: essentially, those of
the geographer and the area specialist. Thus, whilst it may be meaning-
less to differentiate between people on the basis of their credentials as
geographers, mainstream or otherwise, this does reinforce the point
made earlier that differentiation on the basis of degree of areal
specialization may indeed be a worthwhile exercise. If this is the case,
then we could argue that 'regional' geographers who work within a

narrow sub-disciplinary specialism may be more in touch with the grassroots reality that those whose principal preoccupation is with a broader field of enquiry.

Of course, it is a feature of geography that many sub-disciplinary specialists, almost as a matter of course, ply their trade with reference to particular areas or locations. Thus specialist Southeast Asian geographers may differ from, say, their European or Latin American counterparts only on the basis of the contexts within which they operate. On the other hand, there may be significant differences in the extent to which sub-disciplinary specialists 'know their area'. Taking one illustration at random: Rimmer, best known as a transport geographer, has used painstaking historical research to inform his understanding of the evolution of transport provision and policy in Malaya (especially Singapore). On the basis of a thoroughgoing empirical assessment of the transport sector and social relations, he has attempted a theoretical enquiry into the ways in which changes in transportation technology may have precipitated wider social changes in the colonial territory (Rimmer and Allen 1990, 1986a; Rimmer, Drakakis-Smith and McGee 1978). There is, however, an inevitable trade-off between the depth and insight provided by the genuine area specialist and a certain lack of portability of research findings thus derived, so firm is their grounding in a locational context.

Regional geographers

A striking feature of the post-1965 period has been the dearth of general regional geographies of Southeast Asia. Possibly, Fisher's definitive work satisfied the market for quite some time, but it is nevertheless remarkable that such a rapidly emerging and changing region, attracting the increasing attention of geographers, should yield little in the way of general geographies. It is hard to accept that the demise of regional geography should have been responsible, even though it is often publishers rather than scholars who make decisions about the viability of publishing projects. More credible is the suggestion that geographers' growing specialization during the last three decades may have drawn them away from thematic regional overviews towards systematic sub-disciplinary texts.

Two of the main exceptions to the above were Fryer and Donner. Fryer had been quite active in the fields of urbanization and economic geography before the positivist revolution (see e.g. Fryer 1953, 1963). However, in 1970 he published the first edition of *Emerging Southeast Asia: a study in growth and stagnation*, in which he developed the notion of a two-pace Southeast Asia. Interestingly, this book was itself written because 'there are few overall reviews of the region available to the intelligent person seeking to broaden his [sic] understanding of Southeast Asia's pressing problems and their impact on the world at large' (Fryer 1970: preface). A distinction was drawn in the book between the countries that had allowed themselves to be drawn along by the capitalist world economy, and those that had either decided to 'go it alone' or had responded to 'the communist siren-song' (ibid.). He makes very clear his strong distaste for the latter ideological path, and some of his notions about its hollowness and ultimate futility – 'the communists have no effective solution to agrarian ills' – have proven to be remarkably prescient of recent change.

A significant portion of the book was written while Fryer was at the University of Malaya. However, with reference particularly to barriers provided by language and ethnic diversity, he comments that: 'it is impossible for any scholar, however protracted and diligent his field and library research, to be equally authoritative in each political unit or familiarize himself with more than a small part of the region [thus] any overall survey must rely heavily on secondary sources.' Furthermore, in the preface to the 1977 volume *Indonesia*, which he wrote with Jackson, he also conceded the danger of ethnocentric bias, that his knowledge of the country was highly particulate, and that 'a deeper understanding of Indonesian character requires, among other things, a lifetime of work and residence there' (Fryer and Jackson 1977: ix). It would be worth bearing in mind these points when we come to compare the work of the generalist regional geographer with that of the area specialist.

Donner has produced two geographies, one of Thailand (1978), and the other of Indonesia (1987). Both seek to inform a general audience about the role and importance of land and resources in the process of economic development, and are written from the perspective of a former practitioner who worked in the field of technical agricultural assistance. Donner hoped that, by drawing attention to the importance of land as the basis for both economy and society, development planning could be made more appropriate and, ultimately, protective (Donner 1978: xviii–ix). Thailand is presented from a geographical viewpoint via an examination of its five main regions (Bangkok is considered a region in its own right) and although the material is highly statistical and systematic, Donner also manages to convey the insight and knowledge which were derived from almost four years' residence in the country. The book on Indonesia makes an even stronger statement about the ways in which the environment and natural resources are becoming rapidly despoiled and depleted because of the ambivalent and myopic attitude of those who make 'decisions against nature' (Donner 1987: xiii). He was also, however, impressed by the way in which Indonesians at all levels were expressing concern over the rate and scale of environmental degradation, and he produced the volume at least in part as a means of contributing to their and others' efforts in this regard.

Southeast Asia viewed by the area specialist

What is an 'area specialist' and why should the area specialist's approach be any different from that of other geographers whose work has focused on Southeast Asia? I would suggest that Southeast Asian geographers who have been attached to an Areas Studies institution, for at least part of their careers, will have developed certain credentials or tendencies that their counterpart in a mainstream geography department may not. These tendencies, in turn, may have some bearing upon how they approach the human geographical study of Southeast Asia. It seems that the academic environment provided by an Area Studies institution either creates a particular kind of geographer (for instance through regular inter-disciplinary work, or through constant focus on one particular part of the world) or that only a particular kind of geographer is likely to join such an institution in the first place (perhaps someone who has developed strong areal credentials as a result of protracted fieldwork, or mastery of one of a regional language). I noted that Fisher displayed the credentials both of an area specialist and a regional geographer of repute. Now that the discipline has apparently entered a different era, is it possible to say the same about latter day area-specializing geographers?

Jackson is seen by many as an outstanding area specialist and geographer of the post-'revolution' period, even though his contribution was cut short by his death in 1979. A subjective measure of Jackson's standing in the Southeast Asian Studies community is provided by the way that scholars from other disciplines express admiration for his work on, *inter alia*, Chinese and European agricultural enterprise (1968a), the Chinese in the West Borneo goldfields (1970), irrigation and irrigation policy (Jackson and Short 1971) and models of retail development (1979). Jackson's long association with area studies institutions, together with extensive exposure to the region at the University of Malaya, helped him to develop easy conversance with other disciplinary approaches to the study of Southeast Asia. His research frequently strayed beyond the boundaries of an already broad and loosely bounded discipline, but it was a situation he felt comfortable with and, indeed, one he deemed necessary in the interests of his scholarship:

When a field is as uncharted as the economic history or historical geography of Malaya it is frequently necessary to establish the signposts of related disciplines before work can proceed satisfactorily on the task in hand. This the author has not hesitated to do whenever it appeared necessary. The result is a much broader study than was originally intended, a survey which strays constantly beyond the bounds of what is more usually regarded as 'geography'. Nevertheless, as the work of a geographer, this book [*Planters and Speculators*] is more concerned with the effects of social and economic processes on the land than with the processes themselves ...

Adjacent academic disciplines necessarily overlap, and many research topics lie in what might be regarded as the 'no man's land' in between, requiring as they do the application of a mixture of techniques and methods of analysis. In few fields of investigation is this so true as in the study of social and economic phenomena in the past, for here it is virtually impossible, nor does it seem desirable, to disentangle the traditionally-defined spheres of economics, geography and history ... A central point of view can be adopted that is recognized as geographic, but only by probing beyond the limits of a single, traditionally-defined discipline can a satisfactory reconstruction of past social and economic phenomena be achieved.

Although it has become usual to regard geography as the study of the inter-relationships of the 'physical' and 'cultural' environments these are clearly part of a single entity which can only be divided artificially. If it is the task of the geographer to investigate Man's utilization of the earth and its resources, then all those factors which influence this utilization are pertinent to the investigation (Jackson 1968a: xv–xvi).

This tells us much not only about Jackson's approach and philosophy, but also that of area specialists more generally. Not only does Jackson indicate that strict adherence to disciplinary boundaries may severely constrain regional enquiry, but he also stresses the importance of deep historical and cultural insight to a proper understanding of geographical processes and phenomena.

Thus we have finally reached the interface or boundary between geography and area studies. Farmer (1973) observed that (at least in Britain) geographers have played an important role in area studies institutions during the last few decades, in terms both of organization and in helping to provide a fulcrum for interdisciplinary work. They have also continued to contribe usefully to the field of Southeast Asian Studies. I conclude by looking briefly at the work of four specialist Southeast Asian geographers in order to support this immodest claim.

Rigg's *South-East Asia: a region in transition* (1991) provided the first thematic regional geography of Southeast Asia for more than two decades. By focusing on themes of significance to contemporary development problems and processes, it has helped to place the region quite prominently within the undergraduate curriculum. However, Rigg's greater contribution to the field has come in the form of his numerous articles – the majority of which have been published in mainstream geography journals – concerned with such subjects as the green revolution (1985, 1986, 1989a, 1989b, 1995b), migration (1988, 1989c), water (1993, 1995c), grassroots development (1991b) and environment (1995a). Rigg has demonstrated acute understanding of the cultural, political and social context within which development decisions and actions occur, and has shown the difference that deep understanding of a particular area or region can make in geographical enquiry. This does not mean, however, that he is any lesser a geographer as a consequence: indeed his work, like that of the others under consideration here, might also be seen as resting at one of the cutting-edges of development geography – empirically informed theoretical research set within the realist tradition of academic enquiry.

Similarly, Hirsch has been able to demonstrate a sharp understanding of local process as a consequence of extensive field-research in Thailand, allied to exceptional language skills. He too has an area studies background. His earlier work, which laid the foundation for *Development Dilemmas in Rural Thailand* (1990), was concerned with participation and changing social and political relations in the context of agricultural production in a forest area of west-central Thailand. His subsequent work (1990, 1993; Hirsch and Lohmann 1989) has focused particularly on the political economy of environment and resource exploitation in Thailand, where again his familiarity with local context and process, and with the wider political setting, has enabled him to make a valuable contribution to Thai and more general Southeast Asian Studies, as well as to current debates within geography and elsewhere on political ecology.

Dixon first gained his exposure to Thailand through work on a collaborative research project on a major resettlement scheme in northeast Thailand. His earlier work on the problems of this backward, peripheral region (1976, 1977) led to a wider interest in uneven development following capitalist penetration (1981), which in turn laid the foundation for his major work *South-East Asia in the World-Economy* (1991). Whilst Dixon has extensive field experience, he appears most comfortable when working at a level where wider processes impact on national and regional settings.

In contrast, the present writer has given stronger nourishment to his area studies identity whilst continuing to describe himself as a geographer. One consequence of working in a multidisciplinary environment and engaging in collaborative and interdisciplinary research has been a strong tendency towards eclecticism. Thus his research career has ranged from studies of migration and development (1993), rural and regional planning (1988, 1990), tourism (1993), ethnicity (1995b), uneven development (1995a) and environment (1994, 1996), with areal interests including Thailand, Malaysia, Indonesia and, most recently, China.

Southeast Asia viewed by Southeast Asian scholars

We can not complete this general review without mentioning the considerable amount of scholarship on Southeast Asian geography by scholars from the region. Tertiary education institutions in Southeast Asia, particularly in Malaysia and Singapore, and earlier also in Burma, have played an important role in geographical scholarship on the region. Geographers in both 'eras' have used a sojourn as an expatriate member of staff in one of the region's universities as a basis both for their research and for obtaining a deeper understanding of the region's human geography. These universities have also played a crucial role in training local scholars, who now rival in number geographers from outside. In general, there is no justification for viewing the 'insiders' any differently from the 'outsiders' – we are all geographers of Southeast Asia. However, for the present purposes it is useful to make a distinction, because an overview of the evolution of Southeast Asian scholarship in this field is quite instructive in relation to approaches to the subject that have been adopted over time. The central question here is whether it is possible to identify a particular form of indigenous scholarship on the region, or whether the long association of Southeast Asian universities with the Western geographical tradition has stifled its emergence. I shall look particularly at the situation in Malaysia and Singapore.

Geography courses have been available in the region since 1928, when Raffles College was set up in Singapore. Until the mid-1960s, almost all geographical teaching and research in Singapore and Malaysia was undertaken by expatriate staff. Since then a process of 'indigenization' has taken place: a process that McGee (1985) saw as 'a "challenge" to western domination' (cited in Voon and Bahrin 1992: 103). This transformation has not, however, necessarily led to the indigenization of research perspectives. A significant proportion of the local staff in the geography departments in Kuala Lumpur and Singapore were either trained by expatriate staff or trained overseas. In this way, the prevailing traditions of Western geography found new adherents in Southeast Asia, rather than local geographers establishing their own traditions and perspectives. If we look briefly at the orientation of research undertaken by local scholars, we can also begin to assess which traditions found firmest favour in the region.

Using our earlier schema, we can identify a particular tendency towards sub-disciplinary specialization and both practical and applied research. Work has also tended to engage most directly themes which are of particular local interest and importance. In a survey of the research specializations of local staff at the University of Malaya, Voon and Bahrin (1992: 103) identified urban and settlement geography as by far the most prevalent focus of research, followed by demography, agriculture/land use, and more general economic geography. More specifically, Hamzah Sendut has specialized in Malaysian urban structure and form (1965, 1966a), and urban–rural fertility differentials (1966b); and Lee Boon Thong on urban segregation (1976), urban ethnicity (1980), and on new town development in Malaysia (1987). Tunku Shamsul Bahrin has made the Malaysian land development programme a central focus of his research (Bahrin 1968, 1981; Bahrin and Lee 1988); whilst Voon has concentrated on rubber smallholdings (1966), rural land ownership (1977) and the ecological and cultural bases of plantation agriculture in Malaysia (1986). In Singapore, amongst many others, Ooi Jin Bee has specialized in the natural resources of Southeast Asia (1982) and peninsular Malaysia (1990); Chia Lin Sien in environmental management (MacAndrews and Chia 1979; Chia and MacAndrews 1981); Savage in cultural and historical geography (1984); and Wong Poh Poh in coastal tourism (1986, 1988).

From a cursory review of the literature, it appears that less prominence has been given to the classical regional geography – partly because Southeast Asian scholars have tended to focus on their country of domicile – or to the engagement and development of broader theoretical perspectives, Western or otherwise (Douglass, 1993). Savage (1993: 240) has claimed that 'they' (in this case, population geographers) have kept themselves 'firmly entrenched in applied geographical work [and] have not moved beyond empirical description and analytical critique to using theoretical models'. It is difficult to be certain why this should be so, but it could be that the roots of local scholarship have caused it to grow in a particular way. Many of the Western scholars who were associated with local universities represented the regional and applied traditions in geography. Inasmuch as they had an influence on the direction of development by training and working with others, it can be suggested that these traditions were passed down to subsequent generations of geographers in the process (Savage et al. 1993: 243). Because they were unavoidably on the periphery of the Western tradition and without an indigenous tradition of geographical enquiry to replace it, and because of the time-lag that inevitably occurs between change at the core and reaction in the periphery, Southeast Asian institutions may initially have been slower to engage prevailing theoretical discourses. Besides, the practical exigencies of the university system in Southeast Asia may have determined that applied and practical research was the more likely to obtain funding and support.

The local geography scene is changing, however, as recent articles by Kong (1993a, 1993b) clearly indicate. Voon has also suggested (1992: 109) that regional universities are remarkably well placed to meet the research challenges of tomorrow, as the individual countries of Southeast Asia continue to grow apace, in the process creating new tensions, patterns and forms. It is to be hoped that fresh perspectives, approaches and theoretical frameworks will emerge from within and challenge the largely uni-directional flow of influence and ideology that has tended to prevail so far. According to Douglass (1993: 115), the region's geographers 'can teach the rest of the discipline much about serious applied and applicable geography'.

Overview

This chapter has attempted to trace the evolution of Southeast Asian geography from the immediate pre-war period to the present. We have seen how even such a highly focused field of study has spawned a hugely varied array of scholarship, but with certain trends and foci recognizable at particular times. I have also attempted to ascertain whether and how such trends have reflected changes taking place within the mainstream of geography. The diversity of both geography and Southeast Asian geography has made this a challenging task, the outcome of which is not entirely conclusive because, whilst some of our leopards have steadfastly refused to change their spots, others have quite readily engaged in the approaches, methodologies and perspectives of the 'new' geography. It is possible to identify areas where changing trends within geography have had an influence on the area specialist, but harder to discern how the area specialists have influenced mainstream geography. Partly this is because, as we have attempted to show, the self-styled guardians of geography have been insufficiently informed about the quality and diversity of much of the work done within the 'periphery' over the last half-century or so. Yet, with the emergence and consolidation of a New Regional Geography, mainstream geographers are now busily heralding an approach that many of us, and most particularly the genuine area specialists, have been quietly adopting all the while.

Notes

1. The term 'Southeast Asian geography' is used as a convenient, collective means of referring to all forms of geographical study relating to the Southeast Asian region.

2. The objectives of this study determine that there is little value in going back further than the immediate pre-war period, even though the eras of discovery, exploration and early cartography may be considered an important part of the early history of Southeast Asian Geography. Readers are referred to a recent review of the field by Savage, Kong and Yeoh (1993: 229–51) for a brief examination of this earlier period.

3. There are several others to whom I might have referred were it not for constraints of space, including, particularly Drakakis-Smith: see Drakakis-Smith 1992; Dixon and Drakakis-Smith 1993; Drakakis-Smith and Rimmer 1982; Drakakis-Smith et al. 1993.

Bibliography

Bahrin, Tunku Shamsul (1968), 'Land conflicts in the Tanay resettlement projects of Rizal, Philippines', *Journal of Tropical Geography*, 27: 50–8.

— (1981), 'The utilization and management of land resources in Malaysia', *Geojournal*, 5: 557–62.

— and Lee Boon Thong (1988), *FELDA: three decades of evolution* (Kuala Lumpur: FELDA).

Beaver, S. H. (1966), 'Obituary: Sir Dudley Stamp', *Geography*, 51: 388–91.

Bradshaw, Michael J. (1990), 'New regional geography, foreign-area studies and Perestroika', *Area*, 22: 315–22.

Brookfield, Harold C. and Yvonne Byron (eds) (1993), *South-East Asia's Environmental Future: the search for sustainability* (Tokyo: United Nations University Press/Oxford University Press).

— and Abdul Samad Hadi, Zaharah Mahmud (1991), *The City in the Village: the in-situ urbanization of villages, villagers and their land around Kuala Lumpur, Malaysia* (Singapore: Oxford University Press).

Chant, Sylvia and Cathy McIlwaine (1995), *Women of a Lesser Cost: female labour, foreign exchange and Philippine development* (London: Pluto Press).

Chapman, E. C. and Sanga Sabhasri (1978), *Farmers in the Forest: economic development and marginal agriculture in Northern Thailand* (Honolulu: University Press of Hawaii).

Chapman, Graham P. and Kathleen M. Baker (eds) (1992), *The Changing Geography of Asia* (London: Routledge).

Chia Lin Sien (ed.) (1987), *Environmental Management in Southeast Asia: directions and current status* (National University of Singapore).

— and R. D. Hill (eds) (1979), *South East Asia: a systematic geography* (Kuala Lumpur: Oxford University Press).

— and Colin MacAndrews (eds) (1981), *Southeast Asian Seas: frontiers for development* (Singapore: McGraw-Hill).

— and Colin MacAndrews (eds) (1982), *Too Rapid Rural Development: perceptions and perspectives from Southeast Asia* (Athens, OH: Ohio University Press).

Cho, George (1990), *The Malaysian Economy: spatial perspectives* (London: Routledge).

Cleary, Mark C. and Peter Eaton (1992), *Borneo: change and development* (Singapore: Oxford University Press).

Cloke, Paul J., C. Philo and D. Sadler (1991), *Approaching Human Geography: an introduction to contemporary theoretical debates* (London: Paul Chapman).

Courtenay, Percy P. (1985), *Geographical Studies of Development* (Harlow: Longman).

Credner, Wilhelm (1935), *Siam: Das Land der Tai (Eine Landeskunde auf Grund eigener Reisen und Forschungen* (Osnabrück: Otto Zeller).

Delvert, Jean (1961), *Le Paysan cambodgien*, Le Monde d'Outre-Mer Passé et Présent, Etude no. X (Paris: Mouton).

Dicken, Peter (1986), *Global Shift: industrial change in a turbulent world* (London: Harper and Row).

— (1988), 'The changing geography of Japanese foreign direct investment in manufacturing industry: a global perspective', *Environment and Planning A*, 20: 633–53.

— (1992), *Global Shift: the internationalization of economic activity*, 2nd edn (London: Paul Chapman).

Dixon, C. J. (1976), 'Settlement and environment in North East Thailand', *Journal of Tropical Geography*, 46: 1–10.

— (1977), 'Development, regional disparity and planning: the experience of Northeast Thailand', *Journal of Southeast Asian Studies*, 8: 210–23.

— (1981), 'Capitalist penetration, uneven development and government response: the case of Thailand', in M. B. Gleave (ed.), *Societies in Change: studies of capitalist penetration*, Developing Areas Research Group Monograph 2: 65–92.

— (1990), *Rural Development in the Third World* (London: Routledge).

— (1991), *South East Asia in the World-Economy* (Cambridge: Cambridge University Press).

— and David Drakakis-Smith (eds) (1993), *Economic and Social Development in Pacific Asia* (London: Routledge).

— David Drakakis-Smith and H. D. Watts (eds) (1986), *Multinational Corporations and the Third World* (London: Croom Helm).

Dobby, E. H. G. (1939), 'Settlement and land utilization, Malacca', *Geographical Journal*, 94: 469–78.

— (1940), 'Singapore: town and country', *Geographical Review*, 30: 84–109.

— (1942), 'Settlement patterns in Malaya', *Geographical Review*, 32: 211–32.

— (1946), 'Some aspects of the human ecology of Southeast Asia', *Geographical Journal*, 108: 40–54.

— (1950), *Southeast Asia* (London: University of London Press).

— (1951), 'The Kelantan Delta', *Geographical Review*, 41: 226–55.

— (1952), 'Resettlement transforms Malaya', *Economic Development and Cultural Change*, 1: 163–89.

— (1954), 'Malaya's rice problem', *Pacific Affairs*, 27, 1: 58–60.

Donner, Wolf (1978), *The Five Faces of Thailand: an economic geography* (London: Hurst).

— (1987), *Land Use and Environment in Indonesia* (London: Hurst).

Douglas, Ian (1993), 'The tropics: environments and human impacts understood and reinterpreted', *Singapore Journal of Tropical Geography*, 14, 2: 103–22.

Douglass, Mike (1984), *Regional Integration on the Capitalist Periphery: the central plains of Thailand* (The Hague: Institute of Social Studies).

— (1988), 'Transnational capital and urbanisation of the Pacific Rim: an introduction', *International Journal of Urban and Regional Research*, 12, 3: 343–55.

— (1995), 'Bringing culture in: locality and global capitalism in East Asia', *Third World Planning Review*, 17, 3: R3–R9.

Drakakis-Smith, David (1992), *Pacific Asia* (London: Routledge).

— and Peter Rimmer (1982), 'Taming "the Wild City": managing South-East Asia's primate cities', *Asian Geographer*, 1, 1: 17–34.

— and E. Graham, P. Teo and G. L. Ooi (1993), 'Singapore: reversing the demographic transition to meet labour needs', *Scottish Geographical Magazine*, 109: 152–63.

Dwyer, Denis (1964a), 'The problem of in-migration and squatter settlement in Asian cities: two case studies, Manila and Victoria-Kowloon', *Asian Studies*, 2: 145–69.

— (1964b), 'Irrigation and land problems in the central plain of Luzon: comment on a sample study', *Geography*, 49: 236–46.

— (1967), 'The city in the developing world and the example of South East Asia', *Geography*, 35: 353–69.

— (1972), *The City as a Centre of Change in Asia* (Hong Kong: Hong Kong University Press).

— (1975), *People and Housing in Third World Cities: perspectives on the problem of spontaneous settlements* (London: Longman).

— (ed.) (1990), *South East Asian Development: geographical perspectives* (Harlow: Longman).

East, W. G., O. H. K. Spate and C. A. Fisher (1971), *The Changing Map of Asia: a political geography*, 5th edn (London: Methuen).

Fairchild, Wilma B. (1979), 'Two Eastern institutions: the *Geographical Review* and the American Geographical Society', *Annals of the Association of American Geographers*, 69, 1: 33–8.

Farmer, Benny H. (1973), 'Geography, area studies and the study of area', *Transactions of the Institute of British Geographers*, 60: 1–16.

— (1983), 'British geographers overseas, 1933–1983', *Transactions of the Institute of British Geographers*, 8: 70–9.

Fisher, Charles A. (1947), 'Crisis in Indonesia', *Political Quarterly*, 18: 295–312.

— (1964), *South-East Asia: a social, economic and political geography* (London: Methuen).

— (1962), 'South East Asia: the Balkans of the Orient?', *Geography*, 47: 347–67.

— (1973), 'The contribution of geography to foreign area studies: the case of Southeast Asia', in M. W. Mikesell (ed.), *Geographers Abroad*, Department of Geography Research Paper 152: 185–228 (Chicago: University of Chicago).

Forbes, Dean K. (1979), *The Pedlars of Ujung Pandang*, Centre of Southeast Asian Studies, Working Papers 17 (Melbourne: Monash University).

— (1981a), 'Production, reproduction and underdevelopment: petty commodity producers in Ujung Pandang, Indonesia', *Environment and Planning A*, 13: 841–56.

— (1981b), 'Petty commodity production and underdevelopment: the case of pedlars and trishaw riders in Ujung Pandang, Indonesia', *Progress and Planning D: Society and Space*, 16: 105–78.

— (1986), *The Geography of Underdevelopment: a critical survey* (London: Routledge).

— (1995), 'The urban network and economic reform in Vietnam', *Environment and Planning A*, 27: 793–808.

— and Nigel Thrift (1987), *The Socialist Third World: urban development and territorial planning* (Oxford: Blackwell).

— T. Hull, D. Marr, and B. Brogan (eds) (1991), *Doi Moi: Vietnam's renovation: policy and performance* (Canberra: Australian National University, Research school of Pacific Studies).

Fryer, Donald W. (1953), 'The million city in Southeast Asia', *Geographical Review*, 43: 474–94.

— (1963), 'The development of cottage and small scale industries in Malaya and in Southeast Asia', *Journal of Tropical Geography*, 17: 38–48.

— (1970), *Emerging Southeast Asia: a study in growth and stagnation* (London: Philip).

— and James C. Jackson (1966), 'Peasant producers or urban planters? The Chinese rubber smallholders of Ulu Selangor', *Pacific Viewpoint*, 7: 198–228.

— and James C. Jackson (1977), *Indonesia* (London: Benn).

Fuller, T. D., Peerasit Kamnuansilpa and Richard P. Lightfoot (1983), *Migration and Development in Modern Thailand* (Bangkok: Social Science Association of Thailand).

Gilbert, Anne (1988), 'The new regional geography in English and French-speaking countries', *Progress in Human Geography*, 12: 208–28.

Ginsburg, Norton, Bruce Koppel and T. G. McGee (eds) (1991), *The Extended Metropolis: settlement transition in Asia* (Honolulu: University of Hawaii Press).

Gottmann, Jean (1964), 'Obituary: Charles Robequain', *Geographical Review*, 54: 594–5.

Gourou, Pierre (1931), *Indochine française: le Tonkin* (Paris: Exposition Coloniale Internationale).

— (1936a), *Les Paysans du Delta tonkinois: etude de géographie humaine*. Maison des Science de l'Homme, collection de Réimpressions, no. 1 (Paris: Mouton).

— (1936b), *Esquisse d'une étude de l'habitation annamite dans l'Annam septentrioral et central du Thanh Hoa au Binh Dinh* (Paris: Editions d'Art et d'Histoire).

— (1940a), *L'Utilisation du sol en Indochine française* (Paris).

— (1940b), *La Terre et l'homme en Extrême-Orient* (Paris).

— (1948), *Les Pays tropicaux: principes d'une géographie humaine et économique* (Paris: Presses Universitaires de France).

— (1953), *The Tropical World: its social and economic conditions and its future status* (London: Longman).

— (1975), *Man and Land in the Far East* (London: Longman).

Hardjono, Joan (1971), *Indonesia, Land and People* (Djakarta: Gunung Agung).

— (ed.) (1991), *Indonesia: resources, ecology and environment* (Singapore: Oxford University Press).

Hill, R. D. (1977), *Rice in Malaya: a study in historical geography* (Kuala Lumpur: Oxford University Press).

Hirsch, Philip (1989), 'Local contexts of differentiation and inequality on the Thai periphery', *Journal of Contemporary Asia*, 19: 308–23.

— (1990), *Development Dilemmas in Rural Thailand*, South-East Asia Social Science Monographs (Singapore: Oxford University Press).

— (1993), *Political Economy of Environment in Thailand* (Manila: Journal of Contemporary Asia Publishers).

— and Larry Lohmann (1989), 'Contemporary politics of the environment in Thailand', *Asian Survey*, 29: 439–51.

Ho, Robert (1968), 'A major clearing in the jungle: on J. E. Spencer's shifting cultivation in Southeast Asia', *Pacific Viewpoint*, 9: 173–89.

Hodder, B. W. (1953), 'Racial groupings in Singapore', *Malayan Journal of Tropical Geography*, 1: 25–36.

— (1956), 'The economic development of Sarawak', *Geographical Studies*, 3: 71–84.

— (1959), *Man in Malaya* (London: University of London Press).

Hugo, Graeme J. (1978), *Population Mobility in West Java* (Yogyakarta: Gadjah Mada University Press).

— (1982), 'Circular migration in Indonesia', *Population and Development Review*, 8: 59–83.

Jackson, James C. (1968a), *Planters and Speculators: Chinese and European agricultural enterprise in Malaya, 1786–1921* (Kuala Lumpur: University of Malaya Press).

— (1968b), *Sarawak: a geographical survey of a developing state* (London: University of London Press).

— (1969), 'Mining in 18th century Bangka: the pre-European exploitation of a "tin island"', *Pacific Viewpoint*, 10: 28–54.

— (1970), *Chinese in the West Borneo Goldfields: a study in cultural geography*, Occasional Papers in Human Geography 15 (Hull: University of Hull).

— (1974), 'Urban squatters in Southeast Asia', *Geography*, 59: 24–30.

— (1979), *Issues in Malaysian Development*, Asian Studies Association of Australia, Southeast Asia Publications Series 3 (Singapore: Heinemann Educational).

— and David E. Short (1971), 'The origins of irrigation policy in Malaya', *Journal of the Malaysian Branch of the Royal Asiatic Society*, 44: 78–103.

Johnston, R. J. (1993), *The Challenge for Geography: a changing world, a changing discipline* (Oxford: Blackwell).

— J. Hauer and G. A. Hoekveld (eds) (1990), *Regional Geography: current developments and future prospects* (London: Routledge).

Journal of Tropical Geography (1962), 'Studies in the geography of South-east Asia', a selection of papers presented at the Regional Conference of South-east Asian Geographers, Kuala Lumpur (London: George Philip and Son).

Kong, Lily (1993a), 'Ideological hegemony and the political symbolism of religious buildings in Singapore', *Environment and Planning D: Society and Space*, 11: 23–45.

— (1993b), 'Negotiating conceptions of "sacred space": a case study of religious buildings in Singapore', *Transactions of the Institute of British Geographers*, 18: 342–58.

Kunstadter, P., E. C. Chapman and Sanga Saphasri (eds) (1978), *Farmers in the Forest: economic development and marginal agriculture in northern Thailand* (Honolulu: East–West Center).

Lee Boon Thong (1976), 'Patterns of urban residential segregation: the case of Kuala Lumpur', *Journal of Tropical Geography*, 43: 41–8.

— (1980), 'Urban ethnicity and urbanization in peninsular Malaysia', *Prisma*, 17: 58–71.

— (1987), 'New towns in Malaysia: development and planning policies', in David R. Philips and Anthony G. O. Yeh (eds), *New Towns in East and South-East Asia: planning and development*: 153–69 (Kuala Lumpur: Oxford University Press).

Lee Yong Leng (1982), *Southeast Asia: essays in political geography* (Singapore: Singapore University Press).

Lekkerkerker, C. (1916), *Land en Volk van Sumatra* (Leiden: Brill).

— (1938), *Land en Volk van Java* (Groningen: Bij J.B. Wolters' Uitgevers Maatschappij).

Lightfoot, Richard P. (1983), *Circulation and Interpersonal Networks Linking Rural and Urban Areas: the case of Roi-et, northeastern Thailand* (Honolulu: East–West Population Institute).

MacAndrews, C. and Chia Lin Sien (1979), *Developing Economies and the Environment: the Southeast Asian experience* (Singapore: McGraw-Hill International).

McGee, Terence Gary (1967), *The Southeast Asian City: a social geography of the primate cities of Southeast Asia* (London: Bell).

— (ed.) (1970), *Dualism in the Asian City: the implications for city and regional planning* (Hong Kong: University of Hong Kong).

— (1971), *The urbanization process in the Third World: explorations in search of a theory* (London: Bell).

— (1976), 'Beach-heads and enclaves: the urban debate and the urbanization process in Southeast Asia', in Y. M. Yeung and C. P. Lo (eds), *Changing Southeast Asian Cities: readings on urbanization*: 23–36 (Singapore).

— (1982a), *Proletarianization, Industrialization and Urbanization in Asia: a case study of Malaysia*, Flinders Asian Studies Lectures 13.

— (1982b), *Labor Markets, Urban Systems and the Urbanization Process in Southeast Asian Countries* (Honolulu: East–West Population Institute).

— and W. D. McTaggart (1967), *Petaling Jaya: a socio-economic survey of a new town in Selangor, Malaysia*, Pacific Viewpoint Monograph 2 (Wellington).

— and Y.M. Yeung, (eds) (1977), *Hawkers in Southeast Asian Cities: planning for the bazaar economy* (Ottawa: International Development Research Centre).

Murray, P. and I. Szezenyi (1984), 'The city in the transition to socialism', *International Journal of Urban and Regional Research*, 8: 330–50.

Nelson, Howard J. (1985), 'In memoriam: J. E. Spencer, 1907–1984', *Annals of the Association of American Geographers*, 75: 595–603.

Ooi Jin Bee (1982), *The Petroleum Resources of Indonesia* (Kuala Lumpur).

— (1987), *Natural Resources in Tropical Countries* (Singapore).

— (1990), *Development Problems of an Open-Access Resource: the fisheries of peninsular Malaysia* (Singapore: Institute of Southeast Asian Studies, ASEAN Economic Research Unit).

Ormeling, F. J. (1956), *The Timor Problem: a geographical interpretation of an underdeveloped island* (Groningen: Wolters).

Parnwell, Michael J. G. (1988), 'Rural poverty, development and the environment: the case of North-East Thailand', *Journal of Biogeography*, 15: 199–208.

— (1990), 'South-East Asian geography in the United Kingdom', *Area*, 22: 346–52.

— (1993), *Population Movements and the Third World* (London: Routledge).

— (1994), 'Rural industrialisation and sustainable development in Thailand', *Quarterly Environment Journal*, 1: 24–39.

— (ed.) (1995), *Uneven Development in Thailand* (Aldershot: Avebury).

— and Raymond L. Bryant (eds) (1996), *Environmental Change in South-East Asia: people, politics and sustainable development* (London: Routledge).

— and Suranart Khamanarong (1990), 'Rural Industrialisation and Development Planning in Thailand', *Southeast Asian Journal of Social Science*, 18: 1–28.

— and Jonathan Rigg (1995), 'The people of Isan: missing out on the economic boom?', in Denis Dwyer and David Drakakis-Smith (eds), *Ethnodevelopment: concepts and case studies* (London: Longman).

Pelzer, Karl J. (1945), *Pioneer Settlement in the Asiatic Tropics: studies in land utilization and agricultural colonization in Southeastern Asia*, American Geographical Society, Special Publication 29 (New York: Institute of Pacific Relations).

— (1946), 'Tanah Sabrang and Java's population problem', *Journal of Asian Studies*, 5: 133–42.

— (1949), 'Obituary: Willhelm Credner', *Geographical Review*, 39: 333–4.

— (1967), *Man's Role in Changing the Landscape of Southeast Asia*, Yale University Southeast Asian Studies Reprint Series 23.

— (1970), 'Geographical literature on Indonesia', in Howard W. Beers (ed.), *Indonesia: resources and their technological development*, Yale University Southeast Asian Studies Reprint Series 42.

— (1978), *Planter and Peasant: colonial policy and the agrarian struggle in East Sumatra, 1863–1947* (Gravenhage: Nijhoff).

— (1982), *Planters Against Peasants: the agrarian struggle in East Sumatra, 1947–58* (Leiden: KITLV Press).

Pudup, Mary-Beth (1988), 'Arguments within regional geography', *Progress in Human Geography*, 12: 369–90.

Rigg, Jonathan (1985), 'The role of the environment in limiting the adoption of new rice technology in Northeastern Thailand', *Transactions of the Institute of British Geographers*, 10: 481–94.

— (1988), 'Perspectives on migrant labouring and the village economy in developing countries: the Asian experience in a world context', *Progress in Human Geography*, 12: 66–86.

— (1989a), 'The new rice technology and agrarian change: guilt by association?', *Progress in Human Geography*, 13: 374–99.

— (1989b), 'The green revolution and equity: who adopts the new rice varieties and why?', *Geography*, 74: 144–50.

— (1989c), *International Contract Labor Migration and the Village Economy: the case of Tambon Don Han, Northeastern Thailand* (Honolulu, Hawaii: East–West Population Institute).

— (1991a), *Southeast Asia: a region in transition: a thematic human geography of the ASEAN region* (London: Unwin Hyman).

— (1991b), 'Grassroots development in Thailand: a lost cause?', *World Development*, 19: 199–211.

— (1993), 'Rice, water and land: strategies of cultivation on the Khorat Plateau, Thailand', *Southeast Asia Research*, 1: 197–221.

— (ed.) (1995a), *Counting the Costs: economic growth and environmental change in Thailand* (Singapore: Institute of Southeast Asian Studies).

— (1995b), 'Errors in the making: rice, knowledge, technological change and "applied" research in Northeast Thailand', *Malaysian Journal of Tropical Geography*, 26: 19–33.

— (1995c), '"In the fields there is dust": Thailand's water crisis', *Geography*, 80: 23–32.

Rimmer, Peter J. (1971), *Transport in Thailand: the railway decision* (Canberra: Australian National University).

— (1986a), *Rikisha to Rapid Transit: urban public transport systems and policy in Southeast Asia* (Sydney: Pargamon).

— (1986b), 'Changes in transport organisations within Southeast Asian cities: petty producers to statutory corporations', *Environment and Planning A*, 18: 1559–80.

— and Lisa M. Allen (eds) (1990), *The Underside of Malaysian History: pullers, prostitutes, plantation workers* (Singapore: Singapore University Press).

— David Drakakis-Smith and Terence G. McGee (eds) (1978), *Food, Shelter and Transport in Southeast Asia and the Pacific* (Canberra: Australian National University).

Robequain, Charles (1925), 'Deux villes du Mékhong: Luang-Prabang et Vieng-Chane' (Paris).

— (1929), 'Le Thanh Hoá: etude géographique d'une province annamite' (Paris).

— (1935), *L'Indochine française* (Paris: Librairie Armand Colin).

— (1944), *The Economic Development of French Indo-China* (London: Oxford University Press).

— (1954), *Malaya, Indonesia, Borneo, and the Philippines: a geographical, economic and political description of Malaya, the East Indies and the Philippines* (London: Longman).

Savage, Victor (1984), *Western Impressions of Nature and Landscape in Southeast Asia* (Singapore).

— Lily Kong and Brenda S. A. Yeoh (1993), 'The human geography of Southeast Asia: an analysis of post-war developments', *Singapore Journal of Tropical Geography*, 14: 229–51.

Sayer, A. (1989), 'The new regional geography and problems of narrative', *Environment and Planning D: Society and Space*, 7: 253–76.

Sendut, Hamzah (1965), 'The structure of Kuala Lumpur, Malaysia's capital city', *Town Planning Review*, 36: 125–38.

— (1966a), 'City size distributions in Southeast Asia', *Asian Studies*, 4: 268–80.

— (1966b), 'Urban–rural fertility differential, with special reference to Malaysia', *Journal of the Technical Association of Malaysia*, 15.

Spate, O. H. K. (1941), 'Beginnings of industrialization in Burma', *Economic Geography*, 17, 1: 75–92.

— (1945), 'The Burmese village', *Geographical Review*, 35: 523–43.

Spencer, Joseph E. (1954), *Asia, East by South: a cultural geography* (New York: Wiley).

— and Frederick L. Wernstedt (1967), *The Philippine Island World: a physical, cultural and regional geography* (Berkeley and Los Angeles: University of California Press).

Stamp, Lawrence Dudley (1929), *Asia: a regional and economic geography* (London: Methuen).

— (1930), 'Burma: an undeveloped monsoon country', *Geographical Review*, 20: 86–109.

— (1940), 'The Irrawaddy river', *Geographical Journal*, 95: 329–56.

— (1942), 'Siam before the war', *Geographical Journal*, 99: 209–24.

Sternstein, Larry (1976), *Thailand: the environment of modernisation* (Sydney: McGraw-Hill).

Stott, Philip A. (ed.) (1978), *Nature and Man in South East Asia* (London: University of London).

Taylor, Michael J. and Nigel J. Thrift (1986), *Multinationals and the Restructuring of the World Economy* (London: Croom Helm).

Taylor, P. J. (1988), 'World systems analysis and regional geography', *Professional Geographer*, 40: 259–65.

Thrift, Nigel J. (1989), 'The geography of international economic disorder', in R. J. Johnston and P. J. Taylor (eds), *A World in Crisis? Geographical Perspectives* (Oxford: Blackwell).

— (1990), 'For a new regional geography 1', *Progress in Human Geography*, 14: 272–9.

— (1991), 'For a new regional geography 2', *Progress in Human Geography*, 15: 456–65.

— (1993), 'For a new regional geography 3', *Progress in Human Geography*, 17: 92–100.

— and Dean K. Forbes (1985), 'Cities, socialism and war: Hanoi, Saigon and the Vietnamese experience of urbanisation', *Environment and Planning D*, 3: 279–308.

— and Dean Forbes (1986), *The Price of War: urbanization in Vietnam 1954–85* (London: Allen & Unwin).

Uhlig, Harald (1969), 'Hill tribes and rice farmers in the Himalayas and South-East Asia: problems of the social and ecological differentiation of agricultural landscape types', *Transactions of the Institute of British Geographers*, 47: 1–23.

— (ed.) (1984), *Spontaneous and Planned Settlement in Southeast Asia: forest clearing and recent pioneer colonization in the ASEAN countries, and two case studies on Thailand* (Hamburg: Institute of Asian Affairs).

Verstappen, H. Th (1956), *The Physiographic Basis of Pioneer Settlement in Southern Sumatra* (Groningen: Wolters-Noordhoff).

— (1973), *A Geomorphological Reconnaisance of Sumatra and Adjacent Islands (Indonesia)* (Groningen: Wolters-Noordhoff).

Voon Phin Keong (1966), 'Rubber smallholdings – problems and prospects', *Geographica*, 2: 44–8.

— (1977), 'Rural land ownership and development in the Malay reservations of peninsular Malaysia', *Journal of Southeast Asian Studies*, 14: 496–512.

— (1986), 'Plantation agriculture in Malaysia: the ecological and cultural bases of production', *Geography Bulletin of New South Wales*, 18: 218–26.

— and Tunku Shamsul Bahrin (eds) (1992), *The View From Within: geographical essays on Malaysia and Southeast Asia*, Special Edition of the *Malaysian Journal of Tropical Geography* (Kuala Lumpur: University of Malaya, Department of Geography).

Wernstedt, Frederick L. and J. E. Spencer (1967), *The Philippine Island World: a physical, cultural, and regional geography* (Berkeley: University of California Press).

Wong Poh Poh (1986), 'Tourism development and resorts on the east coast of peninsular Malaysia', *Singapore Journal of Tropical Geography*, 7: 152–62.

— (1988), 'Beach resort sites on the east coast of peninsular Malaysia', *Singapore Journal of Tropical Geography*, 9: 72–85.

Yeoh, Brenda S. A. (1991), 'The control of "sacred space": conflicts over the Chinese burial grounds in colonial Singapore, 1880–1930', *Journal of Southeast Asian Studies*, 22: 282–311.

Yeung, Y. M. and T. G. McGee (1986), *Community Participation in Delivering Urban Services in Asia* (Ottawa: International Development Research Centre).

5 Sociology

Victor T. King

An overview of sociological work on Southeast Asia during the last half-century presents a major problem, which is by no means peculiar to the theories and practices of this discipline in relation to one particular part of Asia. There is the general difficulty of distinguishing sociology from cognate disciplines and fields of study such as social anthropology, social and economic history, political economy and development studies. This is hardly surprising in a discipline concerned with the description, analysis and understanding of social relations and processes (see van den Muijzenberg n.d.). We are therefore only able to arrive at rough-and-ready distinctions between sociology and related subject areas, and it is probably more satisfactory to think in terms of a 'sociological perspective' – a perspective that addresses the social dimensions of such crucial issues as poverty, inequality, urbanization, bureaucratization and industrialization and of significant relationships arising from such principles of organization as ethnic difference, class, power, status and patronage. The inspiration for the sociological approach to the understanding of the human condition comes from three main European social theorists – Karl Marx, Max Weber and Emile Durkheim – and their several influences are plain to see in this chapter.

Therefore, in this survey of the sociology of Southeast Asia, I shall also be drawing attention to the work of some writers who are to be found in other related academic disciplines such as anthropology, politics, economics and history, but who are concerned to understand the organization and transformation of human societies. Even given this broader sociological perspective, I am forced to conclude that, in comparison with studies of other regions of the world, the sociological literature on Southeast Asia is not particularly extensive or distinguished. Fifteen years ago the German sociologist Professor Hans-Dieter Evers remarked, in the introduction to his valuable edited book, *Sociology of Southeast Asia. Readings on social change and development*, that 'relatively little progress has been made in furthering the understanding of changing Southeast Asian societies' (1980a: ix). In an appreciative review article of Evers' book, I too observed that:

> Up to now any lecturer faced with the task of teaching Southeast Asian sociology cannot fail to have noted the piecemeal and often 'localized' nature (in content, relevance and orientation) of the sociological literature. With a few notable exceptions ... Southeast Asian sociology has not really distinguished itself (1981: 391).

A few years before this, Evers had also edited a less well-known book, in cooperation with the Singapore sociologist, Peter S. J. Chen, entitled *Studies in ASEAN Sociology. Urban society and social change.* The editors stated then that: 'One common problem faced by all sociology lecturers in Southeast Asia is the lack of local teaching materials' (1978: xiii). More specifically van den Muijzenberg (n.d.: 14) in a review of Dutch sociological work on Indonesia, has noted that it has tended not to engage in the large and important issues of industrialization, the formation of 'new classes' and the influence of expatriate groups on 'the particularities of the Indonesian political system'.

The depressing situation of over a decade ago has improved recently, but the sociological materials are still patchy and we have not seen the emergence of many strong and distinctive schools of study or important internationally recognized academic programmes in particular universities or institutions, although work is being undertaken in the University of Bielefeld under Hans-Dieter Evers, in Otto van den Muijzenberg's department in Amsterdam and in the Asia Research Centre at Murdoch University by Richard Robison and his colleagues. Certain new developments, to which I shall refer later, show some signs of promise (see Anderson 1984 and Doner 1991), but one is still commonly compelled to look outside Southeast Asia and Southeast Asian programmes of study for theoretical insights into such processes as socio-economic change and modernization rather than to indigenous, locally generated or area studies-specific sociologies. Again this situation was one which Evers and Chen had begun to address in the late 1970s when they pointed out that in the discipline of sociology in Singapore:

> Nearly all university text-books are imported from Britain and the United States. Theoretical frameworks, empirical examples and conceptual illustrations, which may be familiar to most academics who were trained in these countries but in most cases are strange to the students, are taught in the classes and transmitted to the students (1978: xiii).

A more recent text on Southeast Asia in the Macmillan 'Sociology of "Developing Societies"' series, edited by John Taylor and Andrew

Turton, reveals the persistence of some of the same problems highlighted a decade before. The editors of the volume phrase the dilemma
in terms of a paradox. Taylor and Turton demonstrate that, from any
point of view, the Southeast Asian region is of crucial political and
economic importance and is socially complex, 'Yet the degree and
quality of much of the research on the region often does not enable
one to address the most important aspects of its current and future
development' (1988: 1). In this regard the authors contrast sociological
research on Southeast Asia with the work of Latin American and
other scholars on dependency and world systems, East African studies
on 'the role of the state and its relation to indigenous classes', and the
analyses of capitalist relations of production in agriculture and the
processes of agrarian differentiation in South Asia. Taylor and Turton
bemoan the fact that Southeast Asian academics, in particular, have
adopted ideas from outside the area 'rather than generating indigenous
explanations of the region and its place in the world economy' (1988:
1). Prior to Taylor's and Turton's remarks, Clark Neher had already
contrasted the 'innovative perspectives of Latin American-oriented
writers with the poor performance of students of Southeast Asian
societies' (1984: 130), and recently Doner has examined the 'relative
weakness' of studies of Southeast Asian political economy (1991: 819).

Comments along very similar lines have also been made by Peter
Preston in his *Rethinking Development. Essays on development and
Southeast Asia* (1987). Preston criticizes the writings of the European
observers, J. H. Boeke and J. S. Furnivall, of Southeast Asian conditions. He attempts especially to counter the claims of Evers, who
reproduces key extracts from the work of Boeke and Furnivall in his
'reader' of 1980, that these two colonial writers represent at least the
beginnings of a distinctively Southeast Asian contribution to sociology.
Preston maintains that, on the contrary, it is an extraordinary claim of
Evers that the work of colonial administrator-scholars can have made
a contribution to an independent Southeast Asian sociological perspective; this is for the simple reason that their analyses have been shaped
by colonial interests. Instead, Preston argues that any 'indigenous'
Southeast Asian sociology 'will only be discovered (if it's there) in the
work of *local* scholars, commentators and activists' (1987: 99). He is
also particularly critical of the contribution of local sociologists such
as Peter Chen, and by extension other sociologists in Singapore, who
are concerned principally with development policy and planning issues
(e.g. Chen 1983). Preston's view is that this stream of local sociology,
which he characterizes as policy science, provides a convenient defence
of government development strategies and serves to maintain the
political status quo.

Preston's criticisms take me a little way from the main concerns in this chapter, but the theme of Western versus indigenous or local perspectives is an important one to which I shall return later. At this point, I should take issue with Preston's criticism of both earlier European observers and applied or policy-oriented Southeast Asian sociologists. In my view there is some value in this work, and I shall argue that it is worth considering the contributions of Boeke, Furnivall and others to the sociology of Southeast Asia. Furthermore, although I am critical of the relatively poor performance of sociologists, both foreign and local, who have been engaged in studies of Southeast Asia, we should not underestimate what has been accomplished and we should be aware of the institutional constraints and historical circumstances of sociological enquiry in the region (cf. Neher 1984: 131).

Two immediate points should be made *contra* Peter Preston's position, before considering some of the reasons for the generally unsatisfactory condition of Southeast Asian sociology. First, Boeke and Furnivall's insights have had greater intellectual value than Preston is prepared to allow. They have stimulated much debate and generated further wide-ranging studies of Southeast Asian societies, and it is by no means the case that distinctive and novel responses to the social and cultural specificities and processes of change in Southeast Asia should necessarily be the preserve of indigenous scholars. Second, there should be a greater recognition of the value of applied social science in Southeast Asia. The practical involvement of local academics in trying to address or help solve the immediate social issues of poverty and underdevelopment have been an important recent element in Southeast Asian sociology. What is more, in my view, Preston fails to give due regard to the context within which local sociologists and other academics study and publish in such countries as Singapore, and to practical social priorities in the region, as against the often radical neo-Marxist perspectives espoused by some Western social scientists.

The underdevelopment of Southeast Asian sociology

Let us now return to the theme of the relatively poor performance of Southeast Asian sociology, and examine briefly the reasons for it. A group of Australian-based political economists have provided us with some clues. In *Southeast Asia. The political economy of structural change* (1985), the editors, Richard Higgott and Richard Robison, argue that scholarship has not responded to the dramatic changes that have been taking place in the region since the mid-1970s. These include:

rapid industrialisation, the emergence of powerful, centralised authoritarian regimes and complex bureaucratic structures together with the accelerated spread of new class relationships in both the town and the countryside (1988: 3).

Working principally in a radical political economy tradition, Higgott and Robison and their colleagues are especially critical of what they perceive to be the generally conservative, empirical writings in Southeast Asian social science. They argue that this situation is:

> largely the consequence ... of the extraordinary influence of positivist and empiricist traditions ... which ... have been constituted by an amalgam of orientalist history, behaviouralism and structural-functional social science (ibid.).

To phrase this quotation in lay-person's language, according to Higgott and Robison, scholars of Southeast Asian Studies have tended to focus on such matters as local cultural traits and overt behavioural patterns; historically important personages and events; the exercise of political skills; political factions and institutionalization as well as regime maintenance; technical aspects of change and growth economics; and on the passage from traditional societies to modern ones. In other words, they have tended towards the descriptive and neglected the analysis of underlying structural conditions of economic underdevelopment and political activity, and the position of Southeast Asian countries in a global economy dominated by capitalism. Furthermore, Higgott and Robison argue that much previous Southeast Asian social science has not given attention to such issues as class formation, conflicting economic and political interests, both inside and outside a given country, and the complexities of the socio-economic and political transformations that Southeast Asian communities have been experiencing during the past forty years. The conceptualization of change as a movement from tradition to a modern society which approximates Western social formations is obviously too simplistic.

Yet even Higgott and Robison do not really explain in detail why this is so. I think the reasons are relatively simple. First, various parts of the Southeast Asian region in the post-war period were effectively closed to most kinds of academic field research (Neher 1984: 131–2). Much of mainland Southeast Asia was embroiled in war and conflict, and after the communist victories in South Vietnam, Cambodia and Laos in the mid-1970s, access to data and permission to undertake fieldwork locally were made virtually impossible to secure. Academic studies of Indochina have commonly concentrated on the fields of politics, history and economics; there has been very little sociological or anthropological research worth mentioning on Indochina during the past thirty years, and not much in the radical tradition either. Part of the reason for this is also located in the 'divisiveness of the Vietnam War in the U.S. academic community' (Doner 1991: 821), and the fact that many activists and radical scholars 'either never secured any academic position, voluntarily left, or were forced out of Asian studies' (Allen 1989: 117, in Doner 1991: 822). On the other hand, various American academics 'of a particular value persuasion' were linked closely to the US government during its active involvement in mainland Southeast Asia. Marr notes that 'the typical American dissertation', most of them written in the 1960s, 'deals with the people of the area [Indochina] as *objects* of the post-World War II political policies of France and, later, the United States' (1973: 97).

What is more, Burma (Myanmar) had essentially severed its ties with the outside world from the early 1960s, and has excluded most foreign scholars since then. Again we have had studies in the politics and history of Burma, which can be undertaken from a distance. But in sociology we have been forced to survive largely with the materials collected prior to 1962, mainly by American cultural anthropologists. As one might expect, these latter used simple paradigms taken from the American anthropology of the time, including such concepts as 'culture', and, as in the case of Manning Nash's *The Golden Road to Modernity* (1965), 'modernization' and the movement from traditional to modern modes of life. Although Nash's analysis is subtle and detailed, his concern to examine the interrelationship of tradition and modernity is plain to see.

In this regard it is instructive that, although the title of Higgott's and Robison's 1985 book of critical articles suggests a broad coverage of the region, it is really only concerned with the ASEAN countries. The sociological neglect of the mainland Southeast Asian countries is then partly a consequence quite simply of the difficulty of gaining access to field sites and data. Yet it is also noticeable that, in general, the radical literature on development and change in Southeast Asia, perhaps because of theoretical and ideological emphases and the fact that capitalism is the object of enquiry and criticism, has paid little attention to the socialist countries, either as components of a world system and interlinked, in various ways, with the capitalist economies, or as forms of political–economic system that might provide contrasting or alternative modes of responding to, managing and generating change from (both theoretically and practically) the Western-oriented, capitalist-dominated economies of the ASEAN countries (King 1986). There are few references to these kinds of issues in Higgott and Robison's compendium, but interestingly, in a footnote, Carol Warren, a contributor to the book, remarks that a 'really thorough comparative analysis of the impact of contrasting approaches to development awaits parallel research on the economic and social transformation of the socialist nations of Southeast Asia – Kampuchea, Laos and Vietnam – as well as Burma which has been least committed to developmentalism in its policies to date' (1985: 145). Of course, recent processes of liberalization in Indochina in particular have tended to shift the grounds of the debate about socialism and its relationship to the political and economic systems of developing countries.

Second, with reference to the ASEAN countries, Higgott and Robison are correct in stating that critical sociological commentary has been virtually excluded by the pre-eminent position of structural-functionalist and modernization approaches. These mainly conceive societies as comprising a set of elements or parts that function to maintain the integrity of the whole. Specifically these perspectives are preoccupied with the ways in which societies sustain an equilibrium, manage conflict, overcome contradictions and tensions, and persist through time. Even modernization analyses that are concerned to examine the transition or change from tradition to modernity posit a gradual and peaceful movement from one kind of integrated society to another. Some examples of these approaches can be seen in Evers' early edited book *Modernization in Southeast Asia* (1973), despite the fact that the volume is presented as a rethinking and re-evaluation of the modernization approach. Other writings in this tradition include Tham Seong Chee's *Malays and Modernization* (1977). The importance of evolutionist assumptions about change and the concern to identify those social elements that either facilitate or retard 'progress' towards modern social institutions are also exemplified, in part at least, in some of the early work of Clifford Geertz, such as his *Peddlers and Princes. Social development and economic change in two Indonesian towns* (1963a).

In my view, the origins of much of this writing can be traced to the important political, economic and academic connections between the USA and the Philippines, Thailand and Indonesia in the post-war period. The dominance of American conservative scholarship in major parts of Southeast Asia during the 1950s and 1960s is exemplified in the overwhelming importance of the Cornell studies of Thailand, dating from 1948 under the direction of Lauriston Sharp (Skinner and Kirsch 1975; Bell 1982), and the Center for International Studies, Massachusetts Institute of Technology research programme in Java from 1952, out of which emerged the substantial writings of Clifford Geertz and his colleagues such as Robert Jay (Higgins 1963; Koentjaraningrat 1975: 198–207). Nowhere is the American academic presence so obvious than in its former colony, the Philippines. What is more, American modernization perspectives and structural-functional analyses are seen not only in the work of the main American exponents, but also in the writings of many Thai, Indonesian and Filipino scholars trained in the United States.

In comparison with other parts of Southeast Asia, the Philippines has enjoyed a long history of teaching and research in sociology. Sociology teaching was introduced into the University of the Philippines some eighty years ago; in contrast, Indonesia appointed its first professor of sociology, T. S. G. Moelia, only in 1950, at the University of Indonesia. In 1938 a Filipino scholar, Sarafin E. Macaraig, published an *Introduction to Sociology*. In 1953 the Philippine Sociological Society was founded, and with it the journal, the *Philippine Sociological Review*. In the same year the very well-known teaching text *Sociology in the Philippine Setting* was published. It was written by Chester L. Hunt, along with two other American scholars and two Filipino collaborators. It came out in a second edition in 1963, and was revised and published again in 1976 as *Sociology in the New Philippine Setting*. Another volume in the same tradition is Cordero and Panopio's *General Sociology* (1969).

Chester Hunt's book has had a tremendous influence in Philippine sociology, and it demonstrates the importance that American sociology and US funding for research had in the Philippines during the formative years of the discipline there. In addition to such American professors of sociology as Chester Hunt, there was also the important presence of Frank Lynch at the Institute of Philippine Culture, Ateneo de Manila (Yengoyan and Makil 1984). Although Lynch was by training an anthropologist, he played a significant role in the development of Philippine sociology. The influence of conservative Parsonian American scholarship of the 1950s and 1960s is obvious. The main paradigm, which can, in part, be traced back to such writers as Durkheim, was behaviourist, positivist and structural-functionalist; there was an interest in norms, social roles and role expectations; processes and mechanisms of social integration and institutionalization, cultural patterns, personality and values.

Early sociological studies of class in the Philippines generally employed integrationist social stratification models, rather than concepts of social conflict (Turner 1978). Importantly, social inequality was translated into analyses of personalistic networks of patrons and clients (Hollnsteiner 1963). Analyses of social change relied very much on modernization paradigms (Carroll 1968); echoes of this influence and concerns with socio-cultural change and diffusion can be found in more recent contributions to Philippine sociology (e.g. Zamora et al. 1982). Hunt and Dizon, in an overview of Philippine sociology (1978), attempt to provide an explanation for the importance of functionalism, and the 'pragmatic and relatively conservative' stance (1988: 107) of scholarship. They argue that at the time it was important to understand 'local customs' and to address practical social problems and policy issues.

On the other hand, in a critical rejoinder to Hunt and Dizon's survey of Philippine sociology, George Weightman argues that Philippine sociology has been dominated by a handful of senior American scholars who were well connected to US-based funding agencies and dictated the research agenda (1978: 178–9; see also Weightman 1975: 43–58). He adds that 'Philippine sociology still finds itself trying to escape from the intellectual strait jacket which sees an idealized American modern urban society as the sole model toward which the Philippines is perceived as approaching, departing, or deviating' (1978: 179). Even though Hunt and Dizon put up a robust defence of the American position, they too had to admit that since the Second World War 'the general trend of the discipline can best be explained as a delayed response to developments in the United States' (1978: 100).

The same can be said for Indonesia. From the 1950s many young Indonesian scholars were trained in America, particularly at Cornell University. There was a heavy concentration on community studies, religion and identity, and problems of agricultural development and national integration, such as in the work of Sunardi Sudarmadi, Tan Giok-Lan (Mely G. Tan), Umar Khayam and Harsja W. Bachtiar (Koentjaraningrat 1975: 225–6). As one might expect, there was a need for basic data collection and therefore a focus on empirical investigation and regional socio-economic surveys. There are also many examples of modernization theory at work in Indonesia, one of the most well-known being Selosoemardjan's *Social Changes in Jogjakarta* (1962). For example, one of his main findings is that 'change from a closed to an open class system tends to turn people's orientation away from tradition and makes them more receptive to other changes', in particular, 'the desire for progress has replaced the security of tradition' (1962: 411–12).

In Thailand, too, American academic influence, particularly up to the early 1970s, has been significant; there was an American emphasis on culture and personality studies, the harmony- and stability-inducing influence of Buddhism, the interpersonal relations of patron–client dyads, the social networks and clusters focused on hierarchy and status, and the preoccupation with the 'looseness' and informality of Thai society. The roots and processes of tension, contradiction, conflict, struggle, exploitation and change played almost no part in this early literature (Phillips 1973; Namsirichai and Vichit-Vadakan 1973).

Finally, there are the remaining areas of Southeast Asia; the former British possessions of Malaya, Sarawak, North Borneo, Brunei and Singapore. In contrast to the granting of political independence to the Philippines and Indonesia in the early post-war period – of course, Thailand was no one's colony – the scatter of British-dominated territories around the South China Sea achieved independence later: Malaya in 1957; Singapore, Sarawak and North Borneo (Sabah) in 1963, and Brunei in 1984. Political autonomy came relatively peacefully, and there was a marked continuity in colonial conservative scholarly perspectives in the early post-colonial era, dominated by colonial historians, linguists, scholars of literature and functionalist anthropologists. We might note in passing that there is no sociology of Brunei, with the partial exception of Brown's historical and sociological/anthropological study of the Brunei Sultanate (1970). The formation of the Federation of Malaysia in 1963 and the establishment of a separate Republic of Singapore in 1965 were followed by major attempts to promote economic growth, while their governments were also preoccupied with the maintenance of political stability, particularly in the ethnically plural society of Malaysia. There was little room for any substantial critical sociology in this environment, and it is therefore of no surprise that sociologists, where they existed, should be concerned with basic data collection and descriptive studies, and with practical issues of development. Van den Muijzenberg remarks that Dutch sociologists of Indonesia have also tended to shy away from critical research in favour of 'less audacious' topics (n.d.: 15).

These concerns are seen very clearly in Evers and Chen's edited book on sociology, to which I have already referred. Apart from some general articles, the book is concerned mainly with Singapore, and to a lesser extent Malaysia, Thailand and Indonesia. There is considerable attention to the characteristics and roles of elites, especially in the context of modernization, development and nation-building. There are empirical studies of different ethnic groups, inter-ethnic relations and ethnic-based institutions; and there are chapters on the consequences of urbanization, especially high-rise living, in Singapore. The research on Singapore is obviously closely associated with the need for the government to collect data on and form conclusions about its public housing policies (Tai 1988). In Malaysia, there has been much empirical work on describing and explaining the relatively disadvantaged status of the Malays (Husin Ali 1981).

A flavour of local empirical sociology can also be had from two very popular and wide-ranging Singapore-based academic journals – the *Southeast Asian Journal of Social Science* and *Sojourn. Social Issues in Southeast Asia.*

Major studies and concepts

This then is the environment in which we must consider the sociological enterprise in Southeast Asia. Let us now examine in rather
more detail some of the major sociological studies and certain important conceptual contributions to the understanding of Southeast
Asian societies, drawing attention to matters of context when necessary.
In my opinion, it is best to start from Evers' reader *Sociology of
Southeast Asia* (1980a) and use this as a springboard for the review.

Evers chooses four concepts that have been developed specifically
in relation to Southeast Asian societies: J. H. Boeke's concept of the
'dual economy/society', J. S. Furnivall's 'plural society/economy' concept, Clifford Geertz's notion of 'involution', and J. F. Embree's
concept, with reference to Thailand, of a 'loosely structured social
system'. As I stated in 1981, Embree's work (in Evers 1980a) has been
inflated out of all proportion to its importance, and, although there
have been some interesting and mainly Thailand-specific debates on
'loose structure' (for example, Evers 1969), it is the theoretical and
empirical yield of the concepts of dualism, pluralism and involution
that has been substantial, and this should be given proper consideration
(King 1981). Doner, too, points to the importance of the works of
Boeke, Furnivall and Geertz in demonstrating the 'mutual influence
of politics and economics' (1991: 819).

A theme in Evers' reader is that of the problems generated by
reliance on theories and concepts 'imported from abroad', particularly
from the industrialized societies, to analyse the 'highly complex, fast
changing, underdeveloped societies of Southeast Asia' (Evers 1980a:
ix). In this connection Evers argues that the concepts he chooses to
highlight were developed to understand sets of social and economic
circumstances created in the context of the penetration of European
colonialism in Southeast Asia. These conditions were considered to be
novel and incapable of satisfactory analysis in terms of the then existing
tools of social science. In my view these creative efforts alone, with the
exception of Embree's work, qualify them for special attention.

All three authors – Boeke, Furnivall and Geertz – stress the destruc-
tive effects of capitalism. For example, Boeke states, with special
reference to Java, that: 'The mass product of the new Western
industries was thrown upon the Eastern market, sweeping away Native
handicrafts, Native trade, and the Native system of distribution' (in
Evers 1980a: 28). Furnivall characterizes the plural society as one that
is 'broken up into groups of isolated individuals, and the disintegration
of social will is reflected in a corresponding disorganization of social
demand'. He notes depressingly that 'in a plural society men are

decivilized' (1948: 31). Like Boeke, he points to the damaging effects of cheap imported Western commodities, which 'smashed the native economic system and straitened the sphere of native arts' so that there was 'an inevitable degradation of native culture' (in Evers 1980a: 92). Geertz too, in tracing the process of involution, concludes that: 'Most of Java is crowded with post-traditional wet-rice peasant villages: large, dense, vague, dispirited communities – the raw material of a rural, nonindustrialized mass society' (1963b: 129).

Boeke and dualism

These contact situations were seen to require new concepts, expressed very clearly in Boeke's call for a new economic theory, 'dualistic economics' – to understand the Oriental condition characterized by a 'sharp, deep, broad cleavage dividing the society into two segments': a Western, modern capitalist segment and an Eastern, traditional, non-capitalist sector (in Evers 1980a: 27; Boeke 1953). Boeke argues that the traditional sector is unresponsive to economic stimuli, particularly that emanating from modern entrepreneurial activity; that traditional communities possess only limited economic needs; and that they are averse to risk-taking, capital accumulation and continuous profit-seeking, and lack discipline and organizational abilities. It is difficult to determine in Boeke's thesis the weight he assigns to the effects of Western capitalism in rendering the non-capitalist Oriental sector passive and risk-averse. Overall, it would seem that he does not give sufficient emphasis to structural and historical factors in accounting for the persistence of tradition, but, in anticipation of modernization theory, he seems rather to rely on explanations in terms of an 'Oriental mentality', an 'Eastern spirit' and the 'force of tradition'. He states that the 'entire life of the [Javanese] village is dominated by religion and semi-religious customs and traditions' (in Evers 1980a: 35), although he does not appear to hold to a view that 'the characteristics of the "Oriental mentality" ... are innate to that mentality' (Koentjaraningrat 1975: 75). The reliance on the concepts of 'traditional culture' and 'personality' and the distinction between 'tradition' and 'modernity' also appear in the models used by modernization theorists. However, Boeke argues, using an evolutionary framework, that dual societies have not moved from a traditional to a modern state. Instead, both social conditions exist side-by-side in a given society.

Boeke's thesis has given rise to a whole series of debates, which were re-examined in detail in a collection of papers edited by James Fox et al. (1980) and reviewed in an edited volume by Hainsworth (1982). However, the concept of dualism continues to exert a powerful

hold on academic and other analyses. It is still used by some economists, for example, in their work on such developing societies as
Malaysia. Indeed, Malaysian planning documents continue to assume
the existence of modern and traditional sectors (King 1988), and the
compulsion to conceptualize societies or social forms as comprising
two parts – large-scale/small-scale; formal/informal; firm/bazaar;
capital-intensive/labour-intensive; urban/rural – is still expressed in
numerous social science publications.

The criticisms of the model are numerous but they can be roughly
categorized into two kinds: the empirical-substantive and the theoretical
(Wertheim et al. 1966; Koentjaraningrat 1975: 73–85). On the basis of
social and economic 'facts' it has been argued that Boeke's depiction
of Eastern society under colonialism is misleading: the economic needs
of villagers were not limited; in various circumstances rural dwellers
were not passive and unresponsive, and their activities did show evidence of organizational abilities. Theoretically it has been proposed that
Boeke has a too narrow, old-fashioned and formal conception of Western economic theories and principles, and that Eastern communities
are not as different from Western ones as Boeke maintains. What is
more, Boeke's stress on a sharp cleavage or distinction between two
different but homogeneous social types is not sufficiently sensitive to
the interconnections between different economic sectors, communities
and groups, to the variations and differences within sectors and communities, and to the dynamic processes of change and response.

Furnivall, pluralism and ethnicity

Moving on to Furnivall's concept of the plural society is clearly more
satisfactory than Boeke's concept of dualism. For Furnivall, like Boeke,
the understanding of 'tropical' societies required new perspectives;
these communities were also considered to be divided by sharp internal
cleavages, in contrast to the assumed homogeneity of Western societies.
However, unlike Boeke, Furnivall inserts another analytical element to
assist us in our understanding of the East, and that is the ethnic
division of labour, or as Furnivall calls them 'distinct economic castes'.
This, in turn, entails an examination of 'alien' Asian, especially Chinese
and Indian, groups and activities, wedged, as it were, between European
capitalist enterprises on the one hand, and the small-scale, largely
agrarian, subsistence-oriented native communities on the other. Furnivall defines a plural society as one that comprises 'two or more
elements or social orders which live side by side, yet without mingling,
in one political unit' (in Evers 1980a: 86; Furnivall 1939, 1948).

Influenced by the Burmese rather than the Javanese experience,

Furnivall views the Burmese peasantry as economically motivated and he notes that Dutch writers, including Boeke, tended to understate the economic values and motivations of Javanese peasants. Indeed, it is a central part of Furnivall's plural society thesis that while

> there is no social demand common to all the several elements, [people from all sections of the plural society] have in common, in greater or less degree, the economic motive, the desire for profit; and they all join, more or less consciously, in forwarding the economic process, the natural law of the survival of the fittest in the economic world, by which the cheaper product tends to supplant the dearer (in Evers 1980a: 87).

Members of the different segments, defined in terms of religion, language, ways of life and position in the economy, 'meet only in the market-place, in buying and selling'. Most significantly, Furnivall notes that 'the conflict between rival economic interests tends to be exacerbated by racial diversity' (ibid.: 88).

Furnivall has drawn attention to the vital principle of ethnic identity and difference in the social organization of Southeast Asia. However, one of the most consistent criticisms of him is that he has a too simple view of the relations between ethnic and economic divisions in the region. The plural society concept assumes a coincidence between ethnicity and social class, in the notion of 'economic castes'. But relations of class, as well as those of status and power, interconnect with those of ethnicity in most complex ways. For example, it is often not the coincidence of economic and cultural cleavage that explains social tensions and conflicts, but rather the breakdown of the monopoly of particular economic positions by given ethnic groups and the consequent economic competition between such groups. What is more, ethnic groups themselves are usually divided along class and status lines; members of different ethnic groups commonly occupy the same class positions, and there are often all kinds of relations between different ethnic groups, expressed in such processes as cultural borrowing, assimilation and intermarriage (Lee 1986: vi). Furnivall's concept is too static to enable analysis of changing inter-group relations, and he assumes, like Boeke, that colonial societies are deeply divided in contrast to Western societies, which are perceived to be relatively homogeneous.

In subsequent debates on pluralism it has been the position of such writers as Wertheim (1964a) and Evers that although we should address issues of ethnicity in Southeast Asia, we should place greater stress on social hierarchy. It is Evers' view, for example, that 'the plural social structure' in urban Southeast Asia is being transformed into one based on 'segregation by social class' (1980b: 122). Wertheim too has noted that the breakdown of residential–occupational–ethnic cleavages through time leads to conflicts between people from different ethnic groups (1964a).

In their analyses of class structures in Southeast Asia, Evers and Wertheim refer back to the classical sociological tradition of Weber and Marx. What is more, Evers formulates the new concept of 'strategic groups' to assist us in our understanding of changing Southeast Asian social structures. Evers identifies three stages in the crystallization of class. First, the 'incumbents of new positions had probably very little in common'; instead, identifications such as ethnicity, cross-cut organizational forms based on occupational position and wealth. Evers refers to these partially formed entities as 'quasi-groups'. These are then transformed into 'strategic groups' as common identity grows, because of such processes as an increase in membership of a quasi-group, which, in turn, results in crisis, conflict and competition. These new social units forged in situations of conflict 'now become of strategic importance as groups for political development'. Examples of these groups are civil servants, the military, teachers, professionals and Chinese businessmen, which presumably for Evers are defined in terms of occupation or economic function. These groups comprise 'a *recruiting field* for political leadership and a political pressure group at the same time' (Evers 1980c: 250). Finally, classes are seen to come about through coalitions between strategic groups, and the increasing restriction or control of mobility into new strata (ibid.: 251). Examples are the coalitions between the military-bureaucratic elite and Chinese businessmen in Thailand, and between the Malay political elite and Chinese entrepreneurs in Malaysia.

Of course, Evers' formulation is not exactly new. It would seem that his concept of 'strategic groups' is similar to the notion of 'class fractions' as used by some neo-Marxist writers. In addition, there are problems in defining and isolating certain 'strategic groups', and, in any case, groups such as 'the military' are themselves complex segments internally differentiated. Nevertheless, Evers' framework does provide a useful starting point in examining social processes of group formation and conflict, in the context of wider international systems of development and dependency.

To add another dimension to the work of Evers, we should also briefly consider Judith Nagata's important studies of ethnicity and class in Malaysia. Like Evers, Nagata argues that an analysis of Malaysian society reveals the development of 'a form of class stratification cross-cutting ethnic boundaries'. Interestingly, however, she argues that Malaysians tend not to *perceive* of their own society in class terms, but that instead 'an ethnic idiom is more common' (in Evers 1980a: 127).

Nagata, therefore, demonstrates that 'Malaysian society is subjectively more plural than objective reality might warrant' (ibid.). She also notes that members of different ethnic groupings commonly have different perceptions of the overall Malaysian social structure.

Nagata's views are supported in a valuable collection of essays on *Ethnicity, Class and Development. Malaysia* (1984) edited by Syed Husin Ali. Husin Ali points out that:

> class conflicts have not occurred between the rich and the poor, although these classes are becoming more discernible now ... ethnic ideology and consciousness are still dominant and act as constraining factors to the development of class ideology and consciousness (1984: 10).

Malaysia, then, according to Husin Ali, is divided horizontally by class and vertically by ethnicity; but although the factor of ethnicity is still strong, ethnic issues and tensions may be generated from politico-economic or class relations (see also Lim Mah Hui 1980). Husin Ali's analysis of the interrelations between ethnicity and class leads him to conclude that class issues and interests will increase, but, at present, the importance of ethnicity in Malaysia requires him to rely on the concept of a multi-ethnic 'elite' and the multi-ethnic 'masses' to demonstrate that class structures are in formation and not yet mature (1984: 13–31).

An interesting analytical development of mainly ethnically grounded perceptions of society in Malaysia is Shamsul's use of the concepts of 'imagined communities' and 'nations of intent' to explore different ethnic agendas (1992):

> Amongst the Malays, the Chinese, the Indians, the Kadazans, the Dayaks, and between them exists a plethora of 'nations of intent' often articulated openly in election manifestos or in debates concerning culture, language, literature and religion' (1992: 13).

The distinction between objective and subjective dimensions of social structures is a useful one, and Malaysian pluralism provides a most appropriate case for exploring these distinctions. But Nagata's, Husin Ali's and Shamsul's work also shows that considerations of ethnicity do not merely operate at the subjective level. Nagata notes, for example, that the groupings of businessmen, professionals and civil servants are still socially divided by ethnicity. In other words, in Evers' terms these groupings are not yet 'strategic groups'.

Clearly, ethnic identity still plays an important organizational role in Malaysia, and it would seem that it is not merely subjective or ideological, but that it also operates, along with economic relations, at the level of action (Lee 1986: viii). Elsewhere in the region, such as in Thailand, the principle of ethnic identity and division appears not to be so socially significant, although this does not thereby imply that there are no problems of ethnic tension and conflict in such countries.

Geertz and involution

We shall return to issues of social class and inequality later. Let us now turn to the important concept of 'involution', formulated by Clifford Geertz, which is also discussed in Evers' compilation. Geertz's definition of 'involution' refers to 'the overdriving of an established form in such a way that it becomes rigid through an inward over-elaboration of detail' (1963b: 82). His very influential study *Agricultural Involution. The processes of ecological change in Indonesia* (1963b) must be read in the context of Boeke's work on dualism, since it is an ecological and historical analysis of the emergence and development of dualism in Java, or more especially 'inner Indonesia' (parts of Java, Bali and Lombok), and its contrast with transformations in the Outer Islands under Dutch colonialism. Geertz's study also has an important bearing on theories of underdevelopment and dependency, although Evers remarks that Geertz's concept 'was somewhat hampered by the Latin American theory of international dependence and dependent reproduction that addressed itself to similar problems' (1980a: 5).

As van Schaik says, '"Agricultural involution" can be considered as the description of a process of adaptation of a socio-economic system to externally induced influences' (1986: 15). Although Geertz's study certainly has some elements in common with analyses of underdevelopment elsewhere, it has particular features of its own. First, it does not attempt to provide a general theory of socio-economic change in contrast to the work on Latin America of such writers as Andre Gunder Frank; it examines a case study in some detail. Second, the neo-Marxist concepts and terms employed in much of the under-development literature are replaced in Geertz's study by the concept of cultural ecology. Geertz examines some of the detailed connections between certain Javanese social and cultural forms, economic organiza-tion and the natural environment, and the ways in which these relations change and develop through time and in the context of a wider set of economic and political relationships. Finally, although Geertz's thesis has affinities with the underdevelopment school, it is also underpinned by certain evolutionary ideas reminiscent of modernization theory. Certainly, if one examines Geertz's study along with his other major contributions such as *Peddlers and Princes*, then there are clear signs of a concern with the passage from tradition to modernity, and the need to identify various facilitators of economic take-off or particular points or elements of growth. Indeed, the notion of involution assumes that the process of evolution is also possible.

Geertz argues that Dutch colonialism integrated Javanese peasant rice agriculture into a system that produced cash crops for the Dutch and also confined the cultivators in the subsistence sector while using some of their land and labour for profit. In effect, the Javanese reproduced their labour power in the subsistence sector which, in turn, supported the cultivation of sugar and coffee on behalf of the Dutch. This reproduction was enabled by the properties of the irrigated wet rice system, which, according to Geertz, could support ever-increasing population densities and the intensification of agriculture. Population increased as a result of the Pax Nederlandica, expansion of infrastructure and modern medicines. Geertz argues that improved irrigation facilities for sugar growing also had a spin-off for the improvement of rice cultivation on adjacent land, and that therefore rice production increased. However, given the growth of population, yield per hectare increased, but not production per capita. Thus, in order to give everyone an economic niche in a situation of increasing numbers, limited resources and restricted alternatives, the Javanese divided up land, work and production so that the result was a high level of socio-economic homogeneity. Rural Java became characterized by 'shared poverty'; it did not develop 'progressively'; it did not 'take off' economically; instead traditional social arrangements were 'ossified'; they became internally overelaborated, intricate and complex, and ultimately incapable of positive transformation.

Such a closely argued and compelling thesis, eloquently expressed and structured, has had a profound influence on Indonesian studies, and has made some impact on general sociological literature (Wertheim 1974) as well as on analyses of rural social structures in other countries such as the Philippines (van den Muijzenberg 1975).

As one might expect, the concept of involution has engendered much debate and the main critical issues are addressed by the Alexanders (1978, 1979, 1982) and White (1983a, 1983b), and then by Geertz in a reply to his critics and in his partial reinterpretation of his own thesis (1984). As van Schaik notes, White is surprised that Geertz's thesis became so popular on the basis of 'so little evidence' (1986: 20). There has subsequently been much attention paid to the evidence and several points need addressing briefly. First, Geertz's views on social homogeneity and shared poverty have been especially criticized since the evidence suggests, on the contrary, that the Javanese village was and is characterized by marked inequalities (Elson 1978; Hüsken 1979). Second, it would seem that rice production gradually stagnated and did not absorb ever-increasing amounts of labour; instead sugar cultivation placed tremendous demands upon local labour. Third, various scholars have demonstrated considerable variations in the relations between population density, rice cultivation, cash crops and Dutch influence across Java, in contrast to Geertz's *general* thesis of involution there (e.g. Elson 1984; Lyon 1970; Stoler 1977). Finally, it has been demonstrated that the wet rice ecosystem does not remain basically unchanged or stable and able to sustain increasing intensification. Following his detailed study of Dutch archives, van Schaik concludes that:

> the natural environment was changed ... less labour and land were available, and ... the water resources of the holding decreased or were limited unproportionately [*sic*] in respect to the total quantity available within the irrigation systems (1986: 28).

Therefore, overall, Geertz's postulated link between high levels of sugar cultivation and wet rice agriculture, as well as high rice yields and population densities, is not borne out generally by the evidence from archival material on east and central Java. Van Schaik concludes that:

> Like the work of the social evolutionists, 'Agricultural Involution' is organized around the comparative method. The suggested change of the social evolutionists however, is not change at all, but variation (ibid.: 36).

This is not to say that Geertz's study is not of importance. It plainly is. Geertz draws attention to the need to take into account the context of colonialism. But he assumes a tightly interrelated ecosystem in parts of rural Java, focused on the properties of wet rice agriculture. Instead, it has been demonstrated by later writers that the impact of Dutch policies was more varied; that there were colonial activities other than sugar cultivation that affected Javanese peasant households; and that the Dutch also restricted the resource base and limited the peasants' incentives to produce both rice and cash crops. Koentjaraningrat, in a balanced review of Geertz's work, also draws attention to Geertz's method of social analysis, in which he constructs 'ideal types of social categories' such as the wet rice and dry rice ecosystems, and compares and contrasts them 'on the basis of a fixed number of characteristics' (1975: 199–200). This tends to sacrifice empirical detail and complexity, and sometimes even inconvenient evidence, in favour of conceptual clarity and theoretical ingenuity.

Although Geertz paid little attention to changing systems of social stratification in his study of involution in rural Java (cf. Utrecht 1973), the subject appears in a more substantial way in *Peddlers and Princes*

(1963a) and *The Social History of an Indonesian Town* (1965). Both these studies relate to problems of social change, and the latter especially can, in part, be seen as the urban companion volume to *Agricultural Involution*. It focuses on the transformation from a colonial social structure comprising a loosely organized set of estate-like and 'self-contained status communities' into post-independent 'strategic groups' and larger 'second-order groups' (*aliran*) of a religio-political kind (see below) (1965: 4). Geertz sees this contemporary system as still 'incomplete', 'vague' and 'ill-defined', which echoes his conclusions in *Agricultural Involution*. This theme of 'permanent transition' also surfaces in *Peddlers and Princes*, in which again the problems in Indonesia of achieving 'take-off' into sustained economic growth and development and the associated institutional arrangements are confronted. The concern with the parallels between Western and Oriental experiences emerges in Geertz's examination of the economic potential of pious Javanese Muslim 'peddlers', which, as Wertheim notes, bears similarities to the Weberian focus on ascetic Calvinist 'burgesses' in Western Europe (1964b: 307–11). The influence of Weber's analyses of religion, social change, and the rise of capitalism on Indonesian sociological studies will be examined in more detail below.

Although it has had less impact on subsequent work, Geertz's analysis of the *aliran* concept has also had some influence on the ways in which Indonesian society has been perceived by social scientists. According to Geertz, these *aliran* (literally stream or current) were a primary focus of political allegiance; they organized different communities into vertically arranged groupings on the basis of such distinguishing criteria as religion and political orientations (1965: 127 ff.). Thus, for example, Geertz demonstrates that important political distinctions were created between Muslims and non-Muslims in Indonesia, which cross-cut social class alignments. These observations, of course, are reminiscent of the analyses of the relations between class and ethnicity in the context of debates about the concept of pluralism in Malaysia, but again Geertz has been taken to task for his ideal typical characterization of the vertical 'streams' and, related to this perspective, for his misleading depiction of Javanese religion in terms of three categories, *santri, abangan,* and *prijaji* (e.g. Bachtiar 1973; Koentjaraningrat 1963; Utrecht 1973).

As Hefner has remarked (1990), overall Geertz has also been subsequently criticized by others for his neglect of class (Anderson 1982), his concentration on ideology and culture at the expense of economic relations and modes of production (Kahn 1982), and his lack of attention to the importance of patron–client linkages in mobilizing political groupings (Wertheim 1969). But Hefner also suggests, and rightly so, that some of these criticisms must themselves be subject to scrutiny, and that importantly Geertz has provided us with a set of studies of social change which have explored, to a greater or lesser extent, the significance of culture with regard to patterns of social behaviour, inter-group alliance and conflict, and social action.

As we have seen, in his study of involution Geertz has certain connections with underdevelopment and dependency theorists. Yet overall his work would appear to come closer to mainstream American social science of the 1950s and 1960s in its concern with the possibilities of and obstacles to modernization, and the importance of culture in understanding human motivations, action and behaviour. That having been said, it is clear that Geertz was hardly an orthodox modernization theorist. Some of Geertz's work has foreshadowed interesting recent developments in sociological analyses of Southeast Asia. There have been more recent calls for incorporating the concept of culture into the formal, structural analysis of situations of development, dependency and socio-economic change (e.g. Worsley 1984), or for moving away from concerns with world systems analysis and macro-sociological studies to local-level and regional social, economic, political and cultural studies (e.g. Hefner 1990).

Wertheim and non-Western sociology

Let us now turn for a moment to other sociological work on Southeast Asia. Geertz's earlier concerns were to be eclipsed by the increasing influence of neo-Marxist writings in the 1970s and 1980s. Even then, in the context of Southeast Asia, structural analyses of under-development and dependency were not as popular as they had become in studies of the rest of the developing world. Nevertheless, one sociologist in particular, who drew on the Asian experience for his empirical data, and who provided a direct bridge between neo-Marxist concerns and those interests of social evolutionists, as well as of Weberian-inspired sociologists, is Professor W. F. Wertheim. Shortly after the Second World War he was appointed to the Chair of Modern History and Sociology of Indonesia at the University of Amsterdam. Wertheim has been a central figure in Dutch non-Western sociology, which has been crucial in combining both historical and sociological perspectives. He has provided us with both theoretical debates in sociology, and with analyses of social transformations in Indonesia in particular (van den Muijzenberg and Wolters 1988). Wertheim's legacy has been maintained in the University of Amsterdam through the work of Professor van den Muijzenberg and his colleagues (on class, patronage and entrepreneurial elites), especially in their studies of the

Philippines (e.g. Wolters 1984). Wertheim also stimulated important local research in Indonesia during the late 1950s, when he was guest professor at the University of Indonesia; among others, Kampto Utomo's (Sajogya's) work on transmigration in Lampung (1957) emerged from this period.

I have argued elsewhere that Wertheim should have been included more centrally in Evers' reader (King 1981), and I wish that he had been featured in Taylor's and Turton's compendium. Furthermore, Higgott and Robison only refer to Wertheim in passing, suggesting instead that his socio-historical approach, along with the work of other Dutch scholars such as Bertram O. J. Schrieke (1955–57) and Jacob C. van Leur (1955), which 'sought to integrate political, social and economic approaches' had been overtaken by other Western writings influenced by 'Orientalist' and 'empiricist' preoccupations (1985: 5). I cannot fully agree with this conclusion.

Wertheim (n.d.) has recently provided ample justification for the importance of the Dutch Weberian-influenced socio-historical tradition in a paper to be published by the *Journal of Southeast Asian Studies*. He notes that 'Weber's sociological studies attracted attention among social scientists in the Netherlands'. He refers to the sociological interpretation of D. M. G. Koch on the Indonesian nationalist movement, and of Bertram Schrieke on the 1927 communist insurrection in Minangkabau and on early Javanese states. In addition, there is Schrieke's important edited book *The Effect of Western Influence on Native Civilization in the Malay Archipelago* (1929). More particularly Wertheim also dwells on the contribution of Jacob van Leur to Indonesian history in his use of Weber's socio-historical methodology, the concept of 'ideal types', and that of 'patrimonial bureaucracy'.

Other significant sociological studies which have been neglected in general text books on Southeast Asia have been those by D. H. Burger (1948–49) on social change in Java and Justus van der Kroef (1954) on Indonesian culture and society in the modern world. One should also not forget the series of Dutch sociological studies which were brought together in translation and for which Wertheim acted as general editor (e.g. 1958).

Among Wertheim's extensive corpus, there are three books that deserve special mention. His *Indonesian Society in Transition. A study of social change* (1956/1959), which drew inspiration from van Leur, provides an early study of the factors underlying Indonesian social change, a discussion of the problems of periodizing and systematizing history, an attempt to indicate probable future developments, and an analysis of the relevance of Weberian and Marxian concepts for the study of process in Indonesian history (see also Wertheim 1962 and

Locher 1961). Wertheim says of this book that he 'attempted to put stress on the continuity of Indonesian social history throughout the period of colonial expansion and colonial rule ... and that this type of treatment was also in agreement with the manner in which Weber viewed Asian societies and civilizations (n.d.: 5). Second, Wertheim's collection of essays *East–West Parallels: Sociological approaches to modern Asia* (1964a) addresses one of the main themes to preoccupy later writers, including Evers, and that is the appropriateness of Western sociological concepts and historical experiences in the study of Eastern society. In this book Wertheim ranges over a diverse set of issues, including ethnicity, class, corruption and bureaucracy, using concepts taken from Western sociological traditions but setting them in the particularities of the Asian context; here he takes both Geertz and Weber to task for their perspectives on the relation between religion and economic growth. In his later reflections on his earlier work Wertheim states that he was concerned 'to investigate to what extent we could establish similarities between developments in earlier European history and developments in contemporary Asian societies'. He confirms that 'such parallel developments could certainly be revealed; but ... in each instance they only hold to some extent' (1993: 2–3).

Finally, there is Wertheim's *magnum opus, Evolution and Revolution. The rising waves of emancipation* (1974), which has been debated substantially in Dutch sociological circles, but which has not commanded the attention it deserves, either in Western social science in general, or in the Asian academic community in particular. It brings together and, in some cases, qualifies and elaborates, the main strands of his thinking on Asian societies into a grand theory of social change. He had already expounded his views about the nature of social structures and the dynamics of change in the 1960s, in his concept of society 'as a composite of conflicting value systems' (1964a and 1973), and this perspective was provided in an earlier form in his analysis of Indonesian social change. In his later work he links this notion of conflict and contradiction in society, which he sees as a central dynamic, to an elaborated and complex version of evolutionary theory. He argues that a clear principle or phenomenon discernible in human history is that of 'emancipation' – emancipation from the 'forces of nature' and from 'human domination'. One can see in this formulation the influence of earlier evolutionary theory, and, in his concerns with dialectical processes, struggle, social conflict and inequality, a clear intellectual debt to Marx. But in his stress on norms and value systems, the importance of ideas in human history, and social institutions as 'nothing but images in the minds of real people' he comes closer to some of the work of Weber and also to Georg Hegel. In my view, there are obvious problems in Wertheim's focus on the conflict between different 'mentalities' and his overly idealistic perception of social structure. Nevertheless, one is presented with a forceful example of the ways in which analyses of the Asian experience can feed into important sociological debates and of how they link back to the founding fathers of the discipline. Furthermore, Wertheim has more recently developed further his thesis on evolution and revolution and emphasized the importance of the state in economic growth (1992); this contrasts with Marx's and Weber's stress on the actions of an 'independent bourgeoisie' or private entrepreneurs, on the basis of a particular interpretation of the Western experience. More specifically, Wertheim explores the role of the state as both a 'motor' of emancipation in certain circumstances, and as a 'brake upon emancipation' in others (1992: 263ff.).

In this connection we should also note briefly that much important work on Southeast Asia has been undertaken on Marx's and Weber's views of the Orient, especially in regard to Marx's concept of the 'Asiatic mode of production' and 'Oriental despotism' and Weber's concept of 'patrimonial bureaucracy' and his writings on Islam and the religions of India and China (e.g. Wiegersma 1982). One of the main aims of these two major social theorists, which, as we have seen, links in with the broad concerns of Boeke, Furnivall, Evers, Geertz, and Wertheim, was to examine the differences between the West and Asia, and the ways in which each can be conceptually brought into relationship with the other (King 1981). More especially Marx and Weber wished to explain why industrial capitalism and a bourgeois class had not apparently emerged in Asia prior to Western intervention. Importantly, the various Marxist concepts of social formation, mode of production and class have been the subject of vigorous debate among, for example, Thai socialists, particularly in regard to the appropriateness of schemes of evolution and the categories 'feudal', and 'Asiatic' in the Thai case (Reynolds and Hong Lysa, 1983; and see Reynolds, 1987). Turning briefly to Weber, his search for explanations in religion and socio-cultural phenomena has, in turn, resulted in a series of debates about the relations between religious belief and practice in Islam and Buddhism on the one hand and economic activity and change on the other. These arguments are well summarized by Von der Mehden (1986; see also Wertheim n.d.: 8–11, and Evers and Siddique 1993). Unfortunately, some of these discussions have been distorted by a reliance on overly simple versions of modernization theory (see Alatas 1972), but there is no doubt that Weber's studies of Islam are inadequate if we wish to explain its role in social change in Indonesia and Malaysia.

Underdevelopment and dependency

As I have already noted, although various concepts of social function and structure and evolutionary theory, emphasizing societal integration and stasis, continued to find expression in studies of Southeast Asia in the 1970s, a gradual shift took place towards a more critical and radical position, influenced by the work of such writers as Gunder Frank on Latin America. Higgott and Robison point to a most important figure in this shift – Rex Mortimer. The volume *Showcase State* (1973), which uses Indonesia as a case study, provided a critique of the prevailing economic and political orthodoxy embodied in modernization theory. In contrast to the eclecticism of Wertheim, Mortimer used neo-Marxist underdevelopment and dependency perspectives to lay bare the consequences of the activities of transnational corporations, military leaders and compradors in Indonesia. A collection of Mortimer's essays, which explores various themes of social inequality, class, patronage and conflict, was later published posthumously under the title *Stubborn Survivors* (1984).

The influence of radical literature was further consolidated in the launching of the *Journal of Contemporary Asia* in 1970, which published both theoretical debates and case studies on Asia – mainly in the Marxist and neo-Marxist traditions – on such matters as class formation and conflict, the nature and role of the state, relations of dependency, authoritarian regimes and transnational corporations and more recently issues of liberalization and democratisation, rapid industrialization, gender and trade unionism. Among others, articles by Resnick on the Philippines (1973), Gordon on Java (1979), Bell (1978) and Elliott (1978a and 1978b) on Thailand, and Bell and Resnick's (1970) and Catley's (1976) general papers on Southeast Asia have been especially important. The equivalent radical publication in the United States is the *Bulletin of Concerned Asian Scholars*, launched in 1968. Although not extensive, other examples of neo-Marxist analyses can also be found in the work of Jonathan Fast and Jim Richardson (1979) on the Philippines; Joel Kahn (1980), Frijtof Tichelman (1980) and Alfons van der Kraan (1980) on Indonesia; Shamsul (1979) and Mohamed Amin and Malcolm Caldwell (1977) on Malaysia; and Grit Permtanjit (1982) on Thailand.

Recent developments

Political economy and macro-level analyses

Since the early 1980s this radical literature has taken new directions, and several interesting developments have recently taken place that deserve note in any sociological survey. Increasingly, neo-Marxist-inspired writers became dissatisfied with the overly general and abstract analyses of underdevelopment and dependency, and the overemphasis on materialist interpretations of history as well as their essentialist and determinist view of capitalism (see Booth 1994). A gradual reorientation has taken place in order to locate concepts of class and processes of exploitation in local level studies and case material. However, there are still differences in emphasis in regard to the level of analysis employed and the factors and processes identified. Let me take three examples. First comes the work of Higgott and Robison and their colleagues in Australia. This group of political economists has been mainly concerned with various international processes of change, but, in the edited book already mentioned (1985), and in a later companion volume, *Southeast Asia in the 1980s* (Robison, Hewison and Higgott 1987), which focuses on economic issues, they choose the nation-state as the unit of analysis (see also Robison 1989). In the latter volume they argue for 'the inseparability of economic, political and social factors' (1987: 15) and the importance of 'globalization' processes in producing 'powerful domestic forces' in the political and economic arena. Higgott and Robison are quite clear about their enterprise. In large part it attempts to carry on the radical tradition, but it re-evaluates previous work and draws attention to 'some of the theoretical difficulties to be overcome in developing a sustained radical analysis of the transformations in the Southeast Asian region in the 1980s' (1985: 5).

Most of the articles in the 1985 book and those in the sequel examine recent changes in the international economy, specifically the emergence of a 'New International Division of Labour' and the shift towards export-oriented industrialization (EOI) strategies. The essential feature of this process is 'the internationalization of production ... including the relocation of entire industries' and 'specific aspects of industrial production ... from industrialized to developing countries' (1985: 45). Given this context, many of the contributors to the book concentrate on class formation and inter-class relations, the nature and role of the state in capital accumulation, especially in regard to debates about political authoritarianism, and the varieties of 'peripheral' capitalist development within particular Southeast Asian nation-states. Despite the continued emphasis on macro-level analyses, the contributors have moved away from general theoretical discourses on dependency and underdevelopment towards analyses of the specific historical conditions and consequences of capitalist penetration; it is very much a 'post imperialist' literature (Doner, 1991: 829). They argue for the importance of 'a much more complex analysis of the structure of capital' (1985: 51) and the need to recognize that 'national bourgeoisies' are 'in an ambiguous relationship, exhibiting both confrontation and alliance with foreign/international capital' (ibid.: 49). Robison has himself explored these complexities in excellent studies on Indonesian political economy and class (1981, 1986, 1988) and Jomo Kwame Sundaram (1988) and Lim Mah Hui (1981, 1985) have done the same for Malaysia. In his general review of political economic studies of Southeast Asia, Doner also argues that in future 'studies should also be cautious in drawing too sharp a contrast between dependency and self-reliance. Most less developed countries (LDCs) are best understood not as one or the other, but as somewhere on a continuum between the two' (1991: 823).

Despite this concern with the particularities of capitalist development in Southeast Asia, one detects a number of loose ends in the analyses of class and class relations. One reason for this difficulty is that most contributors are still operating at the level of the state, rather than at a local or regional level. Yet their concern to examine specific cases does lead to a more realistic appraisal of the economic opportunities and constraints of particular countries in Southeast Asia. Richard Leaver, for example, argues that integration with capital and reformist strategies of economic development can have 'decided advantages' in peripheral states (Leaver 1985: 162). Garry Rodan, in his analysis of Singapore, concludes that 'there is no preordained role for a country in the international division of labour' because 'within certain constraints, governments can set about to shape and influence this integration' (1985: 188). Kevin Hewison demonstrates that the Thai state has supported the development of domestic capital, and therefore that the Thai bourgeoisie is not 'merely a comprador bourgeoisie' (1985: 287; see also Hewison 1989). On the other hand, Wayne Robinson, in his study of Japanese–Indonesian relations, argues that Indonesia's leaders 'proved less able to regulate Japan's economic priorities' (1985: 197), and that 'while the national bureaucratic forces increased their dependence on Japan, Japan decreased its dependence upon them' (ibid.: 220).

More recently Hewison, Robison and Rodan have edited another volume in political economy (1993), specifically to update their *Southeast Asia in the 1980s* (1987). This latest collection concentrates on the political dimensions of the political economy of various countries in the region, more particularly 'to ask whether there was a shift taking place from authoritarianism to democratic [or parliamentary] forms in Southeast Asia' (Hewison, Rodan, Robison, 1993: 3). Although the major countries of ASEAN are examined in this volume as in the earlier texts, Vietnam makes a welcome appearance for the first time, as does Brunei Darussalam. Importantly, the analyses are set in a comparative framework. What the several chapters demonstrate is that the dynamics of capitalism provide the general context within which political power is exercised in Southeast Asia, but as in their previous analyses, the authors also succeed in illustrating the range of outcomes of these dynamics. The editors conclude that:

> different class structures, variations in the relationships between classes and states, as well as related contrasts in economic structures, all serve to complicate, though not necessarily diminish, the significance of capitalist development for the exercise of power (Robison, Hewison and Rodan 1993: 35).

Overall, the collection of essays adopts a framework based broadly on a structural and historical analysis of political power, although the editors also note 'a degree of healthy heterogeneity in theoretical approach' (Hewison, Rodan and Robison 1993: 7). They caution against cultural determinism.

What is clear is that the processes of liberalization in Southeast Asia are moving at different paces in different circumstances and are profoundly contradictory in nature. The challenges to authoritarianism are themselves patchy and uncertain. In their assessments of the arena of the contending forces for democracy and authoritarianism, the contributors to the volume refer variously to continuing struggles (often long and complex), ambiguous victories, ambiguous socio-economic changes, contradictory structures and tendencies, watersheds, insufficient preconditions, and continued accommodation. As one might expect, the analyses are generally pitched at the level of the nation-state, and broader class structures, political groups and interests.

However, these perspectives are far more satisfying in examining the nature of the state and its relationship to social groups and forces than the concept of an autonomous state (or *beamtenstaat*) developed by Anderson and earlier by Benda using Indonesian material. As Gordon has noted, initial responses to Anderson's interpretation of an Indonesian state structure independent of social classes 'seemed likely to turn the notion into a paradigm as fashionable as the "agricultural involution" of Clifford Geertz' (1993: 444). However, Gordon presents a sustained critique of Anderson's analysis on the basis of the historical evidence from Indonesia.

Agrarian and other transformations: the search for continuity

Moving on now to a second strand in recent sociological re-evaluations of radical theory, we have to consider the work of such writers as

Gillian Hart, Joel Kahn, Andrew Turton and Benjamin White (although Joel Kahn had already been pursuing this line of analysis in the late 1970s [1980, 1982]). This approach is exemplified in the important book by Hart et al., *Agrarian Transformations. Local processes and the state in Southeast Asia* (1989). It is here that we see the emphasis on understanding local level processes in the context of 'larger political and economic forces' (1989: 1) and the concern with 'the conceptual and methodological problems of linking local-level institutional arrangements with larger political-economic systems' (ibid.: xiv). These studies bring together the expertise of rural sociologists, anthropologists and agricultural economists. What is more, in focusing on what is increasingly referred to as 'agrarian differentiation', these writers are especially concerned 'to take explicit account of the power structures within which technological change and commercialization occur' (ibid.: 2). Therefore, they are involved in studies of the relations between the state and its representatives and local-level class relations, power blocs and coalitions. As Turton demonstrates in his work on local power structures and agrarian differentiation in Thailand, there is also an increasing body of indigenous Thai scholarship relevant to his concerns (1989: 71).

The spirit and tone of these recent developments in understanding socio-economic change in Southeast Asia are revealed in a particularly apposite statement by White:

> Flexibility and openness in investigations of concrete situations, in contrast with the abstract rigor of theoretical formulations, seems a natural and healthy consequence of the recognition that economic and social changes occur in actual societies with their own configurations of political forces at local and higher levels, with all kinds of complex and sometimes conflicting processes at work both within and beyond the village, whose interaction with general 'tendencies' results in specific patterns of differentiation (1989: 18–19).

A detailed local level study that demonstrated this dictum is Hart's own monograph, which focuses on political power, access to labour and its allocation and the securing of a livelihood in rural Java, and 'the ways in which local processes are both shaped by and act on wider political-economic forces' (1986: xv). Yet another is Philip Hirsch's case study of environmental politics in Thailand, in which he examines 'a range of social groups', particularly rural people, as part of 'a continuing process of incorporating peripheral areas into a wider political economic sphere of action and influence' (1993: 8). The emphasis is on social differentiation, fluidity, complexity and ambiguity. Elements of this concern to explore complexity are also seen in

Taylor's and Turton's volume *Southeast Asia* (1988). This compilation moves from chapters on the more general issues of the role of the state, and the relations of capital and labour, which are provided predictably by such writers as Robison and Hewison, to local-level studies of 'rural transformation and agrarian differentiation', exemplified in the chapters by Stoler on Java (1988: 111–22), Pelzer White on Vietnam (1988: 165–76) and Anan Ganjanapan on Thailand (1988: 123–32). Other significant studies in the volume focus on the realm of culture and ideology and the ethnic identities and social and historical consciousness of minority groups in Southeast Asia.

Sadly, the literature on gender in Southeast Asia is not substantial (Stivens 1991); much of it has been produced by anthropologists in local-level studies. But a good example of work on gender, which shares, in some respects, the concerns of Turton and others, is that of Noeleen Heyzer (1986). Its premise is that 'the forms and bases of women's subordination are influenced by larger systems that produce inequalities and are embedded in the social positions and the social relationships developed through the interaction of economic processes and dominant socio-cultural systems' (Heyzer 1986: ix). This conclusion is reinforced by a collection of essays edited by Chandler et al. (1988) on the deleterious effects of commercialization and the expansion of capitalist relations of production on the roles and statuses of women (see also Ariffin 1992).

Culture, meaning and experience

The various subjects highlighted by Taylor and Turton lead us finally to another recent development in the sociology of Southeast Asia. Turton has been working in both these areas: namely rural differentiation and class formation, and culture and ideology. But one of the best examples of this latter concern is Robert Hefner's studies of the Tenggerese of East Java (1983a, 1983b, 1990). Informed 'by the weighty legacy of Clifford Geertz's work' (1990: xx) he adopts a hermeneutic, or 'meaning-centred' approach to the understanding of social life, which, in turn, can be traced back to the seminal writings of Max Weber and his emphasis on meaningful action. Wertheim too has noted recently 'a kind of revival of the interest in Weber, though it is not particularly noticeable in studies in Southeast Asia' (n.d.: 11). Hefner's study draws on empirical data at the local and regional level, and, like Turton, he locates both the particularities and patterns of local social life in a historical context and in the context of broader political and economic structures and forces. However, Hefner's emphasis is much more on the social experiences, perceptions, understandings and interpretations of the Tenggerese, as well as on 'the circumstances involved in their sustenance and change'. Aside from laying bare 'a Southeast Asian peasantry's experience of politics and economic change from precolonial times to today', Hefner also wishes 'to account for the practical circumstances that have constrained that peasantry's economic actions and conditioned its awareness' (1990: xii).

One can also point to another example of this kind of analysis, although in the field of gender studies. In a thought-provoking analysis of young Malay female factory workers who have moved from a village environment, Ai-hwa Ong (1987) examines the effects on these young women of capitalist discipline. She explores the links between economic organization, power and cultural attitudes and practices. Ong is concerned with the cultural construction of gender and the contradictory images of sexuality generated in the transformation of female villagers to wage-workers. In particular, she shows how these workers respond to and resist in cultural ways the hierarchies and controls of the factory.

This increasing concern with the details of rural social life also requires us to make brief mention of a substantial literature on Southeast Asia, some of which has relevance to sociological analysis, but which has mainly been written by political scientists, political economists, social and economic historians and anthropologists. I am referring to the body of work on peasantries and their responses to change (cf. King 1978). The main contributions have come from Michael Adas (1974), Sartono Kartodirdjo (1973), Ben Kerkvliet (1977), Samuel Popkin (1979), James Scott (1976, 1985), David Sturtevant (1976) and Reynaldo Ileto (1979), as well as Shamsul (1986) and Lim Teck Ghee (1977). However, the key figure in this work must be James Scott. His book *The Moral Economy of the Peasant. Rebellion and subsistence in Southeast Asia* (1976), in which he located peasant perceptions and evaluations of behaviour and action in the context of the constraints and requirements of subsistence economies, provoked much subsequent debate and critical comment from such commentators as Popkin (1979). Scott's later work, some of it in collaboration with Kerkvliet, has continued to explore various of the dimensions of local-level peasant action, behaviour and motivation in the face of social, economic and political transformations generated by technological change, capitalist penetration and the commercialization of agriculture. He has been especially concerned with what he has termed 'everyday forms of peasant resistance' (Scott and Kerkvliet 1986), and the ways in which small-scale rural producers and wage labourers counter, survive and rationalize the processes, events and personalities that are seen to be undermining their very existence. In short, he examines in detail the 'weapons of the weak' (1985).

It is worth noting that Anderson, in a provocative paper on Southeast Asian politics, argued that in the decade 1974–1984 'only three genuinely distinguished books have been published in North America by specialists' in this field; these comprise Scott's *Moral Economy* (1976) and Kerkvliet's *The Huk Rebellion* (1977), in addition to John Girling's text *Thailand* (1981) (Anderson 1984: 41–2).

A further interesting dimension of this literature on peasant social movements is the scope it provides for writing 'history from below'; in my view (and Anderson's), Ileto's excellent examination of the Philippine peasantry's experience of Holy Week and the meaning of the 'pasyon' (Ileto 1979) gives us local perspectives and details on peasant protest. In addition, I still admire Sartono Kartodirdjo's studies of peasant protest in Java (e.g. 1966, 1973); he has also provided a vital contribution to the attempts to construct a 'domestic or local history' of Southeast Asia.

West meets East: the way forward?

Overall, these various strands of analysis, which link the details of social life as it is experienced and acted out at the local level with the larger processes and forces at the national and international levels, are providing most significant ways forward in understanding social change in Southeast Asia. Emphases may vary between different studies, whether it be concern with local power structures, the details of socioeconomic differentiation, or the culture and ideology of rural groups and communities. But these studies do point to promising developments in sociological work on the region.

In my view, the earlier concerns with concepts such as involution, dualism and pluralism, and their applicability to Southeast Asian social realities, are all but past, although they have been important in the development of sociological thinking about the region. There are now hopeful signs that sociological analyses of Southeast Asia, concentrating on national-level issues of the state, capitalist development and class, power structures, globalization, socio-economic differentiation and culture and ideology at the regional and local levels, promise to achieve international recognition and contribute to wider debates in sociology about the processes of change in developing countries. In their concern with understanding local social experiences in the context of wider forces of change, they also show themselves to be sensitive to the need to combine Western-derived concepts such as 'class' with the particularities of Oriental social forms, values, cultures and ideologies. This does not, however, provide evidence of the development of a distinctive indigenous sociology. To be sure, there are local sociologists working in this field of study, although much of the writing has been produced by scholars from outside the region.

There are, of course, exceptions to this, and one can identify various texts by local scholars, often in local languages, which provide depth and subtlety to our understanding of Southeast Asian cultures and the dynamics of social change. In 1984 Anderson noted 'the rise of indigenous studies, typically in the local vernaculars' (Anderson 1984: 50), and assessed this process as a 'healthy' development. Indeed, it is, and the indigenization of scholarship on Southeast Asia continues apace. Yet I am still forced to conclude that in sociology at least local studies have not, in general, provided much in the way of theoretical developments of regional scope. Anderson rightly praises country-specific studies in local vernaculars, but if an analysis of Thai society is not accessible to a Malaysian, or a treatise on Indonesian culture is remote from a Vietnamese, then we still face formidable problems. Nor, as we have seen, does Western scholarship in sociology fare much better, although, as I have maintained, there are promising signs of recent innovation.

Perhaps what I am asking for overall is a coming together, a collaboration of local and foreign scholars to advance our understanding of Southeast Asian societies and the dramatic transformations they are now experiencing. In this I join in Emmerson's hope that the continued development of locally based scholarship 'should permit "Western" and "Eastern" scholars ... to enrich the perceptions, or at least to add to the variety of preconceptions, on both sides of an increasingly obsolete dichotomy' (Emmerson 1984: 57). In this regard a specifically indigenous Southeast Asian sociology is neither desirable, nor, I think, now possible. Local scholarship on Southeast Asia will inevitably continue to grow in substance and stature, but sociologists from the region will, of necessity, engage in dialogues with outside observers, and the sociological study of Southeast Asia will increasingly embrace the perspectives of both indigenous and foreign scholars.

Note

This chapter is a revised version of 'State-of the-art reviews. The sociology of South-East Asia. A critical review of some concepts and issues', originally published in *Bijdragen tot de Taal-, Land- en Volkenkunde*, 150 (1994): 171–206. This version is published with the kind permission of the Royal Institute of Linguistics and Anthropology in Leiden.

Bibliography

Adas, Michael (1974), *The Burma Delta: economic development and social change on an Asian rice frontier, 1852–1941* (Wisconsin: University of Wisconsin Press).

Alatas, Syed Hussein (1972), *Modernization and Social Change* (London: Angus and Robertson).

Alexander, J. and P. Alexander (1978), 'Sugar, rice and irrigation in colonial Java', *Ethnohistory*, 25: 207–23.

— (1979), 'Labour demands and the "involution" of Javanese agriculture', *Social Analysis*, 3: 22–44.

— (1982), 'Shared poverty as ideology: agrarian relationships in colonial Java', *Man*, 17: 597–619.

Allen, Douglas (1989), 'Antiwar Asian scholars and the Vietnam/Indochina War', *Bulletin of Concerned Asian Scholars*, 21: 112–34.

Amin, Mohamed and Malcolm Caldwell (eds) (1977), *Malaya. The making of a neo-colony* (Nottingham: Spokesman Books).

Anderson, Benedict R. (1982), 'Perspective and method in American research on Indonesia', in Anderson and Kahin (1982): 69–83.

— (1984), 'Politics and their study in Southeast Asia', in Morse (1984): 41–51.

— and Audrey Kahin (eds) (1982), *Interpreting Indonesian Politics: thirteen contributions to the debate* (Ithaca, NY: Cornell University, Southeast Asia Program).

Ariffin, Jamilah (ed.) (1992), *Women and Development in Malaysia* (Petaling Jaya: Pelanduk Publications).

Bachtiar, Harsja W. (1973), 'The religion of Java: a commentary', *Madjalah Ilmu-Ilmu Sastra Indonesia*, 5: 85–118.

Bell, Peter (1978), '"Cycles" of class struggle in Thailand', *Journal of Contemporary Asia*, 8: 51–79.

— (1982), 'Western conceptions of Thai society: the politics of American scholarship', *Journal of Contemporary Asia*, 12: 61–74.

— and Stephen A. Resnick (1970), 'The contradictions of post-war development in Southeast Asia', *Journal of Contemporary Asia*, 1: 37–49.

Boeke, J. H. (1953), *Economics and Economic Policy of Dual Societies, as exemplified by Indonesia* (New York: Institute of Pacific Relations).

— (1980), 'Dualism in colonial society', in Evers, 1980a: 26–37.

Booth, David (ed.) (1994), *Rethinking Social Development. Theory, research and practice* (Harlow, Essex: Longman Scientific and Technical).

Brown, D. E. (1970), *Brunei, The Structure and History of a Bornean Malay Sultanate*, Monograph of the Brunei Museum Journal 2-II (Brunei: Brunei Museum).

Burger, D. H. (1948–49), 'Structuurveranderingen in de Javaanse samenleving', *Indonesië* 2: 381–98, 521–37; 3: 1–18, 101–23, 225–50, 381–9, 512–34.

Carroll, John J. (1968), *Changing Patterns of Social Structure in the Philippines 1896–1963* (Quezon City: Ateneo de Manila University Press).

Catley, Bob (1976), 'The Development of underdevelopment in Southeast Asia', *Journal of Contemporary Asia*, 6: 54–74.

Chandler, Glen, Norma Sullivan and Jan Branson (eds) (1988), *Development and Displacement: women in Southeast Asia*, Centre of Southeast Asian Studies Papers 18 (Clayton, Vic: Monash University).

Chen, Peter S. J. (ed.) (1983), *Singapore. Development policies and trends* (Singapore: Oxford University Press).

Cordero, Felicidad V. and Isabel S. Panopio (1969), *General Sociology. Focus on the Philippines* (Quezon City: Ken Incorporated).

Doner, Richard F. (1991), 'Approaches to the politics of economic growth in Southeast Asia', *Journal of Asian Studies*, 50: 818–49.

Elliott, D. (1978a), 'The Socio-economic formation of modern Thailand', *Journal of Contemporary Asia*, 8: 21–50.

— (1978b), *Thailand: origins of military rule* (London: Zed Press).

Elson, R. (1978), *The Cultivation System and 'Agricultural Involution'*, Centre of Southeast Asian Studies Working Paper 14 (Clayton, Vic: Monash University).

— (1984), *Javanese Peasants and the Colonial Sugar Industry: impact and change in an East Java Residency, 1830–1940* (Singapore: Oxford University Press).

Embree, John F. (1980), 'Thailand: a loosely structured social system', in Evers (1980a): 164–71.

Emmerson, Donald K. (1984), 'Beyond Western surprise: thoughts on the evolution of Southeast Asian studies', in Morse (1984): 52–9.

Evers, Hans-Dieter (ed.) (1969), *Loosely Structured Social Systems: Thailand in comparative perspective*, Southeast Asia Studies Cultural Report Series no. 17, (New Haven, CT: Yale University).

— (ed.) (1973), *Modernization in Southeast Asia* (Singapore: Institute of Southeast Asian Studies/Oxford University Press).

— (ed.) (1980a), *Sociology of Southeast Asia: readings on social change and development*, Kuala Lumpur: Oxford University Press.

— (1980b), 'Ethnic and class conflict in urban Southeast Asia', in Evers 1980a: 121–4.

— (1980c), 'Group conflict and class formation in Southeast Asia', in Evers 1980a: 247–61.

— and Peter S. J. Chen (eds) (1978), *Studies in ASEAN Sociology: urban society and social change* (Singapore: Chopmen Enterprises).

— and Sharon Siddique (eds) (1993), *Religious Revivalism in Southeast Asia*, special issue of *Sojourn*, 8, 1.

Fast, Jonathan and Jim Richardson (1979), *Roots of Dependency. Political and economic revolution in 19th century Philippines* (Quezon City: Foundation for Nationalist Studies).

Fischer, Joseph (ed.) (1973), *Foreign Values and Southeast Asian Scholarship* (Berkeley: University of California, Center for South and Southeast Asian Studies).

Fox, James J., Ross Garnaut, Peter McCawley and J. A. C. Mackie (eds) (1980), *Indonesia. Australian perspectives* (Canberra: Australian National University, Research School of Pacific Studies).

Furnivall, J. S. (1939), *Netherlands India: a study of plural economy* (Cambridge: Cambridge University Press).

— (1948), *Colonial Policy and Practice: a comparative study of Burma and Netherlands India* (Cambridge: Cambridge University Press).

— (1980), 'Plural Societies', in Evers (1980a): 86–96.

Ganjanapan, Anan (1988), 'Strategies for control of labour in sharecropping and tenancy arrangements', in Taylor and Turton (1988): 123–32.

Geertz, Clifford (1963a), *Peddlers and Princes: social development and economic change in two Indonesian towns* (Chicago and London: University of Chicago Press).

— (1963b), *Agricultural Involution. The processes of ecological change in Indonesia* (Berkeley and Los Angeles: University of California Press).

— (1965), *The Social History of an Indonesian Town* (Cambridge, MA: MIT Press).

— (1984), 'Culture and social change: the Indonesian case', *Man*, 19: 511–32.

Girling, John (1981), *Thailand: society and politics* (Ithaca, NY: Cornell University Press).

Gordon, A. (1979), 'Stages in the development of Java's socio-economic formations, 700–1979', *Journal of Contemporary Asia*, 9: 129–39.

— (1993), 'Imaginary histories and the real thing: a critique of Anderson and Benda on the "autonomous state" in Indonesia', *Journal of Contemporary Asia*, 23: 444–64.

Hainsworth, Geoffrey B. (ed.) (1982), *Village-Level Modernization in Southeast Asia. The political economy of rice and water* (Vancouver and London: University of British Columbia Press).

Hart, Donn V. (ed.) (1978), *Philippine Studies: history, sociology, mass media and bibliography*, Centre for Southeast Asian Studies, Occasional Paper 6 (De Kalb, IL: Northern Illinois University).

Hart, Gillian (1986), *Power, Labor, and Livelihood. Processes of change in rural Java* (Berkeley and Los Angeles: University of California Press).

— Andrew Turton and Benjamin White, with Brian Fegan and Lim Teck Ghee (eds) (1989), *Agrarian Transformations. Local processes and the state in Southeast Asia* (Berkeley and Los Angeles: University of California Press).

Hefner, Robert W. (1983a), 'The problem of preference: ritual and economic change in highland Java', *Man*, 18: 669–89.

— (1983b), 'Ritual and cultural reproduction in non-Islamic Java', *American Ethnologist*, 10: 665–83.

— (1990), *The Political Economy of Mountain Java. An interpretive history* (Berkeley and Los Angeles: University of California Press).

Hewison, Kevin (1985), 'The state and capitalist development in Thailand', in Higgott and Robison (1985): 266–94.

— (1989), *Bankers and Bureaucrats: capital and the role of the state in Thailand*, Southeast Asia Studies, Monograph Series no. 34 (New Haven, CT: Yale University).

— Richard Robison and Garry Rodan (eds) (1993), *Southeast Asia in the 1990s. Authoritarianism, democracy and capitalism* (St. Leonards, NSW: Allen and Unwin).

— Garry Rodan and Richard Robison (1993), 'Introduction: changing forms of state power in Southeast Asia', in Hewison et al. (1993): 2–8.

Heyzer, Noeleen (1986), *Working Women in Southeast Asia: development, subordination and emancipation* (Milton Keynes and Philadelphia: Open University Press).

Higgins, Benjamin (1963), 'Foreword', in Geertz (1963b): vii–xv.

Higgott, R. and R. Robison (eds) (1985), *Southeast Asia. Essays in the political economy of structural change* (London: Routledge and Kegan Paul).

Hirsch, Philip (1993), *Political Economy of Environment in Thailand* (Manila and Wollongong: Journal of Contemporary Asia Publications).

Hollnsteiner, M. (1963), *The Dynamics of Power in a Philippine Municipality* (Quezon City: Community Development Research Council).

Hunt, Chester L. et al. (1954), *Sociology in the Philippine Setting* (Manila: Alemar's).

— et al. (1963), *Sociology in the Philippine Setting*, revised 2nd edn (Quezon City: Phoenix Publishing House).

— et al. (1976), *Sociology in the New Philippine Setting* (Quezon City: Phoenix Press).

— and Dylan Dizon (1978), 'The development of Philippine sociology', in Donn V. Hart (1978): 98–232, and addendum, 232A–232D.

Husin Ali, S. (1981), *The Malays. Their problems and future* (Kuala Lumpur, Singapore and Hong Kong: Heinemann Educational Books).

— (ed.) (1984), *Ethnicity, Class and Development. Malaysia* (Kuala Lumpur: Parsatuan Sains Sosial Malaysia).

Hüsken, F. (1979), 'Landlords, sharecroppers and agricultural labourers: changing labour relations in rural Java', *Journal of Contemporary Asia*, 9: 140–51.

Ileto, Reynaldo Clemena (1979), *Pasyon and Revolution: Popular movements in the Philippines, 1840–1910* (Quezon City: Ateneo de Manila University Press).

Jomo Kwame Sundaram (1988), *A Question of Class, Capital, the State and Uneven Development in Malaya* (New York: Monthly Review Press; Manila: Journal of Contemporary Asia Publishers).

Kahn, J. (1980), *Minangkabau Social Formations. Indonesian peasants and the world economy* (Cambridge: Cambridge University Press).

— (1982), 'Ideology and social structure in Indonesia', in Anderson and Kahin (1982): 92–193; originally published in 1978 in *Comparative Studies in Society and History*.

Kampto Utomo (Sajogya) (1957), *Masjarakat Transmigran Spontan Didaerah W. Sekampung, Lampung* (Jakarta: Penerbitan Universitas).

Kartodirdjo, Sartono (1966), *The Peasants' Revolt of Banten in 1888: its conditions, course and sequel: a case study of social movements in Indonesia* (The Hague: Nijhoff).

— (1973), *Peasant Movements in Rural Java: a study of agrarian unrest in the nineteenth and early twentieth centuries* (Singapore: Oxford University Press).

Kerkvliet, Benedict, J. (1977), *The Huk Rebellion: a study of peasant revolt in the Philippines* (Berkeley, Los Angeles and London: University of California Press.

King, Victor T. (1978), 'Moral economy and peasant uprisings in Southeast Asia', *Cultures et développement*, 10: 123–49.

— (1981), 'Sociology in Southeast Asia: a personal view', *Cultures et développement*, 13: 391–414.

— (1986), 'Review article. Southeast Asia: essays in the political economy of structural change', *Journal of Contemporary Asia*, 16: 520–33.

— (1988), 'Models and realities: Malaysian national planning and East Malaysian development problems', *Modern Asian Studies*, 22: 263–98.

— (1989), 'Social anthropology and sociology', in V. T. King (ed.), *Research on Southeast Asia in the United Kingdom: a survey* (Hull: Association of Southeast Asian Studies in the United Kingdom): 17–26.

Kloos, Peter and Henri J. M. Claessen (eds) (1975), *Current Anthropology in the Netherlands* (Rotterdam: Netherlands Sociological and Anthropological Society).

Koentjaraningrat (1963), 'Review, the religion of Java, Clifford Geertz', *Madjalah Ilmu-Ilmu Sastra Indonesia*, 1: 188–91.

— (1975), *Anthropology in Indonesia: a bibliographical review*, KITLV Bibliographical Series 8 (The Hague: Nijhoff).

Leaver, Richard (1985), 'Reformist capitalist development and the new international division of labour', in Higgott and Robison (1985): 149–71.

Lee, Raymond (ed.) (1986), *Ethnicity and Ethnic Relations in Malaysia*, Center for Southeast Asian Studies Occasional Paper 12 (De Kalb, IL: Northern Illinois University).

Lim Mah Hui (1980), 'Ethnic and class relations in Malaysia', *Journal of Contemporary Asia*, 10: 130–54.

— (1981), *Ownership and Control of the One Hundred Largest Corporations in Malaysia* (Kuala Lumpur: Oxford University Press).

— (1985), 'Contradictions in the development of Malay capital: state, accumulation and legitimation', *Journal of Contemporary Asia*, 15: 37–63.

Lim Teck Ghee (1977), *Peasants and their Agricultural Economy in Colonial Malaya, 1874–1941* (Kuala Lumpur: Oxford University Press).

Locher, G. W. (1961), 'The future and the past: Wertheim's interpretation of Indonesia's social change', *Bijdragen tot de taal-, land- en volkenkunde*, 117: 64–79.

Lyon, M. L. (1970), *Bases of Conflict in Rural Java*, Research Monograph Series no. 3 (Berkeley: University of California Centre for South and Southeast Asia Studies).

Macaraig, Serafin E. (1938), *Introduction to Sociology* (Manila: Educational Supply Company).

Marr, David G. (1973), 'Institutionalized value imbalances in Vietnam studies', in Fischer (1973): 95–102.

Morse, Ronald A. (ed.) (1984), *Southeast Asian Studies: options for the future* (Lanham, MD: University Press of America).

Mortimer, Rex (ed.) (1973), *Showcase State. The illusion of Indonesia's 'accelerated modernisation'* (Sydney: Angus and Robertson).

— (1984), *Stubborn Survivors: dissenting essays on peasants and Third World development*, Monash Papers on Southeast Asia 10 (Clayton, Vic: Monash University Centre of Southeast Asian Studies).

Nagata, Judith A. (1980), 'Perceptions of social inequality in a "plural society"', in Evers (1980a): 125–39.

Namsirichai, Juree and Vicharat Vichit-Vadakan (1973), 'American values and research on Thailand', in Fischer (1973): 82–9.

Nash, Manning (1965), *The Goldern Road to Modernity. Village life in contemporary Burma* (New York: John Wiley and Sons).

Neher, Clark D. (1984), 'The social sciences', in Morse (1984): 129–36.

Ong Ai-hwa (1987), *Spirits of Resistance and Capitalist Discipline: factory women in Malaysia* (Albany: State University of New York Press).

Permtanjit, Grit (1982), *Political Economy of Dependent Capitalist Development: study on the limits of the capacity of the state to rationalize in Thailand* (Bangkok: Social Research Institute, Chulalongkorn University).

Phillips, Herbert P. (1973), 'Some premises of American scholarship on Thailand', in Fischer (1973): 64–81.

Pieterse, Jan Nederveen (ed.) (1992), *Emancipations, Modern and Postmodern* (London: Sage).

Popkin, Samuel (1979), *The Rational Peasant: the political economy of rural society in Vietnam* (Berkeley and Los Angeles: University of California Press).

Preston, P. W. (1987), *Rethinking Development. Essays on development and Southeast Asia* (London and New York: Routledge and Kegan Paul).

Resnick, Stephen A. (1973), 'The second path to capitalism: a model of international development', *Journal of Contemporary Asia*, 3: 133–48.

Reynolds, Craig J. (1987), *Thai Radical Discourse: the real face of Thai feudalism today* (Ithaca, NY: Cornell University Press).

— and Hong Lysa (1983), 'Marxism in Thai historical studies', *Journal of Asian Studies*, 43: 77–104.

Robinson, Wayne (1985), 'Imperialism, dependency and peripheral industrialization: the case of Japan in Indonesia', in Higgott and Robison (1985): 195–225.

Robison, Richard (1981), 'Culture, politics and economy in the political history of the new order', *Indonesia*, 31: 1–29.

— (1986), *Indonesia: the rise of capital* (Sydney: Allen and Unwin).

— (1988), 'Authoritarian states, capital-owning classes and the politics of newly industrializing countries: the case of Indonesia', *World Politics*, 41: 52–74.

— (1989), 'Structures of power and the industrialisation process in Southeast Asia', *Journal of Contemporary Asia*, 19: 371–97.

— Kevin Hewison and Richard Higgott (eds) (1987), *Southeast Asia in the 1980s: the politics of economic crisis* (Sydney, London and Boston: Allen and Unwin).

— Kevin Hewison and Garry Rodan (1993), 'Political power in industrialising capitalist societies: theoretical approaches', in Hewison et al. (1993): 9–38.

Rodan, Garry (1985), 'Industrialization and the Singapore state in the context of the new international division of labour', in Higgott and Robison (1985): 172–94.

Schrieke, B. J. O. (ed.) (1929), *The Effect of Western Influence on Native Civilization in the Malay Archipelago* (Batavia: G. Kolff).

— (1955–57), *Indonesian Sociological Studies: selected writings of B. Schrieke*, 2 vols (The Hague: Van Hoeve).

Scott, James C. (1976), *The Moral Economy of the Peasant. Rebellion and subsistence in Southeast Asia* (New Haven, CT and London: Yale University Press).

— (1985), *Weapons of the Weak: everyday forms of peasant resistance* (New Haven, CT and London: Yale University Press).

— and Benedict J. Tria Kerkvliet (eds) (1986), *Everyday Forms of Peasant Resistance in Southeast Asia* (London: Frank Cass).

Selosoemardjan (1962), *Social Changes in Jogjakarta* (Ithaca, NY: Cornell University Press).

Shamsul, A. B. (1979), 'The development of the underdevelopment of the Malaysian peasantry', *Journal of Contemporary Asia*, 9: 434–54.

— (1986), *From British to Bumiputera Rule: local politics and rural development in peninsular Malaysia* (Singapore: Institute of Southeast Asian Studies).

— (1992), *Malaysia in 2020. One state many nations? Observing Malaysia from Australia* (Bangi: Universiti Kebangsaan Malaysia Department of Anthropology and Sociology).

Skinner, G. William and A. Thomas Kirsch (eds) (1975), *Change and Persistence in Thai Society. Essays in honor of Lauriston Sharp* (Ithaca, NY and London: Cornell University Press).

Stivens, Maila (ed.) (1991), *Why Gender Matters in Southeast Asian Politics*, Centre of Southeast Asian Studies Papers 23 (Clayton, Vic: Monash University).

Stoler, Ann L. (1977), 'Rice harvesting in Kali Loro: a study of class and labor in rural Java', *American Ethnologist*, 4: 678–98.

— (1988), 'Rice harvesting in Kali Loro: a study of class and labor in rural Java', in Taylor and Turton (1988): 111–22.

Sturtevant, David R. (1976), *Popular Uprisings in the Philippines 1840–1940* (Ithaca, NY: Cornell University Press).

Tai Ching Ling (1988), *Housing Policy and High-Rise Living: a study of Singapore's public housing* (Singapore: Chopmen Publishers).

Taylor, John G. and Andrew Turton (eds) (1988), *Southeast Asia*, 'Sociology of Developing Societies' series (Basingstoke and London: Macmillan Education).

Tham Seong Chee (1977), *Malays and Modernization. A sociological interpretation* (Singapore: Singapore University Press).

Tichelman, Frijtof (1980), *The Social Evolution of Indonesia. The Asiatic mode of production and its legacy*, International Institute of Social History, Amsterdam, Studies in Social History 5 (The Hague: Martinus Nijhoff).

Turner, M. M. (1978), 'Interpretations of class and status in the Philippines: a critical evaluation', *Cultures et développement*, 10: 265–96.

Turton, Andrew (1989), 'Local powers and rural differentiation', in Hart et al. (1989): 70–97.

Utrecht, Ernst (1973), 'American sociologists on Indonesia', *Journal of Contemporary Asia*, 3: 39–45.

Van Den Muijzenberg, Otto D. (1975), 'Involution or evolution in central Luzon?', in Kloos and Claessen (1975): 141–55.

— (n.d.), 'Sociology in the Field of Recent Southeast Asian Studies in the Netherlands: a survey of an academic field' (unpublished paper).

— and Willem Wolters (1988), *Conceptualizing Development. The historical-sociological tradition in Dutch non-Western sociology* (Dordrecht: Foris Publications).

Van Der Kraan, Alfons (1980), *Lombok: Conquest, Colonization and Under-development, 1870–1940*, Asian Studies Association of Australia Southeast Asia Publication Series no. 5 (Singapore: Heinemann Asia).

Van Der Kroef, Justus M. (1954), *Indonesia in the Modern World*, 2 vols (Bandung: Van Hoeve).

Van Leur, J. C. (1955), *Indonesian Trade and Society: essays in Asian social and economic history* (The Hague: Van Hoeve).

Van Schaik, Arthur (1986), *Colonial Control and Peasant Resources in Java: agricultural involution reconsidered*, Netherlands Geographical Studies 14 (Amsterdam: University of Amsterdam Institute for Social Geography).

Von Der Mehden, Fred R. (1986), *Religion and Modernization in Southeast Asia* (Syracuse: Syracuse University Press).

Warren, Carol (1985), 'Class and change in rural Southeast Asia', in Higgott and Robison (1985): 128–45.

Weightman, George (1975), 'Sociology in the Philippines', *Solidarity*, 9: 43–58.

— (1978), 'Comments' [on the chapter on Sociology in Chester L. Hunt and Dylan Dizon], in Hart (1978): 178–9.

Wertheim, W. F. (1956/1959), *Indonesian Society in Transition. A study of social change* (The Hague: Van Hoeve).

— (1962), 'The past revived (reply to G. W. Locher)', *Bijdragen tot de taal-, land-en volkenkunde*, 118: 183–92.

— (1964a), *East–West Parallels: sociological approaches to modern Asia* (The Hague: Van Hoeve).

— (1964b), 'Peasants, peddlers and princes in Indonesia. A review article', *Pacific Affairs*, 37: 307–311.

— (1969), 'From aliran towards class struggle in the countryside of Java', *Pacific Viewpoint*, 10: 1–17.

— (1973), *Dawning of an Asian Dream. Selected articles on modernization and emancipation*, Antropologisch/Sociologisch Centrum, Afdeling Zuid- en Zuidoost Azië, Publication 20 (Amsterdam: Universiteit van Amsterdam).

— (1974), *Evolution and Revolution. The rising waves of emancipation* (Harmondsworth: Penguin Books).

— (1992), 'The state and the dialectics of emancipation', in Pieterse (1992): 257–81.

— (1993), 'Towards a global integration of the social sciences', in W. F. Wertheim, *Comparative Essays on Asia and the West* (Amsterdam: VU University Press): 1–5.

— (n.d.), 'The Contribution of Weberian Sociology to Studies of Southeast Asia' (unpublished paper).

— et al. (eds) (1958), *The Indonesian Town. Studies in urban sociology* (The Hague: Van Hoeve).

— et al. (eds) (1966), *Indonesian Economics. The concept of dualism in theory and practice*, 2nd edn; first published 1961 (The Hague: Van Hoeve).

White, Benjamin (1983a), *'Agricultural involution' and its critics: twenty years after Clifford Geertz*, Working Paper 6 (The Hague: Institute of Social Studies).

— (1983b), '"Agricultural involution" and its critics: twenty years after', *Bulletin of Concerned Asian Scholars*, 15: 18–31.

— (1989), 'Problems in the empirical analysis of agrarian differentiation', in Hart et al. (1989): 15–30.

White, Christine Pelzer (1988), 'Socialist transformation of agriculture and gender relations: the Vietnamese case', in Taylor and Turton (1988): 165–76.

Wiegersma, Nancy (1982), 'Vietnam and the Asiatic mode of production', *Journal of Contemporary Asia*, 12: 19–33.

Wolters, Willem (1984), *Politics, Patronage and Class Conflict in Central Luzon* (Quezon City: New Day).

Worsley, Peter (1984), *The Three Worlds. Culture and world development*, (London: Weidenfeld and Nicolson).

Yengoyan, Aram A. and Perla Q. Makil (eds) (1984), *Philippine Society and the Individual. Selected essays of Frank Lynch, 1949–1976*, Michigan Papers on South and Southeast Asia 24 (Ann Arbor: University of Michigan Center for South and Southeast Asian Studies).

Zamora, Mario D., Donald J. Baxter and Robert Lawless (eds) (1982), *Social Change in Modern Philippines. Perspectives, problems and prospects*, 2 vols (Manila: Rex Book Store for St. Mary's College of Bayombang).

6 Economics

John Walton

The discipline of economics, when looked at within the Southeast Asian context, falls mainly within one branch of the main discipline, namely development economics. Precisely what comprises the field of development economics is open to question, but over time it has spread its wings to encompass a growing number of interests.

In the preface to the first edition of his now widely used economic development text, Todaro noted that the 'very meaning of the term "development" has been altered from an almost exclusive association with aggregate economic growth to a much broader interpretation that encompasses questions of poverty, inequality and unemployment also' (Todaro 1977: xv). In fact the subject matter is far wider and includes problems of rapid population growth, agricultural transformation and rural development, education and human resources, relationships between developed and less developed countries, trade, finance, foreign investment and foreign aid.

Not surprisingly, with the broadening of the subject area there has been an increasing amount of research and writing under the general development umbrella, embracing other disciplines such as sociology, anthropology, politics and geography. This, for the most part, is welcome, since interdisciplinary or multidisciplinary studies have provided and will continue to provide valuable insights into and a greater understanding of the development process. Indeed, in many areas it would be impossible to achieve a rational or realistic perspective without combined studies. However, while not wishing to deny or undermine the importance of interdisciplinary approaches, the concern here is primarily with providing an overview of the dominant issues and debates within the economic context, albeit in a broad rather than narrow view.

Thirlwall, in another widely used economic development text, quotes from Theodore Schultz, the Nobel Prize-winning economist, who has said of development economics:

This branch of economics has suffered from several intellectual mistakes. The major mistake has been the presumption that standard economic theory is inadequate for understanding low-income countries and that a separate economic theory is needed. Models for this purpose were widely acclaimed until it became evident that they at best were intellectual curiosities. The reaction of some economists was to turn to cultural and social explanations for the alleged poor economic performance of low income countries. Quite understandably, cultural and behavioural scholars are uneasy about this use of their studies. Fortunately the intellectual tide has begun to turn. Increasing numbers of economists have come to realise that standard economic theory is just as applicable to scarcity problems that confront low income countries as to the corresponding problems of high income countries (Thirlwall 1983: xiii).

Whilst agreeing that not all standard economic theory is useful or relevant for an understanding of the development process, Thirlwall makes no apology for the use of conventional theory and its application to developing economies.

Likewise, Meier's highly regarded economic development course book *Leading Issues in Economic Development* (1984) – consisting of readings supplemented by contextual notes to give cohesion and direction – concentrates on strategic issues of central concern to economists.

Although such writers as Todaro, Thirlwall and Meier differ in their emphases, or the ways in which they combine descriptive and analytical approaches, each of them nevertheless tends primarily to examine development from the perspective of standard economic theory, or, put another way, from the viewpoint of the trained economist. Unfortunately, while there is a problem of formulating a precise definition of economic development, there is a similar problem in relation to the discipline of economics itself: it can be viewed in a rather narrow sense, or within the bounds of a broader notion of political economy. When economics is opened up to involve the political arena, more radical views are forthcoming. Wilbur and Jameson's book of readings (1992) distils a wide variety of such views. Wilbur notes that:

> Political economy recognises that man is a social being whose arrangements for the production and distribution of economic goods must be, if society is to be livable, consistent with congruent institutions of family, political, and cultural life. As a result, a political economy analysis must incorporate such noneconomic influences as social structures, political systems, and cultural values as well as such factors as technological change and distribution of income and wealth (Wilbur and Jameson 1992: xvi).

Until relatively recently, the economic literature on Southeast Asia has not been particularly extensive, even taking the discipline within its broader definition. It is only over the last twenty-five years or so that a considerable volume of literature has begun to emerge. There are several possible reasons for this. Development economics itself is a relatively new branch of economics, in large measure a response to the efforts of newly established independent governments to diversify their economies away from dependence on the former colonial powers. Another reason for the dearth of early economic literature on Southeast Asia is the relatively late progress of economic development in the region. Although countries such as Burma and Indonesia achieved political independence in the period immediately after the Second World War, political upheavals meant that little development was possible in the strict economic sense, since resources were diverted to military expenditure and attempts to maintain or restore political stability. Malaysia and Singapore did not gain independence from Britain until 1957 and 1963 respectively. Thailand, though never a colony, also remained undeveloped until the late 1950s. Prolonged conflict in Vietnam, Laos and Cambodia precluded a meaningful economic development agenda in Indochina. Paradoxically the Philippines, which in the late 1950s appeared the most promising candidate for economic development, later became embroiled in political problems, which tended to overshadow economic issues, at a crucial time. This was in the 1960s, when it was increasingly recognized that earlier development approaches based on import substitution were inadequate. As a consequence the Philippines failed to transform itself into an economy that could compete in international markets. Meanwhile, South Korea and Taiwan, bolstered by massive flows of military aid from the United States, adopted outward-looking, export-oriented strategies that tended to attract more attention from development economists in this earlier period. It is not until the 1970s that a more substantial flow of economic literature specifically concerning Southeast Asia began. As the region increasingly became associated with economic dynamism, this stimulated a growing amount of economic analysis and commentary.

Another important factor influencing the flow of economic literature concerning the region from the early 1970s was the broadening of the subject area. Earlier arguments that economic growth would inevitably be accompanied by a 'trickle-down effect' that would solve problems of poverty and income distribution lost their credibility when high economic growth rates were paralleled by a growing gap between the rich and the poor. The emergence of the 'basic needs' approach opened up and enlarged the economic debate. The apparent success of the Chinese commune system in the 1950s and 1960s in reducing social inequality and providing basic needs issued a challenge to the capitalist system to prove it could do likewise. As a consequence, economic development strategies became more elaborate and complex, creating the scope for a wider economic debate.

In terms of the economic literature relating to Southeast Asia, three major sources are identifiable. First, there have been a number of important publications from official organizations including the World Bank, the Economic and Social Commission for Asia and the Pacific (ESCAP), the Asian Development Bank (ADB), and government publications such as development plans. Books and articles written by Western scholars have constituted a second important medium for economic debate, and more recently a third source has been analysis by local Southeast Asian scholars. While the latter may often have taken a more parochial view, they have generally tended to follow Western economic thought rather than develop a particularly indigenous approach, probably because most local economists were trained in the United States, Europe or Australia.

The recent expansion of the economic literature relating to Southeast Asia can be traced back to the establishment of the Economic Commission for Asia and the Far East (ECAFE), which was renamed ESCAP in 1974. As early as 1950, ECAFE issued its first *Economic and Social Survey of Asia and the Far East* (ECAFE 1950). Although early issues of this survey were mainly descriptive, they nevertheless provided a useful review of the current situation in Asia not readily available elsewhere. In 1957 ECAFE began producing, in addition to its annual review, studies of some of the major problems of economic development in the region. Initially focused on post-war problems, these studies were expanded to cover many other important facets of development including trade, import substitution and export diversification, agricultural and rural development, human resources and education, finance and foreign investment.

In 1966 the establishment of the Asian Development Bank in Manila initiated another important stream of economic publications on the region. First contributions included the *Asian Agricultural Survey*, *Southeast Asia's Economy in the 1970s*, and the *Regional Transport Survey* (Asian Development Bank 1968; 1971; 1972) Since 1983 it has published the *Asian Development Bank Review*, which provides a forum for both Western and local economists to examine what are perceived to be contemporary and important economic issues or problems. From 1989 *Asian Development Outlook*, another ADB publication, has provided a more detailed analysis of economic conditions within the region, and has focused on particular areas of interest such as poverty and environmental issues.

While the ambit of organizations such as ESCAP and ADB

encompasses the whole Asia–Pacific region, they have nevertheless been able to address economic issues in Southeast Asia more specifically than the widely stretched World Bank. With funds and resources far beyond the dreams of the academic researcher, these organizations were able to recruit professional economists, and indeed other non-economic specialists who because of their official status were able to gain access to data often denied to the individual academic. Perhaps more importantly, economic missions from the organizations stimulated data production that might otherwise not have happened, and set in motion data producing systems which resulted in a wider range of more consistent and reliable statistics.

Initially, many reports on Southeast Asian economies by international organizations were restricted, or classified as confidential, mainly to respect local sensitivities. However, over time, there has been a greater willingness to publish such reports for a wider readership. Thus many important country studies have originated, directly or indirectly, from research conducted by the World Bank, ADB, ESCAP and occasionally other United Nations organizations such as UNIDO (Industrial Development Organization) and FAO (Food and Agriculture Organization).

The resources available to official organizations, and also the more or less guaranteed access to, or cooperation from, governments anxious to receive international loans, permitted comprehensive studies to be produced, and helped to build up economic knowledge of the region. However, official publications also have drawbacks. In the case of country-specific economic appraisals, critical analysis has usually been moderated (or omitted in the case of material made available for general publication), so as not to offend national sensitivities. Furthermore, institutions such as the World Bank suffer from inherent biases that may prejudice their economic appraisals or recommendations. For instance, the president of the World Bank is a United States appointee, and it takes little perception to identify changes in World Bank policy that have coincided with or followed trends in American politics, such as the emphasis on privatization since the 1980s. So long as this is recognized it presents no great problems: most economic literature reflects its author's political beliefs to a greater or lesser extent. Discerning readers should be able to draw their own conclusions, or refer to publications which are critical of World Bank approaches and analyses, in order to achieve a more balanced view.

The watershed for a greater understanding of economic development in Southeast Asia can be traced to the period from the end of the 1960s to the early 1970s. It was at this time that economic development studies begin to come of age. Over the previous twenty to twenty-five years, feedback from experience and the learning process enabled economists to restructure their basic analyses to make them more appropriate to the particular conditions found in underdeveloped countries. In essence, there was a shift away from preoccupation with aggregate economic growth towards greater emphasis on identifying and addressing new emerging problems affecting the economic growth process, such as the unprecedentedly high population growth rates. At an earlier stage, the rapid post-war recovery of Western Europe (based on large inputs of capital under the Marshall Plan) had generated an optimism that similar approaches would succeed in underdeveloped countries. This optimism proved to be unfounded, mainly due to the inability at the time to perceive fully the degree of technological backwardness, lack of absorptive capacity and other growth-inhibiting factors prevailing in the less developed areas. By 1970 the complexities and problems of economic development in Southeast Asian countries were increasingly recognized, though not necessarily thoroughly understood. A major contribution to the understanding of Southeast Asian economies came in 1971 with the ADB's publication of *Southeast Asia's Economy in the 1970s* (Asian Development Bank 1971).

The Fourth Ministerial Conference on the Economic Development of Southeast Asia held in Bangkok in 1969 requested the ADB 'to analyse the nature of the major problems which confront the nations in the region in the seventies and explore the possibilities of individual and cooperative action by governments to effect their solution' (Hla Myint 1972: 15). While the study was not intended to produce detailed or definitive reports on the individual economies it was, however, meant 'to focus attention on key problems of development and study relevant policy alternatives and options open to the countries in dealing with the identified key problems on a national or sub-regional basis' (Hla Myint 1972: 15). The study identified six key sectors: The Green Revolution; The Manufacturing Industry Sector; Foreign Economic Relations (trade); The Impact of Private Foreign Investment; Aspects of Population Policy; and The Impact of the End of Vietnam Hostilities and the Reduction of British Military Presence in Malaysia and Singapore. Appointed consultants supervised and produced reports on the six key areas while the overall report incorporating the consultants findings was drawn up by Hla Myint, who later in 1972 summarized the report with a lucid account and analysis of its main conclusions (published as Hla Myint 1972). As the first large-scale survey of Southeast Asia's economy, the ADB report helped fill a yawning gap in the economic knowledge of the region, as well as broadening the debate to include key problem areas.

Indonesia

If we turn away from economic research primarily generated by official bodies towards academic research, the focus moves on to individual countries. Because of their large resources, official organizations may have greatly enhanced economic research on Southeast Asia, but the academic contribution has in some cases surpassed official coverage, and has made available more detailed analysis. This is particularly true with regard to studies of the Indonesian economy. The first major impact came from North American scholars such as Canadian economist Benjamin Higgins and Bruce Glassburner from Cornell, who in the immediate post-independence years replaced Dutch advisers and intellectuals who were no longer trusted by their former colonial subjects. Higgins had an important influence on economic affairs in Indonesia, at first as economic adviser to the Jakarta government and from 1954 as director of the Indonesia Project at the Massachusetts Institute of Technology (MIT). Despite the presence in Indonesia in the 1950s of talented foreign and upcoming Indonesian economists, Higgins makes a telling point when referring to the disappointing results of the First Five Year Plan (1956–60): 'none of us, Indonesian or foreigner, knew much about the process of economic development' (Higgins 1990: 40). Higgins draws attention to the broad array of social scientists, including Geertz, who were involved in this important period of formulating new directions for Indonesian studies. He notes that the entry of North American social scientists into the field of Indonesian studies produced an explosion of literature, the output of which unfortunately slackened with the deterioration of relations between Indonesia and the United States in the early 1960s (Higgins 1990: 43). Fortunately, however, Australia's growing interest in its large northern neighbour helped fill the gap.

Based at the Australian National University (ANU) in Canberra, Heinz Arndt initiated and directed what has proved to be the most successful and consistent research programme relating to the economy of any Southeast Asian country. Despite the fact that prevailing political and economic conditions gave rise for little optimism regarding economic research, Arndt's initial determination in 1964 was rewarded following the dramatic political changes in late 1965. Suharto's New Order, with its clear priority on economic rehabilitation and development, suddenly attached a new importance and direction to economic issues. Arndt bemoans the fact that the limited number of professional economists interested in Indonesia were either drafted into the government machinery as prominent policy advisers, or were recruited by the World Bank, Ford Foundation and other well-heeled institutions: this limited the number of qualified researchers for the ANU programme (Arndt 1990: 48). A number of Indonesian economic scholars had been trained in the United States and were to become influential in future economic decision-making under Suharto. These economic technocrats became known as 'the Berkeley Mafia', even though many had received their training elsewhere in the United States, including Cornell University. Perhaps one fortunate consequence of Arndt's initial problems in recruiting well-qualified economists was that he himself was compelled to become an active member of the research team, rather than restricting himself to his earlier perceived role as administrator.

Ford Foundation funding enabled Arndt gradually to build up an Indonesia Project within the ANU's Research School of Pacific Studies. The *Bulletin of Indonesian Economic Studies* (*BIES*), launched in June 1965, at the height of economic chaos in Indonesia, eventually became the dominant and leading journal of Indonesian economic research – a position it still maintains. The arrival at the ANU in 1970 of R. M. Sundrum, former professor of economics and statistics at Rangoon University, made up for Arndt's admitted weakness in quantitative techniques, and together they were able to devote considerable effort to enhancing the academic stature of *BIES* (Arndt 1990: 51). However, it was the Indonesia Project's own research students who from the mid-1970s were able to ensure the continued success of *BIES* and Indonesian economic studies in general through a stream of publications initially based on their own empirical research as Ph.D. students, but also later as staff members. Arndt mentions Peter McCawley, Anne Booth and Hal Hill as former students returning 'home' to the ANU to play important roles in its work on Indonesia (Arndt 1990: 52).

While the new political climate in Indonesia after 1965 permitted serious economic research, the legacy of the preceding years under Sukarno presented some immediate problems. Financial chaos, including annual inflation at over 600 per cent, badly run-down infrastructure, massive foreign debts and balance of payment problems provided an unstable background for economic analysis. The lack of economic data (for the most part publication of statistics had been suppressed under Sukarno) seriously compounded economists' difficulties. Longer-established observers of Indonesia such as Jamie Mackie felt able to assess the Sukarno era, and Ingrid Palmer was also able to give some insight into industrial economic conditions based on fieldwork during the later Sukarno period (see Mackie 1967; Palmer 1972). However, the mainstream of economic enquiry became focused on the economic policies formulated to rehabilitate the Indonesian economy and the start of development planning with the introduction of Repelita 1 in 1969.

During the 1970s, as well as its regular Survey of Recent Developments, *BIES* covered an increasingly wide range of both macro-economic and micro-economic issues at a time when little information had been published on the Indonesian economy. By 1981, sufficient time had elapsed since Suharto's accession to power to allow Anne Booth and Peter McCawley to assemble a collection of papers that provided a broad but detailed analysis of important economic issues during this vital period of Indonesian economic development (Booth and McCawley 1981). More recently, Booth repeated the exercise with the publication of *The Oil Boom and After – Indonesian Economic Policy and Performance in the Suharto Era* (1992). This is a similarly valuable reference for both Indonesia specialists and those with broader Southeast Asian interests.

Hal Hill, who took over editorship of *BIES* in 1990, has like Booth contributed prolifically to Indonesian economic literature. Hill (1989) provides a broad understanding of Indonesia's vast and far-stretched economy from regional and provincial perspectives.

Although the ANU has played a dominant role in shaping the course of Indonesian economic studies, especially in the Suharto era, there has also been a steady stream of commentary from Indonesian scholars through the long-established journal *Ekonomi dan Keuangan Indonesia*, launched by Sumitro Djojohadikusumo in the early 1950s. This has been the outlet for a growing number of Indonesian scholars over the last three decades – a far cry from the 1950s when Benjamin Higgins described Sumitro, then minister of finance, as 'virtually the only Indonesian who could be regarded as a fully qualified professional economist' (Higgins 1990: 44). Arndt also acknowledges the contribution of Indonesian scholars to *BIES*, and their helpful cooperation with foreign scholars visiting Indonesia (Arndt 1990: 50). Indonesian scholars are now increasingly providing important contributions to the economic debate concerning their country. Though often trained in the United States, Indonesian academics collaborating with the ANU play a vital role in ensuring that *BIES* remains the leading journal on Indonesian economic affairs. There is also a growing amount of economic literature in *Bahasa Indonesia*. In the first half of the 1990s, Sjahrir, director of the Institute for Economic and Financial Research in Jakarta, has produced seven books containing papers written by himself. In a 700-page volume – *Pemikiran, Pelaksanaan, dan Perintisan Pembangunan Ekonomi* (*Concepts, Implementation, and Pioneering in Economic Development*) – M. Arsjad Anwar, Thee Kian Wie and Iwan Jaya Azis have compiled a collection of readings, mainly by Indonesian authors, which cover a wide range of economic debate concerning Indonesian economic policy since 1966 (Anwar, Thee and Azis 1992).

The Philippines

In the immediate post-war years the Philippine economy attracted more attention than other Southeast Asian countries'. President Roxas' desire to restructure the country away from colonial agrarianism to a diversified industrial economy appeared to be well on course in the 1950s as the process of import substitution brought significant structural change. Meanwhile most other Southeast Asian economies remained within colonial networks, or were embroiled in political struggles that prevented serious attempts to promote economic development. However, the failure to sustain this thrust into industrial development gradually became the principal focus for analysis of the Philippine economy. As John Wong suggests, 'the many problems experienced by the Philippines can be used as examples par excellence to highlight the shortcomings of the import substitution industrialisation strategy' (Wong 1979: 68; Power and Sicat 1971: 102–15).

Unfortunately, during the 1960s and subsequently, the Philippines seemed unable to learn from its earlier problems. By way of contrast, other Southeast Asian countries started to lay the foundations for their later economic success, which increasingly diverted economic attention away from the Philippines. In the 1970s and 1980s, economic literature relating to the Philippines mainly revolves around policies advocated by the International Monetary Fund (IMF) and World Bank. These institutions attempted to correct structural imbalances and put forward policy prescriptions which, however, drew considerable criticism from both indigenous and outside commentators (see Cheetham and Hawkins 1976; World Bank 1980; World Bank 1987). Most critics suggest that far from solving the Philippines economic problems, IMF and World Bank recommendations merely supported the conditions responsible for the Philippines' economic ills, particularly the vested interests of the business oligarchy and transnational corporations. Broad (1988) provides a clear and concise analysis of the criticisms levelled against the World Bank. There are numerous other critiques from both foreign and indigenous scholars who are largely sympathetic to nationalist claims regarding issues of dependency and underdevelopment.

Not surprisingly, given its colonial past, the Philippines has attracted most interest from American economists but there has been a consistent flow of economic debate within the country, and the *Philippine Economic Journal* has provided an outlet for research on a wide variety of topics since 1962. Gerardo Sicat established himself as a leading academic economic writer before joining the Marcos administration. Scholars associated with the Philippine Institute for Development

Studies, such as Alburo and Bautista, have continued to produce analyses of economic performance.

Thailand

Just as Suharto's administration in Indonesia rapidly brought about a major change in economic direction, the accession to power of General Sarit in 1958 had a profound impact on Thailand's economy. Following a period of vacillation with no clear distinction between state and private enterprise, Sarit's clear commitment to private enterprise and foreign investment paved the way for growing outside economic interest in Thailand. Despite frequent changes of government, often by coup d'état, Thailand's economic policy has remained remarkably consistent. In its transition from import substitution to export promotion, Thailand has followed a fairly conventional path and in doing so has generated less controversy than many other countries: this is one reason why the economic literature on Thailand is relatively small compared with that on some other ASEAN countries. Nevertheless, useful World Bank studies include Akrasanee (1977) and Binswanger and Uthaisri (1983). Marzouk (1972) is a good study of Thailand's economy in the 1960s. Jansen (1990) analysed Thailand from a financial perspective rather than using the usual structural approach. Since the late 1980s, however, high economic growth rates based on manufactured exports have stimulated debate over Thailand's potential as a newly industrialized country. There is also considerable interest in the failure of the trickle-down effect to close glaring regional income disparities: much debate has focused on the hegemony of Bangkok and increasing problems of urban congestion, pollution, environment and decentralization.

Economic research on Thailand has suffered from a language barrier to a much more significant extent than has been the case in other ASEAN countries. Thus local scholars, well known within Thailand, have gained less international exposure, or where this has been achieved it has usually been through attachment to international institutions such as the World Bank or ADB. Fortunately this situation is changing and more studies in English are beginning to filter through, especially from the Thailand Development Research Institute (see Loha-unchit 1990; Tambunlertchai 1990).

Malaysia

Since the inauguration in 1971 of Malaysia's controversial New Economic Policy (NEP), which aims to redistribute wealth along ethnic lines, the literature relating to the Malaysian economy has grown immensely. Preoccupation with the ethnic dimension of the NEP has to a large extent tended to overshadow economic issues which in other circumstances would have been the subject of more conventional analysis, such as structural change and industrial diversification. Although Malaysia has not been the beneficiary of a consistent economic analysis similar to that provided by *BIES* for Indonesia, a range of publications have provided a reasonably thorough appraisal of the country's economy. To a considerable extent, the smallness of the country, in terms of both land area and population, makes it a relatively easy task to understand and analyse the main issues, notwithstanding the ethnic complications. This is especially true of Peninsular Malaysia, which tends to be studied separately from the East Malaysian states of Sarawak and Sabah. With the majority of Malays in rural areas, and the main core of poverty also identified as rural, a significant part of the literature has focused on rural development, including the role and achievements of government agencies such as the Federal Land Development Authority (FELDA). Other government bodies promoting *bumiputra* (indigenous) economic interests also figure prominently in the literature. A major theme has been whether the NEP actually achieved its principal redistributional objective of enriching the *bumiputra* community as a whole, or merely succeeded in creating a relatively small wealthy Malay elite. While the ethnic dimension has to some extent diverted attention from other fundamental changes that have occurred within the economy, given the focus on ethnically based issues in the New Economic Policy, it is understandable that socio-economic analysis has received considerable attention.

Since independence, local academics have dominated Malaysian economic analysis. David Lim made an extremely valuable contribution with two books of readings (1975, 1983), which gathered together a wide range of previously published leading articles. More recently, the political economist Jomo K. S. has clearly established himself as the leading academic commentator on economic affairs (see Jomo 1985, 1989, 1990).

Singapore

As a small city-state, analysis of Singapore's economy has required a different approach. Its successful transition to developed country status is well documented (see, for example, Lim Chong-Yah 1984). But the absence of a large, backward agricultural sector has precluded economic analysis conceived within the dualistic framework (comprising modern and traditional sectors) which has often been applied to other Southeast

Asian countries. Many of the thorny economic problems faced by other Southeast Asian countries such as regional or provincial economic development and agrarian reform have not presented themselves, because of the small size of the economy, and therefore many potentially contentious issues have simply not arisen. The dynamic role of the government, its well-managed and efficient public enterprises and the role of multinational corporations in supporting export-led manufacturing growth have attracted most attention in the economic literature on Singapore. Linda Low and Toh Mun Heng from the National University of Singapore (NUS) have been prominent amongst local academic economists, having worked on a broad range of topics relating to Singapore (see Toh and Low 1990). John Wong, also at NUS, has taken a broader view of the region (1979).

The establishment in Singapore of the Institute of Southeast Asian Studies (ISEAS) in 1968 and later that Institute's ASEAN Economic Research Unit (AERU, which has published the *ASEAN Economic Bulletin* since 1983) have greatly enhanced research on Southeast Asian economic affairs in general, rather than Singapore's economy specifically. By providing a well-connected regional base for visiting scholars, from both within and outside the region, ISEAS and AERU have done much to further the economic understanding of Southeast Asia. In addition to the *ASEAN Economic Bulletin*, ISEAS publishes the *Southeast Asian Affairs* yearbook, which contains many items of specialized economic interest.

Southeast Asia's socialist economies

Elsewhere in the region, economic studies have been constrained by the nature of the Southeast Asian socialist states' national economies. The autarkic approach taken by the Burmese regime until the late 1980s, the lack of reliable economic data, and the existence of a thriving parallel economy in the form of a black market have all helped to frustrate economic analysis of Burma (Myanmar). However, Steinberg made a timely contribution (1981), and Hill and Jayasuriya (1986) provide an analysis of the Burmese economy in the 1970s. The commitment since 1988 to follow market principles has stimulated more research, but economic reforms are slow in coming (see Mya Than and Tan 1990). The faster pace of economic reform in Vietnam has generated greater economic discourse (see Fforde and de Vylder 1988; Vo 1990), and limited but nevertheless increasing economic commentary is emerging in relation to Laos and Cambodia (see Asian Development Bank 1994). But a major problem in relation to Myanmar and the Indochinese countries is the continuing lack of reliable data. Conceptual difficulties are also implicit in attempts to analyse the transformation from planned to market-oriented economies.

ASEAN and regional economic cooperation

Most economic research on Southeast Asia has tended to be country-specific rather than comparative. Although a vast amount of literature has been produced on ASEAN within its regional context, this has tended to be written from a political rather than an economic perspective. In assessing the potential for economic cooperation, comparisons between the economies have been drawn, especially in terms of competition or complementarity. However, such analysis has usually been superficial in the sense that it has stated the obvious: there has been little genuine commitment to serious economic cooperation within ASEAN. Many economists realized from an early stage that significant economic integration was unlikely to succeed in an ASEAN context and have subsequently shown only a limited interest in the topic. While there is a substantial literature on ASEAN purportedly with an economic dimension, it is highly repetitious and often written from outside the discipline of economics. ASEAN's commitment to establish AFTA (the ASEAN Free Trade Area) is prompting a further wave of economic analysis – and speculation.

Towards a more critical approach?

It is possible to discern a variety of influences that have shaped the approach to economic research and writing on Southeast Asia. Probably to a greater extent than has been the case with other disciplines, academic economics has suffered from demands by governments, NGOs (such as the World Bank and ADB) and the private sector for the services of competent researchers. This problem of economic brain-drain has been experienced in most Southeast Asian countries. The World Bank's regional presence, and Southeast Asian governments' relative ease of access to its economic advice, may also have marginalized the role of academic economists to some extent. The practice of keeping official economic reports confidential, and the reluctance to share such reports' findings with the academic community, have also helped to constrain economic debate. Partly for these reasons, academic economists (with exceptions such as Jomo K. S.) have not attempted to open up a lively economic debate within Southeast Asian countries, at least not with the conviction or strength evident in Latin America. In most cases, economic analysis and comment have *responded* to major political events, whether external or internal.

Another explanation for less rigorous analysis of the Southeast Asian economies is the lack of reliable data, and the fact that Southeast Asian countries do not have economic frameworks of sufficient maturity to justify the type and depth of economic analysis applied to the mature Western economies. Thus controversial issues debated in relation to the developed economies, such as the merits or appropriateness of a monetarist or Keynesian approach, are generally missing.

Most economic studies on Southeast Asia have been conceived within a neo-classical or rational choice approach, in which consideration of the role of the state, and other political factors, are minimized or isolated, so that analysis can be conducted within a clear economic framework in which economic criteria assume the greatest importance. For some economists this does not necessarily imply that the role of the government is unimportant, or that government policy is perceived to be correct. It does, however, permit neat apolitical analyses based primarily on economic criteria, leaving the assessment of non-economic factors and influences to others. But the neo-classical approach can be used deliberately to play down the role of state-led economic policy, especially when countries adopt market-friendly economic policies. Some scholars have expressed dissatisfaction with what they see as the false distinction between state-led economic interventionism and free-market determinism, particularly in view of the profound role of state intervention in promoting rapid economic change and industrialization in East and Southeast Asia. Such views are succinctly summarized by Richard Robison:

> Whilst recognising, to various degrees, the political necessity for limited state intervention and protection, free market advocates have argued for the removal of 'distortions' in the economy, minimisation of state intervention, 'getting the price right' and identifying and exploiting comparative advantage. It is a voluntarist approach given its implicit assumption that economic success is a matter of economic wisdom (identifying the correct policies) and political will (implementing them). The relationship between policies and social and political interests and power structure is not theorised. The IMF and World Bank (IRBD) have been the most prominent institutional sources for the articulation of this approach (1989: 371).

Robison goes on to argue that the structure of political power, and relationships between the state and social forces are powerful factors decisively shaping economic policies.

The literature based on more radical views of political economy helps to counter views which would have us believe that there has been no government intervention in Southeast Asian economies.

Richard Higgott and Richard Robison help fill this gap for Southeast Asia in general with their edited book (1985). Kunio Yoshihara's *The Rise of Ersatz Capitalism in South-East Asia* (1988) made a particularly useful contribution to the debate. At the country level there are now a number of books that offer the broader analysis of political economy. Rodan (1989), for example, provides an interesting but highly analytical country study of Singapore.

The long-standing criticism of the World Bank's neo-classical economic policy prescriptions prompted the Japanese government, as a major shareholder but also an advocate of state intervention, to provide funding for a major research programme to undertake a comparative study of economic growth and public policy in East Asia. The World Bank study identified eight high-performing economies: Hong Kong, Indonesia, Japan, Korea, Malaysia, Singapore, Thailand and Taiwan (World Bank 1993). The main conclusion was that rapid growth was primarily due to the application of a set of market-friendly economic policies that led to both higher accumulation and better allocation of resources. It also argued, with qualifications, that some selective state interventions contributed to growth. Critics have welcomed the admission that intervention can contribute positively to the growth process, and point to the qualified conclusions as an attempt to explain why World Bank policies may not be consistent with East Asian experience (Awanohara 1993). The debate is likely to continue, but meanwhile China's growing acceptance of market forces and the demise of socialist planning in Eastern Europe have firmly established the hegemony of market-oriented policies, and consequently financial liberalization, deregulation and privatization are the order of the day in most of Southeast Asia, including previously planned economies such as those of Indochina and Myanmar. It seems likely, therefore, that in the foreseeable future most economic literature on the region will closely follow the pattern established over the last three decades, with most work conceived and analysed within the framework of neo-classical analysis.

The growth of direct foreign investment, identified as a major determinant of recent export manufacturing growth in Southeast Asia, will no doubt reinforce conventional economic analyses. However, increased reliance on foreign investment may also stimulate more critical literature from political economists. With Southeast Asia assuming increasing economic importance both within the Asia–Pacific region and within the wider world economy, there is a growing interest in cultural influences on business relationships. Moreover, supposed 'Asian values' of thrift and hard work are frequently identified as major influences underpinning economic performance (see, for example,

Whitley 1992). This means there is considerable scope for inter-disciplinary studies on Southeast Asian economics.

Where do these developments leave the study of economics in relation to Southeast Asia? The unequivocal answer is in a much stronger and more exciting position than twenty-five years ago. Since 1970 there has been a proliferation of economic literature that permits both a deep and broad understanding of the economic processes responsible for economic growth in Southeast Asia. Rapid economic growth and structural change are continually opening up further opportunities for both micro-economic and macro-economic studies. Improved statistical data and expanded research by indigenous academic economists should allow more penetrating analyses. In addition, the fact that Southeast Asia and the wider Pacific Rim are clearly acknowledged as the world's most dynamic economic region implies that they will continue to attract great attention from foreign scholars.

Bibliography

Akrasanee, N. (1977), *Industrial Development in Thailand* (Washington, DC: World Bank).

Alburo, F. A. et al. (1986), *Economic Recovery and Long-Run Growth: agenda for reforms* (Manila: Philippine Institute of Development Studies).

Anand, S. (1983), *Inequality and Poverty in Malaysia. Measurement and decomposition* (New York: Oxford University Press).

Anwar, Arsjad, Thee Kian Wie and Iwan Jaya Azis (1992), *Pemikiran, Pelaksanaan, dan Perintisan Pembangunan Ekonomi* (Jakarta: Fakultas Ekonomi, Universitas Indonesia).

Arndt, H. W. (1984), *The Indonesian Economy: Collected Papers* (Singapore: Chopmen).

— (1990), '25 Years of BIES', *Bulletin of Indonesian Economic Studies*, 26: 45–58.

Asian Development Bank (1968), *Asian Agricultural Survey* (Manila: Asian Development Bank).

— (1971), *Southeast Asia's Economy in the 1970s* (London: Longman).

— (1972), *Regional Transport Survey* (Singapore: Straits Times Press).

— (1994), *Asian Development Outlook 1994* (Hong Kong: Oxford University Press).

Awanohara, Susumu (1993), 'The magnificent eight', *Far Eastern Economic Review*, 22 July: 79.

Bautista, R. M. et al. (1979), *Industrial Promotion Policies in The Philippines* (Manila: Philippine Institute for Development Studies).

Bello, W., D. Kinley and E. Ellinson (1982), *Development Debacle: the World Bank in The Philippines* (San Francisco: Institute for Food and Development Policy).

Binswanger, H. and R. Uthaisri (1983), *Thailand: rural growth and employment* (Washington, DC: World Bank).

Booth, A. (ed.) (1992), *The Oil Boom and After: Indonesian economic policy and performance in the Soeharto era* (Singapore: Oxford University Press).

— and P. McCawley (eds) (1981), *Indonesian Economy During The Soeharto Era* (Kuala Lumpur: Oxford University Press).

Boyce, J. K. (1993), *The Philippines: the political economy of growth and impoverishment in the Marcos era* (Honolulu: University of Hawaii Press).

Broad, R. (1988), *Unequal Alliance: the World Bank, the IMF and the Philippines* (Berkeley: University of California Press).

Buang, A. (ed.) (1990), *The Malaysian Economy in Transition* (Kuala Lumpur: National Institute of Public Administration).

Cheetham, R. J. and E. K. Hawkins (1976), *The Philippines: priorities and prospects for development* (Washington, DC: World Bank).

Economic Commission for Asia and the Far East (1950), *Economic and Social Survey of Asia and the Far East* (Bangkok: ECAFE).

Fforde, A. and S. de Vylder (1988), *Vietnam: an economy in transition* (Stockholm: Swedish International Development Authority).

Fry, M. (1993), *Foreign Direct Investment in Southeast Asia* (Singapore: Institute of Southeast Asian Studies).

Higgins, B. (1990), 'Thought and action: Indonesian economic studies and policies in the 1950s', Bulletin of Indonesian Economic Studies, 26: 37–47.

Higgott, R. and R. Robison (eds) (1985), *Southeast Asia: essays in the political economy of structural change* (London: Routledge).

Hill, H. (1988), *Foreign Investment and Industrialisation in Indonesia* (Singapore: Oxford University Press).

— (ed.) (1989), *Unity and Diversity: regional economic development in Indonesia since 1970* (Oxford: Oxford University Press).

— and S. Jayasuriya (1986), *An Inward-Looking Economy in Transition: economic development in Burma since the 1960s* (Singapore: Institute of Southeast Asian Studies).

Hla Myint (1972), *Southeast Asia's Economy*, Modern Economics Series (Harmondsworth: Penguin).

Jansen, K. (1990), *Finance, Growth and Stability: financing economic development in Thailand* (Aldershot: Avebury).

Jomo, K. S. (1985), *A Question of Class: capital, the state and uneven development in Malaysia* (Kuala Lumpur: Oxford University Press).

— (1989), *Beyond 1990: considerations for a new national development strategy* (Kuala Lumpur: University of Malaya).

— (1990), *Growth and Structural Change in the Malaysian Economy* (London: Macmillan).

— and Ishak Shari (1986), *Development Policies and Income Inequality in Peninsular Malaysia* (Kuala Lumpur: University of Malaya).

— et al. (1987), *Crisis and Response in the Malaysian Economy* (Kuala Lumpur: Malaysian Economics Association).

Khor Kok Peng (1983), *The Malaysian Economy in Transition* (Kuala Lumpur: Marican).

Lim, D. (ed.) (1975), *Readings on Malaysian Economic Development* (Kuala Lumpur: Oxford University Press).

— (1983), *Further Readings on Malaysian Economic Development* (Kuala Lumpur: Oxford University Press).

Lim Chong-Yah (1984), *Economic Restructuring in Singapore* (Singapore: Federal Publishers).

— et al. (1988), *Policy Options for the Singapore Economy* (Singapore: McGraw Hill).

Loha-unchit, Chesada (1990), *Policies, Instruments and Institutions for Rural Development* (Bangkok: Thailand Development Research Institute).

McCawley, P. (1979), *Industrialisation in Indonesia: development and prospects* (Canberra: Australian National University).

Mackie, J. A. C. (1967), *Problems of Indonesian Inflation* (Ithaca, NY: Cornell University Press).

Marzouk, G. A. (1972), *Economic Development and Policies: a case study of Thailand* (Rotterdam: Rotterdam University Press).

Meesook, O. A. (1975), *Income Distribution in Thailand* (Bangkok: Thammasat University).

Mehmet, O. (1986), *Development in Malaysia* (London: Croom Helm).

Meier, G. M. (1984), *Leading Issues in Economic Development* (New York: Oxford University Press).

Mya Than and Joseph L. H. Tan (1990), *Myanmar Dilemmas and Options: the challenge of economic transition in the 1990s* (Singapore: Institute of Southeast Asian Studies).

Nasution, A. (1983), *Financial Institutions and Policies in Indonesia* (Singapore: Institute of Southeast Asian Studies).

Palmer, I. (1972), *Textiles in Indonesia: problems of import substitution* (New York: Praeger).

Panglaykim, J. (1983), *Japanese Direct Investment in ASEAN: the Indonesian experience* (Singapore, Maruzen Asia).

Power, J. H. and G. P. Sicat (1971), *The Philippines: industrialisation and trade policies* (London: Oxford University Press).

Robison, R. (1986), *Indonesia: the rise of capital* (Sydney: Allen and Unwin).

— (1989), 'Structures of power and the industrialisation process in Southeast Asia', *Journal of Contemporary Asia*, 19: 331–97.

Rodan, G. (1989), *The Political Economy of Singapore's Industrialisation* (London: Macmillan).

Sicat, G. P. (1974), *New Economic Direction in The Philippines* (Manila: National Economic and Development Authority).

Silcock, T. H. (ed.) (1961), *Readings in Malayan Economics* (Singapore: Eastern Universities Press).

Sjahrir (1986), *Basic Needs in Indonesia: economics, politics and public policy* (Singapore: Institute of Southeast Asian Studies).

— (1995), *Persoalan Ekonomi Indonesia* (Jakarta: Pustaka Sinar Harapan).

Snodgrass, D. R. (1980), *Inequality and Economic Development in Malaysia* (Kuala Lumpur: Oxford University Press).

Steinberg, D. I. (1981), *Burma's Road towards Development: growth and ideology under military rule* (Boulder, CO: Westview).

Tambunlertchai, Somsak (1990), *A Profile of Provincial Industries* (Bangkok: Thailand Development Research Institute).

Tan Tat Wai (1982), *Income Distribution and Determination in West Malaysia* (Kuala Lumpur: Oxford University Press).

Thirlwall, A. P. (1983), *Growth and Development* (London: Macmillan).

Todaro, M. P. (1977), *Economic Development* (London: Longman).

Toh Mun Heng and L. Low (1990), *An Economic Framework of Singapore* (Singapore: McGraw Hill).

Vo Nhan Tri (1990), *Vietnam's Economic Policy since 1975* (Singapore: Institute of Southeast Asian Studies).

Whitley, R. (1992), *Business Systems in East Asia* (London: Sage).

Wilbur, C. K. and K. P. Jameson (1992), *The Political Economy of Development and Underdevelopment* (New York: McGraw-Hill).

Wong, J. (1979), *ASEAN Economies in Perspective: a comparative study of Indonesia, Malaysia, the Philippines, Singapore and Thailand* (London: Macmillan).

World Bank (1978), *Thailand: towards a development strategy of full participation* (New York: World Bank).

— (1980), *Philippines: industrial development strategy and policies* (Washington, DC: World Bank).

— (1987), *Philippines: a framework for economic recovery* (Washington, DC: World Bank).

— (1990), *Indonesia: strategy for a sustained reduction in poverty* (Washington, DC: World Bank).

— (1993), *The East Asian Miracle* (New York: Oxford University Press).

Yoshihara, K. (1988), *The Rise of Ersatz Capitalism in South-East Asia* (Singapore: Oxford University Press).

— (1994), *The Nation and Economic Growth: the Philippines and Thailand* (Kuala Lumpur: Oxford University Press).

Young, K. W., C. F. Bussink and P. Hasan (1980), *Malaysia. Growth and equity in a multiracial society* (Baltimore, MD: Johns Hopkins University Press).

7 Politics

Duncan McCargo and
Robert H. Taylor

The relationship between politics as a subject of study and the countries and peoples of Southeast Asia as objects of study poses a number of difficult but intriguing issues for students of both. Politics itself is a highly complex subject, at once both theoretical and applied. As a social science, it is rooted in the language and culture of its practitioner, who attempts to explain and categorize political life as if standing apart from the world being explained. In North America there developed a distinct discipline of 'political science', which aspires in many instances to equivalency with the natural sciences, while in most of Europe vaguer, more eclectic terms 'politics' and 'political studies' are preferred. The literature coming from the region itself shares both of these tendencies.

The problem of defining both the key elements and the outer parameters of the study of politics is mirrored by the difficulty of identifying the central comparative features in politics of a region as diverse as Southeast Asia. There is no obvious model for the analysis of Southeast Asian polities: the region contains ten countries, ranging from the tiny Sultanate of Brunei to the huge archipelago of the Indonesian Republic, from the industrialized city-state of Singapore to the predominantly peasant polity of Vietnam. Looked at through contemporary eyes, previous historical experiences, at a superficial glance, explain little about current conditions and institutions. For example, Myanmar (formerly Burma), Malaysia and Singapore have a common heritage of British colonial rule, but while the military wields immense power in Myanmar, the Malaysian and Singaporean armed forces are amongst the least politicized in the region. Southeast Asian cultures, religions and economies are extremely divergent and rarely correlate with each other and prevailing regime types. For example, there are both predominantly Buddhist and Islamic states in Southeast Asia where the military has had immense political power, but one can also point to equally Buddhist or Islamic countries where the military is not particularly powerful politically. Thus the politics of Southeast Asia cannot readily be explained in the same general terms as more homogeneous areas of the world, such as the Middle East or Latin America. It is striking that many edited volumes and textbooks on comparative political questions omit to deal with Southeast Asian cases – perhaps because the region does not easily conform to the general principles being expounded. For example, Randall (1988) contains case studies from Africa, the Caribbean, Latin America, the Middle East and South Asia, but none from Southeast Asia.

Comparative politics and Southeast Asia

The study of Southeast Asian politics is a branch of the wider field of comparative politics. Comparative politics may be seen as a development of the political thought of the French theorists Montesquieu and de Tocqueville, who drew upon related subjects such as law and history (see Montesquieu 1989; de Tocqueville 1969). These founders of comparative politics sought to understand the relationship between the constitutional principles and institutional practices of other nations with their dominant societal characteristics. At the outset, the underlying aim of these thinkers was to gain a superior understanding of their own societies, but their growing interest in the political systems of other countries marked the beginning of a line of intellectual enquiry which was to lead towards the political scrutiny of the non-Western world.

Comparative politics is not a subject that can be studied easily in societies where freedom of debate and analysis are constrained. The subject involves three main elements: detailed observation of political conditions and events, analysis of the phenomena observed, and debate about the conclusions to be drawn. In societies where publicly acceptable conclusions may only be arrived at by reference to tradition or to higher political authority, rather than by open debate, the methodology of comparative politics can not be readily utilized. While foreign academics have frequently used comparative approaches to develop their own insights into the nature of Southeast Asian societies, the academic study of politics has not flourished in all parts of the region itself. In so far as Southeast Asian politics has developed locally as a discipline, it has generally been heavily influenced by American traditions of political science. In countries such as Thailand and the Philippines, the great majority of academics who have studied politics abroad have done so in the United States. Even in Singapore, with its traditional educational links to the British system, a similar pattern may be identified. Although some Southeast Asian academics gained their graduate degrees from political science departments with a well-established interest in the region, many others studied in more conventional, domestically oriented departments, where they were sometimes encouraged to apply American social science paradigms to their home societies. General theories, popular within the framework of American strategic interests and popular understandings – such as those advanced by Samuel Huntington in *Political Order in Changing Societies* (1968) – were often uncritically received. Similarly, American concepts of politics and analytical methods appropriate to the study of American questions were imported into Southeast Asia often without a critical appraisal of their utility in a different context. A parallel phenomenon can be seen in Britain and Australia, where in the 1960s and 1970s universities lacking a local tradition of Southeast Asian political studies hired staff trained in the United States to teach this 'new' subject.

The influence of American scholarship

The quality of teaching and research into the politics of Southeast Asia has until recently been extremely dependent upon the quality of American scholarship in the field. Yet the dominant intellectual traditions of American political science have not been comparative in scope; nor have they given a central place to the understanding of societies that do not accord with liberal democratic paradigms (see Crick 1959; Ricci 1984). American political science had its origins in a moral enterprise, an attempt to foster an understanding of American institutions and practices in such a way as would contribute to the continuation and development of democracy. In other words, the academic discipline is part and parcel of a training in citizenship. When this discipline turns its attention to the non-Western world, it often does so with a particular purpose, looking to identify evidence of incipient liberalism and to nurture democratic thoughts. However, these terms of reference are not always appropriate to the central analytical issues at the heart of most polities – European, American, African or Asian. American-trained political scientists have often been inclined to approach Southeast Asian polities with questions such as 'How democratic is this polity?' rather than the more fundamental question for political analysis of 'How is power distributed in this society?' The concepts of liberalism, rationalism and individualism that lie at the heart of American political thought militate against an accurate understanding of Southeast Asian political realities.

The academic study of politics in Europe is closer to the spirit of historical and philosophical enquiry that characterized the writings of

Montesquieu and de Tocqueville. British academics, for example, have neither been obliged, nor have felt it necessary, to teach politics as a training course for citizenship: like the unwritten constitution, the requirements of British citizenship are implicit in the prevailing order, rather than explicitly promulgated by educators. Whilst recent developments in the discipline – such as the empirical study of contemporary politics – have been added to the curriculum, they have not undermined the more eclectic ethos of British and European political studies.

In the decades following the end of the Second World War, universities on both sides of the Atlantic established academic programmes in 'area studies', designed to teach a detailed understanding of non-Western societies, particularly at post-graduate level. The United States led the way in these developments, largely because during the Cold War period an understanding of Africa, Asia and Latin America appeared essential if American global hegemony was to be ensured. For Southeast Asian studies, these concerns were closely connected with the Vietnam War: Americans hoped that a knowledge of Southeast Asian societies and political systems would enable them to prevent the region falling into communist hands. Although the programmes established in North America during the 1950s were imitated in Britain a few years later, the British had previously seen the study of Asian and African languages and cultures as a training for the administration of colonies, and, with the winding-down of the British Empire, there was little rationale for investing substantially in area studies (see Smith 1986).

The American tradition of political studies relating to Southeast Asia developed after the Second World War, building upon earlier historical work. Given the Cold War imperatives that underlay its expansion, Southeast Asian studies was particularly concerned with contemporary political questions; most scholars worked within the area studies paradigm, which stressed the distinctiveness of each country's culture, history and language. Rather as the British colonial district officer was directed to 'know his patch', American scholars working on Southeast Asian politics carved out niches of expertise which were both intellectually and geographically delineated. As a result, most of their publications were country-specific rather than comparative. This approach was based partly on a scepticism about theoretically led research on a complex and extremely diverse region. An exceptional work of this genre is *Governments and Politics of South East Asia*, edited by George McT. Kahin (1964). The volume contains contributions by eight authors and is organized entirely by country, from an atheoretical perspective. Kahin's book set the pattern for most subsequent work, which tended to adopt a country-specific format:

good examples are Girling (1981a) and Wurfel (1988). This pattern helps explain why Southeast Asian studies has made few significant contributions to the theoretical debates pursued in the broader field of politics. Although some subsequent studies have adopted a more comparative perspective, they have tended to use limited theoretical frames of reference that offered few useful insights. When Southeast Asian studies is compared in this regard with, say, Latin American studies, the contrast is striking. Southeast Asian political studies has yet to produce any convincing comparative framework to account for regional developments, let alone models with a broader application.

In more recent years, the study of Southeast Asian politics has been enlarged by a series of country-specific studies written and edited by scholars from the countries under study themselves. Organized to bring together research on particular topics and issues by leading authorities on their topics, the volumes have provided useful indigenous accounts of topics of interest to students in their own and neighbouring countries. One such series was inspired by the Institute of Southeast Asian Studies in Singapore, which established itself as a leading research centre within the region during the 1970s and 1980s (see Quah, Chan and Seah 1985; Xuto 1987; Ahmad 1987; de Guzman and Reforma 1988).

The study of the politics of Southeast Asia was able to develop effectively only after decolonization and the rise of autonomous political movements and governments within the region. Consequently, the earliest research on the politics of the region centred on questions of nationalism: other issues such as religion, ethnicity and communism were seen as components of nationalism. The path-breaking study was George McT. Kahin's *Nationalism and Revolution in Indonesia* (1952). As has been noted, 'American sympathy for Asian nationalists can be seen as a logical continuation of the anti-colonial interpretation of the United States' own historical experience' (Smith 1986: 16). Nationalism was not initially analysed in broader ideological terms, and there was no systematic attempt to distinguish between the various manifestations of nationalism that emerged during the late colonial and immediate post-colonial periods. Not until the 1970s was the nationalist model of Southeast Asian politics subjected to serious critical scrutiny.

Behaviourism and the failure of constitutional democracy

Another key issue in the early research on the politics of the region was the failure of constitutional democracy to establish itself as the dominant pattern during the 1950s and early 1960s. Scholars sought to understand why democracy had not flourished in countries such as Burma and Indonesia, and why military and authoritarian regimes were so prevalent in the region. A classic work dealing with such questions was Feith's *The Decline of Constitutional Democracy in Indonesia* (1962), which gave rise to an intense scholarly debate on the appropriateness of the questions being raised by such research (see Anderson and Kahin 1982). At Cornell, where Feith did his initial research, and at other American universities, Indonesia, Thailand and the Philippines were the main focus of academic study. Indonesia then seemed to offer perhaps the most useful paradigm of Southeast Asian political history: a traditional society which had undergone Western colonization, then experienced a resurgent nationalism that led to independence; yet the post-colonial state had numerous parallels with its pre-colonial predecessor, leading to the demise of democratic politics. However, this model was less appropriate to other Southeast Asian societies, such as Thailand (which had never been formally colonized) and Vietnam.

Rather than question the relevance of their liberal democratic ideals to the societies they were studying, many scholars fell back upon ill-defined notions of political culture as the primary explanatory variable. The use of quantitative methods (such as attitude surveys) to analyse the politics of non-Western societies was occasionally also attempted, borrowing from the methodological paraphernalia of the so-called behaviourist approach that was the dominant paradigm in American political science during the 1960s. But as Ruth McVey observed:

> The difficulty of using quantitative methods to study political behaviour is compounded when we address ourselves to societies with very different cultures, inadequately described histories and institutions, few reliable social statistics, and no open system of expressing public opinion. As these comprise most of the countries of the world, the behavioralist is faced with the prospect of restricting himself to home territory or having an inadequate base on which to set up his experiments (McVey 1981: 261).

Far from being a 'value-free' social science approach, behaviourism was based entirely upon a set of Western assumptions.

The diversification of research on Southeast Asian politics

Since the 1960s, research has been published on a wider variety of issues in Southeast Asian politics, including the bureaucracy, the military, leadership, ideology and political parties. However, most of this research has remained country-specific, with explanations based upon broad notions of political culture or 'modernization'. One of the most important contributions to Southeast Asian political studies from this period was Fred W. Riggs' *Thailand: the modernization of a bureaucratic polity* (1966). What makes Riggs' work so unusual in its period was the analytical stance he assumed. Though starting from the developmentalist assumptions common in American political science at the time, Riggs discovered that the Thai bureaucracy did not function as it was assumed it should within the models of politics derived from European and American historical experience. Rather than being a mere instrument of government, the bureaucracy, including the armed forces, was the government. The 'bureaucratic polity' concept was later appropriated to the study of other regimes that were perceived to have developed sufficiently to be no longer explicable primarily in terms of nationalism and its variants (see Jackson 1978; Girling 1981b).

Since the 1970s a number of scholars working on Southeast Asian politics have used more intensely local research methods similar to those of anthropologists, such as in-depth interviewing and participant observation. Using these methods, scholars such as James Scott (1985) and Benedict Tria Kerkvliet (1977, 1990) were able to challenge the widespread simplistic assumptions about the nature of politics in Southeast Asian societies.

Political economy

Since the early 1980s, another new area of research has concerned political economy in its classical, non-Marxist tradition. In these explorations, the study of 'mature' post-colonial states and societies in Southeast Asia can be linked with theoretical concerns that have resonance beyond the region itself. However, the relationship between Southeast Asian studies and political economy is a problematic one. Richard Doner has identified three main areas of research that may be classed as 'political economy': the application of neoclassical assumptions to non-market situations, for example by analysing the behaviour of elected officials in terms of their desire for short-term personal gain; the study of the relationship between economic and political power and resources; and an analysis of 'the failure of markets to operate according to strict neoclassical assumptions', as manifested in the emergence of institutionalism (Doner 1991: 825). Those students of politics who are primarily interested in ascertaining who exercises political power, and how that power is exercised, may feel that the new political economy scholarship is interested more in matters of economics than in issues of politics.

Some political economists working on Southeast Asia have, however, succeeded in bringing economic perspectives to bear on genuinely political questions. Their work generally falls into the second category of scholarship identified by Doner – studies of the relationship between economic resources and political power. Such political economists include Anek Laothamatas (1992), Gary Hawes (1987), Kevin Hewison (1989) and Andrew MacIntyre (1991). Gary Hawes, for example, demonstrated the extent to which Ferdinand Marcos owed both his political longevity and his eventual downfall to the 'crony capitalism' that thrived during his regime, whilst Anek Laothamatas has shown that the rise of influential business associations in Thailand challenges the received view that the Thai public policy process is dominated by bureaucrats. As yet, however, there are very few studies offering detailed and thoroughly satisfactory socio-economic explanations for the changing patterns of political participation evident in contemporary Southeast Asia. If more political economists would attempt to provide economic explanations for political change, major breakthroughs might well be made in the understanding of Southeast Asian politics; like those who work on public policy, political economists are frequently in danger of concentrating on specific issues, rather than on broader analytical questions of interest to the non-specialist.

The rise of the so-called East Asian 'developmental state' as a possible model for the would-be newly industrializing economies of Southeast Asia has attracted considerable interest, in view of the remarkable economic growth achieved by several Southeast Asian countries during the 1970s and 1980s. Political economists have increasingly looked towards Southeast Asia in an attempt to find solutions for development problems in regions such as Africa. Whilst some political economists have used neo-Marxist dependency approaches to analyse developments in the region, these approaches, which draw upon Wallerstein's view that international capitalism operates as a 'world system', are unacceptable to many area specialists, who emphasize the need to understand the internal political dynamics of individual countries. The 'world system' argument, which sees the developed nations of the Western world as the 'centre' of the global economy, and Asian countries as part of the 'periphery', is profoundly Eurocentric. The high levels of growth experienced by the developing nations of Southeast Asia may be cited to challenge the notion of a monolithic international economic system (Doner 1991: 825). Just as political scientists working on Southeast Asia have tended to regard particular countries as exceptions to accepted theoretical generalizations, so political economists who work on the region have tended to challenge the wider orthodoxies of their discipline, rather than developing new and more broadly applicable theoretical perspectives (Doner 1991: 819).

Democratization

A good deal of the literature on Southeast Asian politics has been influenced by academic fashions in the West. In the late 1940s and early 1950s, nationalism was seen as an all-embracing explanation for the emergence of new forms of politics in the region. By the late 1950s, culture had taken over as the key determining factor, only to be replaced within a decade or so by ideas of developmentalism. At certain times and for certain countries during the 1960s and 1970s, ideas of revolution and class conflict appeared to be of central political significance, as the United States failed to defeat communist forces in Indochina, and left-wing movements played a prominent role in countries such as Indonesia, Thailand and the Philippines. Marxist-inspired literature on Southeast Asian politics, which emphasized the potency of left-wing insurgency movements, began appearing during the 1970s (see, for example, Turton, Fast and Caldwell 1978). This literature stressed the degree and variety of class and other conflicts existing in Southeast Asian societies: previously, area specialists had been overly inclined to regard individual societies as relatively conflict-free, self-regulating political orders. Yet by the early 1980s most of the left-wing movements that had inspired this literature were moribund: in so far as the radical tradition lived on, it was mainly in the writings of neo-Marxist political economists such as Richard Robison (1986). By the early 1990s, the dominant paradigm was that of democratization. Scholars working on Southeast Asia saw evidence of a resurgence of more open forms of political participation, with greater levels of opposition, protest and debate (see Diamond, Linz and Lipset 1989).

Mass uprisings against unpopular authoritarian governments in the Philippines (1986), Myanmar (1988) and Thailand (1992) seemed to some to symbolize a tide of liberalism sweeping across the region. Indeed, the phenomenon of democratization has been seen in terms of a global trend, evident also in other parts of Asia, Africa, Latin America, Eastern Europe and the former Soviet Union states. Few specialists on Southeast Asian politics, however, believe that fully fledged Western-style democracy is likely to take root in the region in the immediate future, though the rise of new urban, 'middle-class' business and professional groups is generating pressures in that direction.

A number of different arguments are put forward to support the view that the transition from authoritarian to pluralist political orders is inevitable. One standard interpretation is that the emergence of liberalism has a direct correlation with economic development: once a country achieved a certain level of gross national production, pluralism follows (Dahl 1976: 89). Another common view sees the authoritarian regimes that emerged in many Southeast Asian states during the post-colonial period as an aberration from 'normal' democratic conditions, or as a necessary transitional stage before the emergence of a more liberal order. Related to this view is the popular belief that all socialist, communist and other state-led economic systems are now defunct – an argument that fails to recognize the central role played by the state in the economic development of newly industrialized countries such as Singapore. An alternative, radical argument is that the rise of liberalism is the result of a profound crisis of Western hegemony. But all these explanations are extremely general, and fail to take account of country-specific rather than 'global' reasons why politics may have became more open in certain societies and at particular times.

It could well be argued that attempts to understand and explain the politics of the region through crude dichotomies (military/civilian, democratic/authoritarian, free market/planned economy) serve only to obfuscate analysis. Many Southeast Asian states have semi-military, semi-democratic regimes, and semi-planned economies. To criticize these states on the grounds that they do not conform to Western social science paradigms is to impose a set of values – essentially, American liberal values – upon them. Does the defect lie in the states, or in the paradigms themselves? The current Eurocentric preoccupation of the discipline of political studies with ideas of democratization is unlikely to produce many useful insights into the nature of politics in Southeast Asia.

State and society

A more valuable way of examining Southeast Asian politics from a disciplined theoretical perspective might be to focus upon the relationship between the state and society. Joel Migdal's *Strong Societies and Weak States* offers a comparative framework for such analyses; Migdal is centrally concerned with the capacity of states and leaders 'to use the agencies of the state to get people in the society to do what they want them to do' (Migdal 1988: xii). The distinction between 'strong' and 'weak' states is an extremely problematic one in the Southeast Asian context, since even relatively authoritarian states are frequently 'weak' in terms of their practical ability to govern – and to tax – their populations. However, analytical questions of this kind are not laden with value judgements so much as questions about the degree of democratization achieved by particular societies. Questions based around a discussion of state–society relations can make use of insights from other disciplines such as anthropology and economics, examining the extent to which social and political change is occurring at the instigation of the state, and the extent to which this change is beyond the control of political leaders. It might be argued, for example, that a strong society coupled with an authoritarian but weak state (Thailand under the 'Anand I' premiership, 1991) could offer the individual the same range of human choice as a strong state with Western-style representative institutions (Singapore during the same period). Institutional arrangements for political participation may be far less important than the *de facto* operation of politics. What are the informal channels and networks through which political power and influence are exercised? Are there non-institutionalized agencies that compete with formalized agencies for effective control? Are elections held to ensure the representative sharing and rotation of power, or to consolidate the political grip of the ruling elite? What are the strategic groups that mediate between state interests and those of key sectors such as the business community? Who controls information reaching the public, and to what political effect? What holds states in Southeast Asia together, beyond entrenched bureaucratic authority? How do these states operate, and how can they be understood? Questions such as these offer more appropriate ways of analysing the changing nature of politics in Southeast Asia than do questions that assume the inevitable dawning of liberal democracy.

However, undertaking a comprehensive comparative study of politics in the various Southeast Asian states based upon questions such as these would be a formidable task, requiring extensive access to government data not normally made available to academics, as well as large-scale opinion surveys. Although all Southeast Asian societies place limitations upon the extent to which foreign scholars are permitted to conduct politically sensitive research, some countries allow indigenous political scientists greater leeway. But it is rare for home-grown research to examine comparative questions about the nature of state–society relations, since the results of such research might challenge political orthodoxies propounded by the state. Questions about sensitive issues – the political influence of the military, the relationship between politics and religion, the degree of power enjoyed by particular ethnic groups, the political role of the monarchy – are usually off-limits to local academics. Instead, political scientists are encouraged to focus their attentions on particular issues or policy questions of current interest to the government (see Uchida 1984: 69–224). Unless properly channelled, the academic study of politics poses a threat to those who hold power. Just as American political scientists have tended to engage in the promotion of American liberal values, so Southeast Asian political scientists have often been co-opted into the public policy process. In some countries, leading political scientists are frequently aligned with particular politicians and parties, functioning in an advisory capacity, either officially or unofficially. Although there is interesting and important work on politics being done by academics in several Southeast Asian countries, little of this has yet filtered out to enrich the discipline beyond the region.

The discourse of Southeast Asian politics

One area of research that might fruitfully be explored is a return to the underlying theoretical and constitutional questions out of which political studies originally developed. In doing so, it would be necessary to recognize the shortcomings of employing Western-derived concepts such as the state, society and bureaucracy for the analysis of Asian politics. Where central institutions such as the military are pursuing their own independent policy objectives by political means, can they properly be regarded as part of the state? When the foreign minister and the prime minister of a country have adopted entirely different foreign policy goals, for example, which is the authentic state policy? When civil servants are in the pay of capitalist cronies of the president, how can the bureaucracy be distinguished from the executive, or from the private sector? Political science, which uses definitions highly specific to Western culture, is ill-equipped to address questions of this kind. In this respect, scholars working within an area studies tradition have the potential to contribute to a broadening of the intellectual scope of political science, making it relevant to the study of non-Western societies.

Where scholars have succeeded in marrying the cultural sensitivities of Southeast Asian studies with the theoretical concerns of the discipline of politics, they have tended to do so by understanding Southeast Asian societies as continually developing political 'texts'. By engaging with the discourse of politics in these societies such scholars have produced some highly original research, which is not vitiated by Eurocentrism or intellectual determinism. Nor do these scholars insist upon the 'exceptionalism' of the particular societies they study – an argument that weakens and marginalizes so much political research on Southeast Asia. Outstanding examples of such work include James C. Scott's book (1985) on the forms of 'everyday resistance' practised by Southeast Asian peasants, Benedict Anderson's 'The Idea of Power in Javanese Culture' (1972) on the way President Sukarno sought to legitimate his rule by tapping into traditional Javanese notions of kingship, and Ruth McVey's 'The *Wayang* controversy in Indonesian communism' (1986), which examined the use for political purposes of shadow puppet theatre by the Indonesian Communist Party. Works such as these successfully convey to the contemporary student a sense of what Southeast Asian politics is all about, and how such politics differs from and resembles the politics of European societies. Southeast Asia emerges neither as uniquely and entirely 'other', nor as a region predestined to follow in the historical and political tracks of the West. The politics of Southeast Asia is given clear comparative relevance. However, although written from very different perspectives, all three of these examples are virtuoso performances on a particular theme, rather than extended studies of the politics of one or more Southeast Asian society. Anderson, for instance, has since argued that his piece on Javanese notions of power was excessively ingenious and over-stated. There is no outstanding example of scholarship on Southeast Asian politics which has undertaken the systematic exegesis of an entire political 'text'.

The challenge for those studying Southeast Asian politics is to develop a more systematic and rigorous approach to research, an approach which, while acknowledging the near universality of Western political forms such as the concept of 'stateness', must address the manifestations of these forms in Southeast Asia in the political languages of the societies under examination. This may best be accomplished by returning to the philosophical and constitutional roots of comparative politics, approaching Southeast Asian societies in a genuine spirit of enquiry, without attempting to subject those societies to a list of questions more relevant for other countries with different historical experiences and varied cultural traditions.

Bibliography

Ahmad, Zakaria Haji (ed.) (1987), *Government and Politics of Malaysia* (Singapore, New York and Oxford: Oxford University Press).

Anderson, Benedict (1972), 'The idea of power in Javanese culture', in Holt (1972): 1–70.

— and Audrey Kahin (eds) (1982), *Interpreting Indonesian Politics: thirteen contributions to the debate*, Modern Indonesian Project: Interim Report Series no. 2 (Ithaca, NY: Cornell University, Southeast Asia Program).

Bassett, D. K. and V. T. King (eds) (1986), *Britain and South East Asia*, Occasional Paper 13 (Hull: University of Hull, Centre for South-East Asian Studies).

Crick, Bernard (1959), *The American Science of Politics: its origins and conditions*, (Berkeley: University of California Press).

Dahl, Robert (1976), *Modern Political Analysis*, 3rd edn (Englewood Cliffs, NJ: Prentice-Hall).

De Guzman, Raul P. and Mila A. Reforma (eds) (1988), *Government and Politics of the Philippines* (Singapore, Oxford and New York: Oxford University Press).

Diamond, Larry, Juan J. Linz and Seymour Martin Lipset (eds) (1989), *Democracy in Developing Countries: Volume 3, Asia* (Boulder, CO: Lynne Rienner).

Doner, Richard E. (1991), 'Approaches to the politics of growth in Southeast Asia', *Journal of Asian Studies*, 50: 818–49.

Feith, Herbert (1962), *The Decline of Constitutional Democracy in Indonesia* (Ithaca, NY and London: Cornell University Press).

Girling, John L. S. (1981a), *Thailand: society and politics* (Ithaca, NY and London: Cornell University Press).

— (1981b), *The Bureaucratic Polity in Modernizing Societies*, Occasional Paper 64 (Singapore: Institute of Southeast Asian Studies).

Hawes, Gary (1987), *The Philippine State and the Marcos Regime* (Ithaca, NY: Cornell University Press).

Hewison, Kevin (1989), *Bankers and Bureaucrats: capital and the role of the state in Thailand* (New Haven, CT: Yale University, South East Asian Studies).

Hobart, Mark and Robert H. Taylor (eds) (1986), *Context, Meaning and Power in Southeast Asia* (Ithaca, NY: Cornell University, South East Asia Program).

Holt, Claire (ed.) (1972), *Culture and Politics in Indonesia* (Ithaca, NY and London: Cornell University Press).

Huntington, Samuel P. (1968), *Political Order in Changing Societies* (New Haven and London: Yale University Press).

Jackson, Karl D. (1978), 'Bureaucratic polity: a theoretical framework for the analysis of power and communications in Indonesia', in Jackson and Pye (1978): 3–22.

— and Lucien W. Pye (eds) (1978), *Political Power and Communications in Indonesia* (Berkeley and London: University of California Press).

Kahin, George McT. (1952), *Nationalism and Revolution in Indonesia* (Ithaca, NY and London: Cornell University Press).

— (1964), *Government and Politics in Southeast Asia*, 2nd edn (Ithaca, NY and London: Cornell University Press).

Kerkvliet, Benedict J. (1977), *The Huk Rebellion: a study of peasant revolt in the Philippines* (Berkeley and London: University of California Press).

— (1990), *Everyday politics in the Philippines: class and status relations in a central Luzon village* (Berkeley and London: University of California Press).

Laothamatas, Anek (1992), *Business Associations and the New Political Economy of Thailand: from bureaucratic polity to liberal corporatism* (Boulder, CO: Westview Press).

MacIntyre, Andrew (1991), *Business and Politics in Indonesia* (Sydney: Allen and Unwin).

McVey, Ruth (1981), 'Islam explained', *Pacific Affairs*, 54: 260–87.

— (1986), 'The *Wayang* controversy in Indonesian communism', in Hobart and Taylor (1986): 79–92.

Migdal, Joel (1988), *Strong Societies and Weak States: state–society relations and state capabilities in the Third World* (Princeton and London: Princeton University Press).

Montesquieu (1989), *The Spirit of the Laws*, trans. and ed. Anne M. Cohler, B. C. Miller and H. S. Stone (Cambridge: Cambridge University Press).

Quah, Jon S. T., Chan Heng Chee and Seah Chee Meow (eds) (1985), *Government and Politics of Singapore* (Singapore, New York and Oxford: Oxford University Press, 1985).

Randall, Vicky (ed.) (1988), *Political Parties in the Third World* (London: Sage).

Ricci, David (1984), *The Tragedy of Political Science: politics, scholarship and democracy* (New Haven and London, Yale University Press).

Riggs, Fred W. (1966), *Thailand: the modernization of a bureaucratic polity*, (Honolulu: East–West Center Press).

Robison, Richard (1986), *Indonesia and the Rise of Capital* (London: Allen and Unwin).

Scott, James C. (1985), *Weapons of the Weak: everyday forms of peasant resistance* (New Haven, CT and London: Yale University Press).

Smith, Ralph (1986), 'The evolution of British scholarship on South East Asia, 1820–1970: is there a "British tradition" in South East Asian studies?', in Bassett and King (1986): 1–28.

Tocqueville, Alexis de (1969), *Democracy in America*, trans. G. Lawrence and ed. J.P. Mayer (Garden City, New York: Doubleday).

Turton, Andrew, Jonathan Fast and Malcolm Caldwell (eds) (1978), *Thailand: the roots of conflict* (Nottingham: Spokesman Books).

Uchida, Takeo (ed.) (1984), *Political Science in Asia and the Pacific: state reports on teaching and research in ten countries* (Bangkok: UNESCO Regional Office for Education in Asia and the Pacific).

Wurfel, David (1988), *Filipino Politics: development and decay* (Ithaca, NY and London: Cornell University Press).

Xuto, Somsakdi (ed.) (1987), *Government and Politics of Thailand* (Singapore, New York and Oxford: Oxford University Press).

8 International relations[1]

Tim Huxley

The study of the international relations of Southeast Asia is essentially a post-1945 phenomenon. This should not be surprising, given the relative youth of the international relations discipline, which began to take on a self-conscious existence as a prescriptive social science differentiated from the study of diplomatic history only in the aftermath of the First World War. Moreover, the expansion of the modern society of states into Southeast Asia did not occur until after the Second World War, with the ending of Dutch, French, British and American colonial rule in the region.

Inter-state relations in pre-colonial Southeast Asia

The absence of a modern states-system in the region at the time of international relations' genesis as a self-conscious discipline does not fully explain the lack of interest in Southeast Asia on the part of writers on international politics before the 1950s. International relations was a strongly Eurocentric discipline even as late as the 1940s, when even the United States and Japan were still sometimes seen by leading international relations scholars as rather peripheral to the supposed European focus of the international system.[2] While there was an almost excessive concern amongst early international relations writers with 'learning the lessons' of modern European history, they evinced little interest in the extensive and varied pre-colonial inter-state relations of non-Western regions of the world such as Southeast Asia.

The clear origins of the modern states system in early-modern Europe after the dissolution of medieval Christendom may justify international relations specialists' lack of interest in Southeast Asia's pre-colonial inter-state relations. However, more conventional *historians* of Southeast Asia, both local and Western, have also generally lacked great interest in the overall pattern of relations between pre-colonial

Southeast Asian states and between these states and outside powers. This is a great pity because while it has been widely argued that the notion of 'Southeast Asia' as a political region is a twentieth-century construct, it seems incontestable that there was an intense pattern of relationships between Southeast Asia's pre-colonial states for between five hundred and a thousand years before the colonial impact. These relations were particularly intense in mainland Southeast Asia, where there were numerous and complex power struggles involving Thai, Lao, Vietnamese, Cham, Khmer and Burmese states. Geographical factors restricted political interaction between the mainland and maritime Southeast Asia. However, the fourteenth-century competition between the mainland (Thai) state of Ayutthaya and the maritime (Javanese) state of Majapahit for dominance of the Straits of Malacca demonstrates that there was no absolute divide between the inter-state relations of Southeast Asia's two spheres. Moreover, while it is true that the geographical bifurcation of Southeast Asia was reinforced by the cultural division that emerged by the fourteenth century between the mainland (where Theravada Buddhism assumed cultural dominance except in Vietnam) and maritime Southeast Asia (much of which was Islamicized), there was no clear-cut differentiation in the relations of the two spheres with the outside world. Most parts of Southeast Asia, mainland and maritime, were involved in tributary relations with China. Indian traders maintained links with the Burmese and Thai coasts as well as with ports in the Malay peninsula and Indonesian islands.

While many aspects of these relations, together with those between Southeast Asian states and non-state peoples, have been examined in considerable detail in the various histories of the pre-colonial states, the focus has been on bilateral relationships. An authoritative, geographically extensive and chronologically wide-ranging study of pre-colonial Southeast Asia's inter-state relations remains to be written, although McCloud's work (1986: 92–116; 1995: 89–111) represents a tentative step in this direction. The absence in the region of an indigenous tradition of historically orientated scholarship comparable to that of India or China precluded the emergence of a 'classical' Southeast Asian philosopher interested in inter-state relations equivalent to Kautilya or Mencius. However, the empirical substance of relations amongst the culturally diverse Southeast Asian states before the European impact might nevertheless yield patterns of interest to modern international relations theorists: Wolters (1994: 11) suggests that 'the skills of diplomacy are part of the Southeast Asian tradition'.

The colonial impact

The European powers' intrusion into Southeast Asia from the early sixteenth century led ultimately to the wholesale suspension of indigenous sovereign statehood in the region. Although Acehnese resistance to Dutch domination continued into the first few years of the twentieth century, there was a short-lived Philippine Republic in 1898–99, and Siam remained nominally independent all through the colonial era, by the late nineteenth century virtually the whole of Southeast Asia had been subjugated to European rule. One outstanding feature of the colonial period was the lack of contact between the various European powers' administrative units in Southeast Asia. The principal economic and political orientation of these colonial territories was towards their respective metropolitan capitals rather than their geographical neighbours. However, inter-state politics were not removed from Southeast Asia. While colonial rule was still being extended during the nineteenth century, apart from the intense relations between European powers and the Southeast Asian states that were being encroached upon (including Siam, which used diplomatic skills to retain a modicum of sovereignty), Britain competed fiercely with the Netherlands and France for spheres of economic influence and political control. But the cumulative impact of the conclusion of the Treaty of London (1824) between Britain and the Netherlands, the Anglo-Dutch Treaty of Sumatra (1871), and the Anglo-French Entente Cordiale (1904), together with the increasing reliance of the Netherlands East Indies on British military protection against the growing spectre of an expansionist Japan, was that relations between the three major colonial powers became stable and uncontroversial during the first four decades of the twentieth century. Perhaps surprisingly, while sections of a number of the standard histories of Southeast Asia cover diplomatic aspects of the colonial impact in some detail, and others investigate the regional policies of the individual powers, there are few region-wide analyses of colonial Southeast Asia's international relations. The most important recent work is Tarling's *The Fall of Imperial Britain in South-East Asia* (1993). Though his focus is on British policy in the region, Tarling incidentally provides an excellent overview of the interplay of the European powers' Southeast Asian policies in the nineteenth and twentieth centuries.

The creation of 'Southeast Asia'

Japan's onslaught against and rapid destruction of colonial Southeast Asia in 1942 paved the way for the re-introduction of relations between indigenous Southeast Asian states. By providing outlets for the pent-up nationalist pressures that had built up in British and Dutch Southeast Asia during the 1920s and 1930s, and by provoking armed nationalist revolt there and in French Indochina in 1945, the Japanese had helped to ensure that colonial rule could not be re-established on a permanent basis. The Indian historian K. M. Panikkar provided one of the first assessments of the likely impact of the Japanese occupation. Panikkar's monograph, *The Future of South-East Asia* (1943), looked forward to a post-war Southeast Asia that would inevitably be composed of independent states. While Panikkar argued for a system of 'collective security' in Southeast Asia based on the 'regional authority' of both India and Indonesia, and involving Australian and British 'co-operation', his argument that 'the defence [of the region] has to be based in India' suggested an Indian sphere of influence in the region. Incidentally, Panikkar seems to have been the first writer on international relations to use the term 'South-East Asia'.

Panikkar's vision of post-war Southeast Asia was realized only to a limited extent. By the end of the 1940s, several newly independent entities – the Philippines, Indonesia, Burma – formed, with Thailand, a new constellation of sovereign Southeast Asian states. After the 1954 Geneva agreements established sovereign states in north and south Vietnam, Cambodia and Laos, and the Malayan Federation became independent in 1957, the only Southeast Asian territories remaining under colonial control were West Papua (until 1962), Singapore, Sarawak and North Borneo (until 1963), and Portuguese Timor (until 1975). But in the face of internal and external communist threats (unforeseen by Panikkar, who envisaged post-war China as a powerful but cooperative non-communist republic which would have a 'special responsibility' for the defence of Indochina and Thailand), much of the region came to depend on security guarantees from Britain and the United States, and ultimately on American military intervention in the case of the anti-communist states of Indochina. India's role in the security of post-war Southeast Asia actually turned out to be relatively insignificant.

Nevertheless, Panikkar was vindicated in the sense that the Western powers' wartime conceptualization of Southeast Asia as an important and to some extent discrete strategic region[3] was carried into the post-1945 era. Particularly after the victory of the Chinese communists in 1949, both the West and the communist powers came to see Southeast Asia – with its strategically significant location between the Pacific and Indian Oceans, its massive natural resources, its relative proximity to China, and its large ethnic Chinese minority populations – as an important battleground in the Cold War. According to Russell H.

Fifield, writing in 1958, 'Geography and politics have combined on the international level to make Southeast Asia one of the most strategic areas of the world' (Fifield 1958: 2).

International relations in Cold War Southeast Asia

The Western powers saw the political fate of the individual Southeast Asian states as being inextricably interlinked. When President Eisenhower claimed, a month after the fall of Dien Bien Phu to the Viet Minh in 1954, that 'the loss of Indochina will cause the fall of Southeast Asia like a set of dominoes', he was expressing a view that would not only underlie American policy in the region for the next twenty years, but in the long-term would also profoundly influence the attitudes of non- and anti-communist Southeast Asian governments. From the late 1940s, Southeast Asia's 'strategic importance' in the Cold War made it the focus for considerable attention from Western – and particularly American – international relations writers, who were especially concerned with how the security of the region's non-communist states could be bolstered in the face of the 'communist threat'.

Like Broek (1944: 195) before him, the British political geographer Charles Fisher compared Southeast Asia with the Balkans. Writing in 1949, Fisher suggested that 'the present phase of comparative friendliness among the peoples of Southeast Asia may be ... the prelude to a renewal of strife, should the Europeans finally withdraw' (Fisher 1950: 235), arguing that Southeast Asia's equivalent to the First Balkan War (that is, the anti-imperialist struggle) might be followed by a local version of the Second Balkan War in which the liberated nations of the region would turn on each other. In 1962, when he enlarged on his earlier comparison of two regions, Fisher had to explain why Southeast Asia had not, after all, followed the Balkan pattern of intra-regional conflict. Fisher reasoned – not altogether convincingly – that while 'Balkanization' was a 'very real threat' within the new Southeast Asian states, it had not extended across international borders in the region because of the original focus of Southeast Asia's various nationalisms against a *variety* of colonial powers rather than a common imperialist foe (Ottoman Turkey) as in the Balkans. But he argued that Southeast Asian statesmen's 'sense of responsibility', shown in their commitment to maintaining a regional order based on the sanctity of treaties and respect for the principles of the United Nations, was a more important explanatory factor (Fisher 1962: 366). He might have added that most Southeast Asian governments had been so busy contending with domestic Balkanization and communist insurgency that they had perhaps had little inclination or surplus energy for pursuing disputes with neighbours.

The most substantial work on the new international relations of Southeast Asia published during the 1950s was Fifield's *The Diplomacy of Southeast Asia: 1945–1958*. In the course of writing this book, Fifield personally interviewed or corresponded with many of the key leaders and personalities who shaped the making of foreign policy within the region, including Magsaysay and Quirino (the Philippines), Sukarno, Hatta, Sastroamidjojo, Sjahrir and Aidit (Indonesia), U Nu and Ba Maw (Burma), Pibul Songgram (Thailand), Ngo Dinh Diem (South Vietnam), Souvanna Phouma and Souphanou Vong (Laos), Prince Sihanouk (Cambodia), and Tunku Abdul Rahman (Malaya). As Fifield pointed out, the period his book covered was particularly significant because it represented the formative phase of most of these countries' foreign policies; the Asian leaders he interviewed were 'often the George Washingtons and Simón Bolívars of today' (Fifield 1958: 12). Though writing at the height of the Cold War, Fifield was hardly a strident 'Cold Warrior'. Indeed, despite the recent conflicts in Korea, Indochina, Malaya and the Philippines, he was careful not to overemphasize the 'real threat of Communist imperialism' (Fifield 1958: 496). Instead, he concentrated on explaining Southeast Asian states' individual foreign policy orientations, fully acknowledging that, to the particular discomfort of the West, nationalism was the 'consistently strongest force' in Southeast Asia. Fifield saw 'neutralism' as an increasingly important force in Southeast Asia, arguing that the establishment of the Western-sponsored Manila Pact and its military organization, the South-East Asia Treaty Organization (SEATO), in 1954–55 had helped to divide rather than unite the region, by tending 'to push the uncommitted states into greater independence of attitude' (Fifield 1958: 498).[4] Fifield argued that Southeast Asian 'regionalism' might become a powerful force in the future, but pointed out that 'little basis presently exists for effective regional coöperation' (Fifield 1958: 498–9). This scepticism regarding the usefulness of SEATO and equivocation over Southeast Asia's future as a politically cohesive region echoed doubts expressed by many other Western writers during the 1950s. For example, Nathaniel Peffer argued that 'a Southeast Asia organization in 1954 is a rhetorical device, not a political fact' and that 'Southeast Asia is not a region that can be conceived as an effective entity in world politics' (1954: 311–15).

The Vietnam War era: questions of conflict and cooperation

The escalation of the conflict in Indochina in the early 1960s heightened Western and particularly American interest in many facets of the social sciences and humanities in relation to Southeast Asia, and over the following two decades generated a considerable volume of valuable writing on the modern history and politics of individual Southeast Asian countries and to a lesser extent on the region's international relations. While some of the writing on international relations focused on Indochina, many writers looked at other parts of Southeast Asia, and some attempted overviews of the whole region. Overall, there were three principal themes: the foreign policies of individual Southeast Asian states, the relationships of extra-regional powers with the region and with particular states within it, and the question of how a system of regional order (which was so clearly absent) might be constructed.

The most important general survey of Southeast Asian international relations written during the Vietnam War era is almost certainly Bernard K. Gordon's *The Dimensions of Conflict in Southeast Asia* (1966). Gordon, whose book included detailed case studies of the Philippine–Malaysian dispute over North Borneo, Cambodia's relations with her neighbours, and Indonesia's confrontation with Malaysia, stressed that despite the attention given to the communist threat to Southeast Asia, 'those conflicts which have little to do with communism often seem to be by far the most important considerations to the states involved' (1966: xi). But Gordon's crucial argument was that, despite these and other conflicts, and in contrast to the situation in the 1950s, Southeast Asia now constituted a 'political region'. Indeed, Gordon proposed that the widespread existence of conflict in Southeast Asia was one of three important factors which made it a region, the other two factors being the awareness by Southeast Asian leaders of 'the many similar problems they share' and the 'incentive' provided by the communist view of Southeast Asia as a region of great revolutionary potential (1966: 1–3).

In a path-breaking analysis, Gordon investigated in some detail the pressing problem of how the states making up this conflict-ridden 'political region' could be brought into an institutionalized pattern of regional cooperation. Gordon's starting point was that 'any suspicion that the idea [of regional cooperation] is generated outside the region is the kiss of death', and that this was now well appreciated in the West as well as in Southeast Asia (1966: 161). Gordon looked in some detail at the most important effort to institutionalize Southeast Asian regional cooperation: ASA (Association of Southeast Asia), established in 1961 by Malaya (from 1963 Malaysia), the Philippines and Thailand with the primary intention of fostering economic development as a means of bolstering political stability in the face of the communist challenge. Before it could register any significant achievements, ASA was effectively crippled by the Philippines' claim to sovereignty over the territory of Sabah (formerly North Borneo), which was incorporated into Malaysia in 1963. But Gordon pointed out that, although ASA was suspended because of the Philippine–Malaysian dispute, the fact that Manila and Kuala Lumpur continued to communicate and by mid-1964 had resumed consular relations was 'in large part, a result of the intensive communications paths established in the wake of ASA'. Gordon's description of ASA as an 'instrument for absorbing some of the region's conflicts' (1966: 185–7) foreshadowed the most important role of ASA's larger successor, the Association of South-East Asian Nations (ASEAN) which was established in 1967. Looking to the future of Southeast Asian regional cooperation, Gordon saw Indonesia's potential role as pivotal. He argued that a broader regional organization was needed in order to 'channel and accommodate' Indonesia's 'destabilizing' aspirations and resources. He suggested an 'Association of Southeast Asian New Emerging Forces', which would combine the membership of ASA and Maphilindo,[5] and 'perhaps even Burma and Cambodia' (1966: 188–93).

Despite their great diversity of scope, the plentiful writings on the international relations of Southeast Asia produced during the 1960s and 1970s were often characterized by several significant common features. In the first place, these writings were largely not theoretically self-conscious. They were permeated with implicit realist assumptions regarding the nature of the international system,[6] but seldom referred directly to the work of international relations theorists. While this might be explained in part by the generally weak linkage between the mainstream discipline and international relations specialists working on non-Western regions, it also arguably reflected the rather narrow parameters imposed on Southeast Asian research by the contemporary Cold War and 'Limited War' context. Nevertheless, Bernard Gordon, who did refer to the writings of Ernst Haas, Karl Deutsch and Harold Guetzkow on regional integration, as well as proposing his own quantitative model to explain the international political implications of Southeast Asian leaders' personalities (1966: 163–5, 186), was one of the first to attempt to conceptualize the international relations of Southeast Asia to some extent in theoretical terms. It was this and subsequent efforts to relate Southeast Asian developments to international relations theory which since the 1970s (and more particularly since the late 1980s) have increasingly tended to differentiate writing on the international *relations* of Southeast Asia from writing on the region's international *history*. International historians such as R. B. Smith (1983, 1985) and Buszynski (1983) have, nevertheless, continued to produce authoritative work on modern Southeast Asia.

A second characteristic of writing on Southeast Asia's international relations during the 1960s and 1970s was that it was produced almost entirely by non-Southeast Asian writers, most of whom were American, British or Australian. Given the acutely felt strategic interests of the United States, the United Kingdom and Australia in the region, and the still relatively low level of non-governmental interest in international matters within Southeast Asia, this should not have been surprising. But this changed with the large-scale withdrawal of American and British forces from the region by the mid-1970s, and with the concurrent maturing of various Southeast Asian institutions of higher learning at a time when when it was becoming imperative for Southeast Asians to play a greater role in shaping their region's destiny. Singaporeans (such as Lau Teik Soon, Chin Kin Wah and Lim Joo-Jock), Malaysians (for example, K.K. Nair and M. Rajendran), Indonesians (like Jusuf Wanandi), as well as Thai and Philippine scholars, all contributed significantly to the growing literature on Southeast Asian international relations as their countries adjusted to new regional realities in the 1970s and early 1980s.

Interestingly, most of the important writing by Southeast Asians on the region's international relations was available in English. By this time it was clear that English (rather than Malay or Indonesian, as some had anticipated or hoped during the 1960s) would be the language of Southeast Asian 'high politics': this was reflected in choice of English as the official language of ASEAN.[7] Even the Centre for Strategic and International Studies in Jakarta published both a journal (*Indonesian Quarterly*) and monographs in English. A related feature of Southeast Asians' writing on international relations was the extent to which it usually conformed to the realist tradition that dominated North American, British and Australian international relations thinking and writing, and in which most Southeast Asian academics working on international relations were trained. The generally illiberal nature of the ASEAN states' political systems tended to reinforce the local scholars' realist assumptions.

The third common feature of pre-1975 analyses of Southeast Asian international relations was a preoccupation with how the region's non-communist states should adjust their foreign policies in the light of the changing balance of great power involvement in the region. Announcements from London in 1967–68 that Britain's Southeast Asian military presence would be drastically reduced, President Nixon's enunciation in 1969 of his 'Guam Doctrine' (which anticipated a reduced direct United States' involvement in providing for the security of Southeast Asian allies, and foreshadowed Washington's military disengagement from Indochina), and the spectre of an assertive China produced particular interest in the idea of 'regional neutralization' as a means of ensuring the security of Southeast Asia. This interest culminated in the ASEAN governments' 1971 Kuala Lumpur Declaration, which proposed a Southeast Asian Zone of Peace, Freedom and Neutrality (ZOPFAN) 'free from any ... interference by outside Powers'. But the ZOPFAN proposal lacked practicality for several reasons. In particular, the consensus amongst regional states which was necessary if they were to assume responsibility for managing regional order in Southeast Asia would clearly be absent as long as the war in Indochina continued.

The 1970s: questions over the future of Southeast Asia's regional order

Concern amongst specialists in the Southeast Asian international relations in the early 1970s with questions related to the role of outside powers often camouflaged a frequent unwillingness or inability to get to grips with a critical problem confronting non-communist Southeast Asia: how to integrate Indochina into some sort of indigenously managed regional order. From the time of the Vietnamese communists' Tet offensive in 1968, it had been clear that the anti-communist side could not expect to win the war in the South. But beyond that, nothing seemed certain: a central problem for analysts was the inherent unpredictability of the course of the war in Vietnam.

Deep uncertainty over the future of Indochina was naturally reflected in a reluctance on the part of academic observers to commit themselves to a clear vision of future relations between the ASEAN and Indochinese states. When twenty leading specialists in the international relations of Southeast Asia from both inside and outside the region presented papers at a conference on 'New Directions in the International Relations of Southeast Asia' in Singapore in 1972, there was surprisingly little specific discussion of the future orientation or role of the Indochinese states (see Lau 1973a). There was also little unanimity in the viewpoints that were tentatively expressed. Some of the conference papers argued that Vietnam was likely to remain divided in circumstances of either continuing war (Nugroho 1973: 18) or peace (Nguyen 1973: 144), and that the continuing political conflicts were likely to prevent the Indochinese states (Devillers 1973: 127) or at least North Vietnam (Nguyen 1973: 144) from joining ASEAN. Others forecast accurately that the communists would ultimately reunify Vietnam by force, and that a unified Vietnam would seek to control Laos and Cambodia, thus threatening Thailand's security, and even provoking China's opposition (Goh 1973: 102; Stargardt 1973: 109). One participant argued that by the year 2000 Southeast Asia would be divided into two political regions: a Chinese-dominated continental Southeast Asia (comprising Indochina, Thailand and Burma) and an insular Southeast Asia or 'Greater Malaysia' comprising the former Maphilindo countries (Fernandez 1973: 29, 35). As it turned out, a more accurate prediction was Lau Teik Soon's, which foresaw 'two sub-regional groups, namely a non-communist ASEAN and a group involving the Indochina states', with diplomatic and trade contacts continuing between the two groups (Lau 1973b: 109).

A similar absence of focus on intra-regional relations was evident in the published proceedings of other conferences and seminars on Southeast Asian international relations held in the early 1970s, such as the University of British Columbia's Institute of International Relations' 1972 seminar (see Zacher and Milne 1974). Even Dick Wilson, in his otherwise extremely useful book on the ZOPFAN proposal, published shortly before the communists seized control of South Vietnam, Cambodia and Laos in 1975, was reluctant to predict the nature of Vietnam's post-war role in Southeast Asia beyond observing that: 'If at any time the two halves of this war-torn country become reunited, then Vietnam would play a crucial role in the affairs ... of the entire region' (Wilson 1975: 93–4).

With the unexpectedly rapid collapse of the anti-communist Indochinese regimes in 1975 and the consequent consolidation of communist regimes throughout Vietnam and in Cambodia and Laos, the issue of how to integrate communist Indochina into the regional order assumed a higher profile in writing on Southeast Asian international relations (see, for example, Lyon 1980: 110–14). Much continued to be written about the relationships between regional states and outside powers and particularly the growing strategic interest of the Soviet Union in the region (Buszynski 1986; Gregor 1989), but over the following twenty years the focus of thinking and writing about Southeast Asian international relations noticeably shifted from issues of great power involvement to issues of regional cooperation.

Regional cooperation: the focus on ASEAN

The first extended analysis of regional cooperation in Southeast Asia was Arnfinn Jorgensen-Dahl's, published in 1982 but based on a doctoral dissertation completed in 1975 (Jorgensen-Dahl 1982).

Jorgensen-Dahl traced the evolution of Southeast Asian regional organizations (and particularly ASEAN), paying particular attention to ASEAN's role in 'securing adherence to peaceful modes of conflict resolution' in relation to intramural disputes. He concluded that co-operation within ASEAN represented 'a significant move towards' a '"sense of community" in the Deutschian conception' within non-communist Southeast Asia (ibid.: 236).[8] But ASEAN performed wider roles: it was also 'an organisational expression of a regional polarisation process which has as its other principal pole the communist states of Indochina' and performed a 'defensive function' against extraregional powers – especially China (ibid.: 238). Although Jorgensen-Dahl credited ASEAN with important achievements, he concluded that 'the existing interstate order in Southeast Asia is clearly a precarious one', pointing out that intra-ASEAN order rested on a 'very tenuous' degree of domestic order in ASEAN's members (Jorgensen-Dahl 1982: 240).

Despite the clear strains that emerged within the organization during the 1980s (see Nair 1984; Huxley 1985), ASEAN's image as a successful regional organization benefited enormously from its leading role in opposing Vietnam's subjugation of Cambodia after 1979 and in keeping the issue on the international agenda for almost a decade after Vietnam's invasion. This image apparently contradicted Jorgensen-Dahl's rather pessimistic assessment of ASEAN's prospects. Although some analyses of ASEAN's security role during the 1980s (Simon 1982; Tilman 1987) were perhaps overly sanguine about the actual and potential depth of security cooperation between ASEAN members, others were more careful to distinguish between the organization's superficial image of strength and cohesion and the underlying reality of fragility and intramural tensions. Michael Leifer concluded that while the organization's 'primary concern' had been with 'politically expressed security co-operation', its 'natural defects ... cannot be overcome by any indulgence in symbolic forms of achievement'. Looking to the future, Leifer argued that ASEAN's 'collective enterprise' could not be taken for granted (1989: 150, 158–9). Michael Antolik took a similar line, pointing out that: 'ASEAN is truly a myth in the classical sense; under its facade of smiles and stories of friendship lie the basic truths. It is the acceptable public expression for cooperation between governments that have yet to overcome feelings of suspicion and rivalry.' Antolik argued that in future the ability and willingness of ASEAN member governments to continue with their 'diplomacy of accommodation' might be threatened by 'the rise of new powers, the arrival of new leaders or domestic instability, or modifications in diplomatic procedures' (1990: 160–1).

While there were doubts over ASEAN's viability, cooperation

between the Association's members in the late 1970s and 1980s nevertheless provided a stark contrast with the conflict between the parties
to the international level of the war in Cambodia. During the 1980s,
a sophisticated discourse developed concerning the Third Indochina
War, which in 1978–79 involved the first examples of large-scale, open
warfare between communist states (Democratic Kampuchea and Vietnam, and Vietnam and China) as well as subsequently developing into
a major theatre in the second Cold War of the 1980s. The resultant
literature contributed substantially to the understanding of the regional
foreign policies of China and the Soviet Union, and of Vietnam's
relations with its Indochinese neighbours as well as with these two
great powers (see Evans and Rowley 1984; Chang 1985; Chanda 1986;
McGregor 1988).

International relations theory and Southeast Asia: security complex, security community and security regime

Although some earlier writers had made efforts to relate their analyses
of Southeast Asia's international relations to relevant international
theory, it was only at the end of the 1980s that regional specialists
began to focus as a matter of course on theoretical issues. One particular stimulus for this development came from the writings of Barry
Buzan, a British international relations theorist who attempted to lend
a degree of theoretical rigour to discussion of Southeast Asian regional
security by applying the idea of the 'security complex'. Buzan defined
such a complex as 'a relatively self-contained pattern of security
relationships among a geographically coherent group of states', and
argued that there existed a Southeast Asian security complex, composed
of the three Indochinese states and the six ASEAN members. According to Buzan, the Southeast Asian security complex demonstrated 'the
destabilizing effect that weak states can have on the international
anarchy when whole regions are dominated by them' (1988: 3–4, 14).

Buzan did not – and could not reasonably have been expected to –
foresee the way in which the end of the second Cold War would
transform Southeast Asia's international relations at the end of the
1980s. This transformation involved, most notably, the withdrawal of
Vietnamese forces from Cambodia during 1988–89, the run-down of
the Soviet naval deployment in Vietnam from 1989 to 1991, the
comprehensive international political settlement of the Cambodian
dispute in Paris in 1991, and the ending of the US military presence
in the Philippines in 1992. These dramatic developments had the
incidental effect of liberating consideration of the region's international
relations from the fixation with the Cambodian issue which had become

dominant during the 1980s. In the new, more fluid regional environment, scholars were forced to step back and ask more profound questions about the past, present and future of Southeast Asia as a regional security complex.

One important question concerned the nature of ASEAN as a security organization. During the late 1980s and early 1990s discussion of this issue became increasingly sophisticated. Following Noordin Sopiee's description of ASEAN as a 'quasi-security community' (1986: 229), Buzan argued that 'the ASEAN states seem to trust each other enough to have created a security community among themselves' (1988: 11). Sheldon Simon claimed that ASEAN was 'a security community, in Karl Deutsch's sense, in which there no longer is an expectation of the use of force by one member against another' (1988: 68). In Amitav Acharya's view, 'ASEAN has indeed become a security community in the sense that its members do not foresee the prospect for resorting to armed confrontation among themselves to resolve existing bilateral disputes' (1991: 172–3). These were rather optimistic viewpoints, which failed to take into account the seriousness of bilateral tensions involving certain combinations of ASEAN members, such as Malaysia and Singapore or Malaysia and the Philippines (see Huxley 1991; David 1995). However, after a more rigorous assessment of both the relevant theory and the actual state of bilateral relations between ASEAN members, Acharya soon revised his position and argued that: 'While ASEAN has come a long way in reducing tensions between its members, it has not yet reached the stage of a "security community"' (1992: 12), which would require 'not only the absence of armed conflicts ... but also the absence of interactive weapons acquisition and contingency-planning in anticipation of ... conflict' (1993: 33). And Michael Leifer pointed to ASEAN's failure to invoke its own 'dispute settlement machinery' (in the form of a High Council) (1992: 169). It soon came to be widely accepted amongst interested international relations specialists that ASEAN constituted an 'emerging' or 'limited' security *regime* rather than a true security community (Wiseman 1992: 46; Leifer 1992: 167–9; Huxley 1993).

Southeast Asia: does it still exist?

Another important question concerned the extent to which Southeast Asia remained valid as a discrete and coherent regional framework of international analysis in the 1990s. In view of the changing pattern of threat perceptions and security linkages, various alternative frameworks to Buzan's Southeast Asian security complex were suggested. Sheldon Simon and Richard Stubbs both proposed that a bifurcated pattern of intra-regional relations was emerging in Southeast Asia along maritime and continental lines, with Malaysia, Singapore, Indonesia and Brunei being drawn together by a common preoccupation with maritime security as well as economic complementarities. Thailand, it was argued, was becoming increasingly preoccupied with 'continental' issues, in both economic and security spheres (Simon 1992: 112–14; Stubbs 1992: 397–410). Charles McGregor, however, criticized Simon's analysis on two grounds: that it tended to 'overestimate the degree of cohesion that could be created in each of these groupings'; and that it underestimated the increasing shared emphasis on maritime security within the whole region (McGregor 1992: 17). Indeed, N. Ganesan's analysis was much more convincing: he discussed the emergence of a 'Malay Archipelago complex' comprising Indonesia, Malaysia, Singapore and Brunei and characterized by competition and latent conflict as much as by cooperation (1994: 458–60).

McGregor also argued that 'the boundaries of Buzan's Southeast Asian security complex should be extended to encompass China', because of the intensity of that power's involvement in Indochina and the South China Sea (1992: 16–19). McGregor and Huxley subsequently suggested that 'the distinctiveness of the Southeast and Northeast Asian security complexes is diminishing ... we can begin to talk in terms of an East Asian security complex' (1993: 2). These arguments in favour of a broader East Asian security complex paralleled the evolution of policy: during the early 1990s, Southeast Asia's declining significance as a discrete security complex was being reflected in the ASEAN governments' efforts to place the Association at the centre of efforts to construct a new security 'architecture' in the form of the ASEAN Regional Forum (ARF) for the wider East Asian region. Paradoxically, though, if the ARF or a similar body were to become a significant security forum it seemed likely that it would undermine the importance of ASEAN. Similarly, the evolution of an 'Asia-Pacific community' based in the first instance on the Asia-Pacific Economic Cooperation (APEC) conference might potentially 'engulf ASEAN' (Ganesan 1994: 464).

Regional challenges to realism?

From the 1980s, the state-centred, realist assumptions that have underlain the mainstream of the international relations discipline since 1945, and infused most writing on Southeast Asian international relations, have increasingly been challenged by proponents of international relations theories that might usefully be referred to as constituting the 'world society approach'. This approach stresses the notion of global interdependence, the role of non-state actors as well as states, the importance of human needs as well as national interests, and the significance of cooperation as well as conflict. It 'emphasizes the importance of ideas, images and ideological preferences, as opposed to "facts" whose validity is questionable' (see Booth 1991: 375). Reflecting this reevaluation of the discipline's working assumptions, some regional specialists began to look at contemporary East (including Southeast) Asian security and international relations from this perspective. In the late 1980s and early 1990s, it became voguish to argue that a distinctly 'Asian' style of international relations was emerging which stressed regional interdependence in economic, political and security terms, avoidance of confrontation, mutual non-interference in domestic affairs, and informal confidence-building and political networking. Some writers argued that this 'Asian' style of international relations helped to explain East Asia's increasing wealth as well as its relative tranquillity in security terms in the 1980s and 1990s. ASEAN was held up as the exemplar of the Asian way to peace and prosperity, and it was pointed out that ASEAN initiatives had paved the way for the creation of wider regional organizations (APEC and the ARF respectively) in both economic and security spheres (Haas 1989; Mahbubani 1995: 105–20). One writer – a senior Singapore government official – went so far as to draw unflattering comparisons between the 'strategically incoherent' attempts to evolve a satisfactory post-Cold War regional order in Europe and the 'relatively sound strategic decisions' made by East Asian countries (Mahbubani 1995: 109).

Proponents of what Michael Haas called 'the Asian way to peace' interpreted the absence of a formal, institutionally based security architecture in East Asia as a strength rather than a weakness. Far from East Asia needing its own equivalent to Europe's strong but 'exclusive' institutions (principally the North Atlantic Treaty Organization, the European Union and the Organization for Security and Cooperation in Europe), it was suggested that Europe could learn from Asia's more inclusive networking processes (Mahbubani 1995: 117).[9] In contradiction to Donald Emmerson's argument that 'the preoccupation of Southeast Asianists with cultural factors had prevented Southeast Asian studies from contributing to the field of international relations' (see Keyes 1992: 16), it was argued that these successful networking processes in Southeast Asian and wider East Asian international relations owed much to supposedly 'Asian' cultural values – such as cultural tolerance, respect for 'face', consensus decision-making and ready acceptance of hierarchy (Haas 1989: 5–10; Mahbubani 1995: 116–17). Personal relationships between premiers and between foreign and defence ministers were supposedly 'the basis for positive security relations' amongst countries which shared 'a growing and collective pride in being Asian' (Kerr 1994: 407).

But there were critics of this line of argument, which sometimes seemed to suggest that Southeast Asian states were themselves at the leading edge of the fashionable attack on realism in international relations. Kanishka Jayasuriya highlighted the reality that Singapore and other ASEAN members have effectively rejected challenges from both sub-national non-governmental organizations and from supranationalism to the dominance of state-centred realism in their foreign policies. Jayasuriya discussed a fundamental problem involved in attempting to transfer ideas about a supposed paradigm shift towards a greater role in international relations for non-state 'policy networks' from a liberal Western political environment to an authoritarian Southeast Asian political environment. Jayasuriya claimed that, in contrast to the situation in western Europe, supposed non-state actors in Southeast Asia (essentially think-tanks, such as the Institute of Southeast Asian Studies in Singapore and its equivalents in Indonesia and Malaysia) actually have little or no autonomy: their role has 'not been as policy or ideas innovators but as "cheer leaders" for government policy' (1994: 414–19). He also asserted that in contrast with 'societal' European regionalism, Southeast Asian regionalism is 'statist', being intended to reinforce rather than diminish state power (1994: 419).

Another critic was Michael Leifer, who, while acknowledging that 'bureaucratic and ministerial consultation is very deeply entrenched' within a 'virtual quasi-familial' ASEAN, proposed that arguments about the relevance of 'common security' approaches to Southeast Asian security needed to recognize 'the persistence of the realist persuasion amongst ASEAN's policy makers despite their willingness to pay more than lip-service to the virtues of common security' (1992: 169). In practice, the ASEAN states continued to rely on realist means of ensuring their security in the more multi-polar and less predictable regional strategic environment of the 1990s. These realist means included efforts by the ASEAN states to maintain or enhance defence links with the United States and to improve their own military capabilities. But William Tow wisely pointed out that there is not necessarily any contradiction between what he called 'realist/bilateralist' and 'institutionalist/multilateralist' approaches to regional security, and argued in favour of 'gradual transition to an Asia-Pacific security regime incorporating both types of relationships' (1993: 107–8). Similarly, Simon argued that the ASEAN states were pursuing a 'dual-track strategy' on regional security, combining realism and 'neoliberalism' (1995: 20–1).

The underlying realist agenda of Southeast Asian governments was reflected in the continuation of Southeast Asian international relations scholars' overwhelmingly realist approach to questions of regional security. Through their employment by or association with the rapidly growing 'think-tank' sector during the 1980s, Southeast Asian scholars became increasingly preoccupied with policy-related agendas directly or indirectly dictated by their own country's governments.[10] While not denying the importance of certain contributions to the literature on national foreign policies in the region (for example, Anwar 1994), the concentration of many Southeast Asian international relations scholars on national issues may in turn have reinforced the relative lack of 'interest in or tradition of theoretical scholarship' (Kerr 1994: 400). One result of this was that, although Southeast Asians had begun to contribute to the literature on their own region's international relations during the 1970s and 1980s, in the early and mid-1990s there was surprisingly little input from within the region into the debates with which many outside international relations specialists (located mainly in North America, Australia and Britain) were concerned. The growth of local international relations specialists' influence on policy (see Jayasuriya 1994: 414–15) seems to have been paralleled by a degree of estrangement from international academic debates over Southeast and East Asia's international relations.[11]

Conclusion

Fifty years ago, 'Southeast Asia' was just coming into being as a region of international political analysis. Since then, the study of Southeast Asia's international relations has been concerned with two main issues: relations amongst regional states, and relations between these states and outside powers. The emphasis has varied over time. During the 1950s, the stress was on relations with extra-regional powers. There was a growing sense of 'region' during the 1960s (both despite and because of the United States' deep involvement in the Vietnam War), but in the late 1960s and early 1970s the focus remained on the implications for the region of outside powers' changing roles. Deep uncertainty over the future pattern of regional order in the early 1970s was superseded in mid-decade by a clear emphasis on regional cooperation and particularly ASEAN's role. This emphasis on regionalism continued into the 1980s. Since the late 1980s there has been considerable interest in relating international relations theory to Southeast Asia, and particularly to security issues. During the 1990s, fundamental questions have been raised which challenge the future relationship between the international relations discipline and the region. Notwithstanding the evidence pointing to the continuing dominance of realist considerations in Southeast Asian states' foreign policies, there has been a serious questioning of the realist assumptions that have underlain most previous international relations' scholarship in relation to the region. And, paradoxically, at a time when many mainstream international relations specialists are beginning to take more than polite interest in the contribution of Southeast Asian states to international cooperation, the late 1980s and 1990s have brought questioning of Southeast Asia's very meaning as a 'region' in economic and security terms.

The strong arguments pointing to Southeast Asia's diminishing identity as a discrete strategic and economic region do not necessarily imply that there is now less need for specialists in Southeast Asian international relations. There is scant evidence amongst international relations scholars working on the broader East Asian, 'Asia Pacific' or 'Western Pacific Rim' region of any profound understanding of the specific factors that continue to influence relations between Southeast Asian states, and between these states and the rest of the world. This is where input from specialists in Southeast Asian international relations (whether they are Southeast Asians or outsiders) remains vital. But for such specialists to make a significant contribution to the mainstream debates relating to the region's international relations, it is becoming increasingly important for them to place their Southeast Asian expertise in the context of the wider region as well as developments in international relations theory.

Notes

1. A version of this chapter has been published in the journal, *Pacific Review*.

2. See, for example, Wight's statement that 'we might define a world power as a great power which can exert effectively *inside* Europe a strength that is derived from sources *outside* Europe' (Wight 1979: 56).

3. The Anglo-American 'South-East Asia Command' (SEAC) was set up in 1943. Under the command of Admiral Mountbatten, SEAC's headquarters were established in New Delhi (later moving to Ceylon). The Command was charged with liberating Burma, Malaya, Sumatra and Thailand; after the Japanese surrender, its boundaries were expanded to include Cambodia, southern Vietnam, Borneo and the rest of the Netherlands East Indies.

4. The Southeast Asian signatories to the Manila Pact were Thailand and the Philippines. The obligations of the Pact's signatories extended to Laos, Cambodia and the Republic of Vietnam through a protocol to the Pact.

5. Maphilindo was an extremely short-lived attempt to promote cooperation between Indonesia, Malaya and the Philippines in 1963. Based on the supposed 'Malay' ethnicity of the three countries, Maphilindo only lasted three months,

because of Indonesian and Philippine objections to the creation of Malaysia in September 1963.

6. 'Realists tend to accept a world divided into independent sovereign states in constant competition with each other for scarce resources as being the normal, if not the permanent condition of international society' (Garnett 1984: 30).

7. ASEAN was established in 1967 by Indonesia, Malaysia, the Philippines, Singapore and Thailand.

8. Deutsch (1957: 5–6) defined a 'security community' as a grouping of states in which all disputes between members are resolved to such an extent that none fears, or prepares for, either political assault or military attack by any of the others. For an earlier discussion of Deutsch's security community concept in relation to Southeast Asia, see Lyon (1973): 163–4.

9. There certainly was willingness on the European side to at least investigate and possibly to learn from Asian networking. For example, in 1994 a team at Manchester University secured a grant of £120,000 from Britain's Economic and Social Research Council to pursue research on 'Identity, policy networks and international policy coordination in Pacific Asia'. See ASEASUK News (Newsletter of the Association of Southeast Asian Studies in the United Kingdom), No. 16 (Autumn 1994): 2.

10. In the case of international relations scholars in communist Vietnam, this of course had always been the case. Even as Hanoi moved towards ASEAN membership in the early 1990s, there was no evidence of any significant deviation from the Party line in Vietnamese writing on regional (or other) international relations. See, for example, Hoang (1993): 280–91.

11. There were, of course, exceptions. See, for example, Ganesan (1994): 457–68.

Bibliography

Acharya, Amitav (1991), 'The association of Southeast Asian nations: "security community" or "defence community"?', Pacific Affairs, 64: 159–78.

— (1992), 'Regional military–security cooperation in the Third World: a conceptual analysis of the relevance and limitations of ASEAN (Association of Southeast Asian Nations)', Journal of Peace Research, 29: 7–21.

— (1993), A New Regional Order in South-East Asia: ASEAN in the post-Cold War era, Adelphi Paper 279 (London: International Institute for Strategic Studies).

Antolik, Michael (1990), ASEAN and the Diplomacy of Accommodation (Armonk, NY: M. E. Sharpe).

Anwar, Dewi Fortuna (1994), Indonesia in ASEAN. Foreign policy and regionalism (Singapore: Institute of Southeast Asian Studies).

Booth, Ken (1991), 'War, security and strategy: towards a doctrine for stable peace', in Ken Booth (ed.), New Thinking about Strategy and International Security (London: HarperCollins Academic): 335–76.

Broek, Jan O. M. (1944), 'Diversity and unity in Southeast Asia', Geographical Review, 34: 175–95.

Buszynski, Leszek (1983), SEATO: the failure of an alliance strategy (Singapore: Singapore University Press).

— (1986), Soviet Foreign policy and Southeast Asia (London: Croom Helm).

Buzan, Barry (1988), 'The Southeast Asian security complex', Contemporary

Southeast Asia, 10: 1–15.

— (1991), *People, States and Fear*, 2nd edn (Hemel Hempstead: Harvester Wheatsheaf).

Chanda, Nayan (1986), *The War after the War* (San Diego: Harcourt Brace Jovanovich).

Chang Pao-Min (1985), *Kampuchea between China and Vietnam* (Singapore: Singapore University Press).

Chin Kin Wah (1974), *The Five Power Defence Arrangements and AMDA* (Singapore: Institute of Southeast Asian Studies).

David, Harald (1995), *Die ASEAN nach dem Ende des Kalten Krieges. Spannungen und Kooperations-probleme* (Hamburg: Institut für Asienkunde).

Deutsch, Karl et al. (1957), *Political Community and the North Atlantic Area* (Princeton, NJ: Princeton University Press).

Devillers, Philippe (1973), 'A neutralized Southeast Asia?', in Lau (1973): 114–28.

Evans, Grant and Kelvin Rowley (1984), *Red Brotherhood at War. Vietnam, Cambodia and Laos since 1975* (London: Verso).

Fernandez, Alejandro M. (1973), 'On the future of Southeast Asia', in Lau (1973): 27–35.

Fifield, Russell H. (1958), *The Diplomacy of Southeast Asia: 1945–1958* (New York: Harper & Brothers).

Fisher, Charles W. (1950), 'Southeast Asia', in W. Gordon East and O. H. K. Spate, *The Changing Map of Asia: a political geography* (London: Methuen): 179–246.

— (1962), 'Southeast Asia: the Balkans of the Orient? a study in continuity and change', *Geography*, 47: 347–67.

Ganesan, N. (1994), 'Taking stock of post-Cold War developments in ASEAN', *Security Dialogue*, 25: 457–68.

— (1995), 'Rethinking ASEAN as a security community in Southeast Asia', *Asian Affairs* (Washington, DC), 21: 210–26.

Garnett, John C. (1984), *Commonsense and the Theory of International Politics* (London: Macmillan).

Goh Cheng Teik (1973), 'The United States and Southeast Asia: past, present and future', in Lau (1973b): 98–103.

Gordon, Bernard K. (1966), *The Dimensions of Conflict in Southeast Asia* (Englewood Cliffs, NJ: Prentice-Hall).

Gregor, A. James (1989), *In the Shadow of Giants. The major powers and the security of Southeast Asia* (Stanford, CA: Hoover Institution Press).

Haas, Michael (1989), *The Asian Way to Peace: a story of regional cooperation* (New York: Praeger).

Hoang Anh Tuan (1993), 'Why hasn't Vietnam gained ASEAN membership?', *Contemporary Southeast Asia*, 15: 280–91.

Huxley, Tim (1985), *ASEAN and Indochina. A study of political responses 1975–81*, Canberra Studies 19 (Canberra: Australian National University, Department of International Relations).

— (1991), 'Malaysia and Singapore: a precarious balance?', *Pacific Review*, 4: 204–13.

— (1993), *Insecurity in the ASEAN Region*, Whitehall Paper 23 (London: Royal United Services Institute for Defence Studies).

Jayasuriya, Kanishka (1994), 'Singapore: the politics of regional definition', *Pacific Review*, 7: 411–20.

Jervis, Robert (1982), 'Security regimes', *International Organization*, 36: 173–94.

Ji Guoxing and Hadi Soesastro (eds) (1992), *Sino-Indonesian Relations in the Post-Cold War Era* (Jakarta: Centre for Strategic and International Studies).

Jorgensen-Dahl, Arnfinn (1982), *Regional Organization and Order in South-East Asia* (London: Macmillan).

Kerr, Pauline (1994), 'The security dialogue in the Asia-Pacific', *Pacific Review*, 7: 397–409.

Keyes, Charles F. (1992), 'A conference at Wingspread and rethinking Southeast Asian studies', in Charles Hirschmann, Charles F. Keyes and Karl Hutterer (eds), *Southeast Asian Studies in the Balance: reflections from America* (Ann Arbor, MI: Association for Asian Studies).

Lau Teik Soon (1973a), 'ASEAN and the future of regionalism', in Lau (ed.) (1973b): 165–72.

— (ed.) (1973b), *New Directions in the International Relations of Southeast Asia: the great powers and Southeast Asia* (Singapore: Singapore University Press).

Leifer, Michael (1989), *ASEAN and the Security of South-East Asia* (London: Routledge).

— (1992), 'Debating Asian security: Michael Leifer responds to Geoffrey Wiseman', *Pacific Review*, 5: 167–9.

Lim Joo-Jock (1979), *Geo-Strategy and the South China Sea Basin* (Singapore: Singapore University Press).

Lyon, Peter (1973), 'ASEAN and the future of regionalism', in Lau (ed.) (1973b): 156–64.

— (1980), 'ASEAN after ten years: problems and prospects for regional and functional cooperation within Southeast Asia', in S. Matsumoto (ed.), *Southeast Asia in a changing world. Proceedings and papers of a Symposium held at the Institute of Developing Economies on March 15–17, 1978* (Tokyo: Institute of Developing Economies).

McCloud, Donald G. (1986), *System and Process in Southeast Asia: the evolution of a region* (Boulder, CO: Westview).

— (1995), *Tradition and Modernity in the Contemporary World* (Boulder, CO: Westview).

McGregor, Charles (1988), *The Sino-Vietnamese Relationship and the Soviet Union*, Adelphi Papers 232 (London: International Institute for Strategic Studies).

— (1992), 'Southeast Asia and new international relations: forces for change', paper presented at the annual conference of the British International Studies Association, Swansea, December 1992.

— and Tim Huxley (1993), 'Security in Southeast Asia: frameworks of analysis', paper presented at the British Pacific Rim Research Group workshop, Liverpool, May 1993.

Mahbubani, Kishore (1995), 'The Pacific impulse', *Survival*, 37: 105–20.

Nair, K. K. (1984), *ASEAN-Indochina Relations since 1975: the politics of accommodation*, Canberra Papers 30 (Canberra: Australian National University, Strategic and Defence Studies Centre).

Nguyen Man Hung (1973), 'The two Vietnams and the proposal for a neutralized Southeast Asia', in Lau (1973b): 137–45.

Nugroho (1973), 'Southeast Asian perceptions of the future of the region', in Lau (1973b): 7–19.

Panikkar, K. M. (1943), *The Future of South-East Asia* (London: George Allen & Unwin).

Peffer, Nathaniel (1954), 'Regional security in Southeast Asia', *International Organization*, 8: 311–15.

Rajendran, M. (1986), *ASEAN's Foreign Relations. The shift to collective action* (Kuala Lumpur: Arenabuku).

Simon, Sheldon W. (1982), *The ASEAN States and Regional Security* (Stanford, CA: Hoover Institution Press).

— (1988), *The Future of Asian-Pacific Security Collaboration* (Lexington, MA: Lexington Books).

— (1992), 'The regionalization of defence in Southeast Asia', *Pacific Review*, 5: 112–24.

— (1995), 'International relations theory and Southeast Asian security', *Pacific Review*, 8: 5–24.

Smith, R. B. (1983), *An International History of the Vietnam War.* Volume I: *Revolution versus Containment, 1955–61* (Basingstoke: Macmillan).

— (1985), *An International History of the Vietnam War.* Volume II: *The Struggle for South-East Asia, 1961–65* (Basingstoke: Macmillan).

Sopiee, Noordin (1986), 'ASEAN and regional security', in Mohammed Ayoob (ed.), *Regional Security in the Third World: case studies from Southeast Asia and the Middle East* (London: Croom Helm).

Stargardt, A. W. (1973), 'Neutrality within the Asian system of powers', in Lau (ed.) (1973): 104–13.

Stubbs, Richard (1992), 'Subregional security co-operation in ASEAN: military and economic imperatives and political obstacles', *Asian Survey*, 32: 397–410.

Tarling, Nicholas (1993), *The Fall of Imperial Britain in South-East Asia* (Oxford: Oxford University Press).

Tilman, Robert O. (1987), *Southeast Asia and the Enemy Beyond. ASEAN perceptions of external threats* (Boulder, CO: Westview).

Tow, William T. (1993), 'Contending security approaches in the Asia-Pacific Region', *Security Studies*, 3: 75–116.

Wanandi, Jusuf (1979), *Security Dimensions of the Asia-Pacific Region in the 1980s* (Jakarta: Centre for Strategic and International Studies).

Wight, Martin (1979), *Power Politics* (Harmondsworth: Pelican).

Wiseman, Geoffrey (1992), 'Common security in the Asia-Pacific region', *Pacific Review*, 5: 42–59.

Wilson, Dick (1975), *The Neutralization of Southeast Asia* (New York: Praeger).

Wolters, O. W. (1994), 'Southeast Asia as a Southeast Asian field of study', *Indonesia*, 58: 1–17.

Zacher, Mark W. and R. Stephen Milne (eds) (1974), *Conflict and Stability in Southeast Asia* (Garden City, NY: Anchor).

Index